Praise for
Investing 101
Updated and Expanded
by Kathy Kristof

"*Investing 101* is a sensible, well-written, and comprehensive guide to investor options. I learned much from this book and am certain you can to."

Stephen Brobeck
Executive Director
Consumer Federation of America

Praise for the first edition

"*Investing 101* by Kathy Kristof is a reader-friendly introduction to the basics of investing and personal finance. . . . If I had to suggest a book on investing and personal finance to an absolute beginner, it would be *Investing 101*."

BookPage

"… [an] excellent primer about investing. Investors will get a clearer idea of how markets work and what you can realistically expect from your retirement funds."

The Boston Globe

"Kristof's down-to-earth style and clear prose gives her writing a decidedly user-friendly quality. . . . The vast majority of us worker drones who haven't yet made complete sense of things will find *Investing 101* an easy way to get started."

Miami Herald

"In *Investing 101*, Kathy Kristof skillfully guides the novice investor, step-by-step, along the path to investment success. It's an ideal primer for anyone who wants to enter the financial world and would like a helping hand."

Myron Kandel
Founding Financial Editor, CNN

"Not only is this book more simple and straightforward than the typical book on investing, it's also more humorous and personal."

Today's Librarian

"Too many of us give too little thought to the underpinnings of investing: how much risk to shoulder, when to sell, etc. Kathy Kristof explains these basics in language we all can understand. *Investing 101* is sure to become a great reference guide for novices and longtime investors alike."

Steve Dinnen
Personal Finance Columnist
The Des Moines Register

"Kathy Kristof knows investing inside and out. She can take even the most complicated information and make it easy to understand—and entertaining."

Ilyce R. Glink
National Syndicated Columnist
Author of *100 Questions You Should Ask about Your Personal Finances*

"If you're just getting started in the investing world, this is the book you need. Kathy Kristof's smart, sensible advice demystifies the markets and shows you exactly what you need to know to achieve your financial goals. *Investing 101* offers a road map to financial success without gimmicks or secret formulas—and it's a whole lot of fun to read, besides."

Liz Pulliam Weston
Personal Finance Columnist
Los Angeles Times

Investing 101

Updated and Expanded

Also by Kathy Kristof

Taming the Tuition Tiger:
Getting the Money to Graduate—with 529 Plans,
Scholarships, Financial Aid, and More

———

A complete list of our titles is available at

www.bloomberg.com/books

Investing 101

Updated and Expanded

Kathy Kristof

BLOOMBERG PRESS
NEW YORK

BLOOMBERG, BLOOMBERG ANYWHERE, BLOOMBERG.COM, BLOOMBERG MARKET ESSENTIALS, *Bloomberg Markets,* BLOOMBERG NEWS, BLOOMBERG PRESS, BLOOMBERG PROFESSIONAL, BLOOMBERG RADIO, BLOOMBERG TELEVISION, and BLOOMBERG TRADEBOOK are trademarks and service marks of Bloomberg Finance L.P. ("BFLP"), a Delaware limited partnership, or its subsidiaries. The BLOOMBERG PROFESSIONAL service (the "BPS") is owned and distributed locally by BFLP and its sub-sidiaries in all jurisdictions other than Argentina, Bermuda, China, India, Japan, and Korea (the "BLP Countries"). BFLP is a wholly-owned subsidiary of Bloomberg L.P. ("BLP"). BLP provides BFLP with all global marketing and operational support and service for these products and distributes the BPS either directly or through a non-BFLP subsidiary in the BLP Countries. All rights reserved.

This publication contains the author's opinions and is designed to provide accurate and authori-tative information. It is sold with the understanding that the author, publisher, and Bloomberg L.P. are not engaged in rendering legal, accounting, investment-planning, or other professional advice. The reader should seek the services of a qualified professional for such advice; the author, publisher, and Bloomberg L.P. cannot be held responsible for any loss incurred as a result of specific investments or planning decisions made by the reader.

Updated and expanded edition published 2008;
First edition published 2000
1 3 5 7 9 10 8 6 4 2

Library of Congress Cataloging-in-Publication Data

Kristof, Kathy.
    Investing 101 / Kathy Kristof.—Updated and expanded ed.
        p. cm.
    Includes index.
    Summary: "The fully updated and expanded edition of Investing 101 offers basic advice to market newcomers. Subjects include: stocks, bonds, mutual funds, retirement planning, college savings, and tax strategies. This new edition removes roadblocks and offers low-maintenance portfolios that put investors on the path to investment success"—Provided by publisher.
    ISBN 978-1-57660-307-9 (alk. paper)
    1. Investments. 2. Stocks. 3. Mutual funds. 4. Bonds. 5. Finance, Personal. I. Title.

HG4521.K738 2008
332.6—dc22

                                                                                  2008021592

To Mom and Dad

You taught me everything of great value—and none of it was about money. For that reason, and about a thousand more, you are my heroes. Yesterday, today, and always.

CONTENTS

ACKNOWLEDGMENTS

I never planned to write a book about investing. I really didn't think I could be that dull. But my former editor at the *Los Angeles Times*, Bill Sing, insisted that consumers were in desperate need of solid advice on how to pick individual stocks, how to diversify their assets, when they should invest in bonds, and how they could get started. They needed this information and they needed it in a form that actually wouldn't be dull, he argued. Informative, interesting, and short. Just the facts. No jargon. It was a tall order, but he's the boss.

So I wrote a series of investing tutorials, then another series, then another. After responding to hundreds of requests for hard copies, we added yet more information and made it all into this book. In the process, I learned that Bill was right, again. (I hate that.) Yet, again, I'm indebted. Thanks, Billy.

It's often said that a reporter is only as good as his or her sources. I'm grateful to mine. There are literally hundreds of experts—analysts and money managers from the likes of Merrill Lynch, Oppenheimer & Co. Inc., Neuberger Berman LLC, Fidelity Investments, the Vanguard Group Inc., T. Rowe Price Group Inc., and others—not to mention literally dozens of brilliant and highly paid tax accountants and financial planners who spent hours chatting about markets, economics, trading strategies, and asset allocation. Some of them are quoted in the following pages; some aren't. Their wisdom contributed greatly to the creation of *Investing 101*.

Much more difficult to thank are my friends and family, who contribute to everything I do in ways both obvious and subtle. With their help and support, it seems as if anything is possible. For you, I am truly blessed. Thank you.

INTRODUCTION

Before we get started with the serious financial stuff, I'd like to share one of my favorite stories about investing. It's true, and it illustrates a point that you need to remember while you're reading this book—particularly if you're a little nervous about your ability to invest wisely.

The story starts one dark October day on Wall Street, when the so-called "Asian Currency Crisis" struck. The Dow Jones Industrial Average—a key indicator of market health—plunged more than 300 points. I, like every other financial reporter on the planet, was charged with making some sense of it all for the readers of a general circulation newspaper.

Luckily for me, I work for the *Los Angeles Times*, where dozens of skilled reporters mobilize whenever there's a major news event. As a result, I didn't need to do the straight story—the story replete with numbers and specific details of which stocks fell the most and why. Instead, I was charged with figuring out whether individual investors were in a panic (as the professional investors assumed they would be). Given the fast-paced trading and the rapid decline in stock prices, it was clear that *somebody* was panicking.

First I called the professional investors. Beads of sweat were forming under their starched white collars and gray pinstriped suits. They didn't talk. They sputtered, blurting out incomplete sentences, such as "The Asian financial crisis . . . spreading . . . could create global crisis. Market meltdown . . . It may be time to sell." Yes, this could be called panic.

Then I called dozens of individual investors. A few were home. A few were at work. Some were at the baseball game. They were not breathless. They were not sweating. (Well, in the interest of accuracy, I don't know for sure about the sweating thing. It's sometimes hot in Los Angeles, even in October. But they didn't *sound* as if they were sweating.)

Were any of them frantically calling their brokers trying to sell? Not a one. Instead, the individual investors said what the professionals should have said: Markets go up; markets go down. As long as your investments are appropriate for your goals, you don't need to sweat the day-to-day movements. You can go about your business. Take in the baseball game. Relax.

The next day, the wisdom of the guy and girl on the street won out. Stocks climbed right back. Within a few days, they were higher than they'd been before the onset of the "crisis."

What did the professionals have to say about the currency crisis that had them screaming "sell, *sell, SELL*" the day before? Ahem. "It's better."

The moral of this story: You can invest every bit as wisely—and sometimes more wisely—than a professional. Why? The professionals were in a panic for one very good reason: If you manage money for a mutual fund, your gains or losses show up in the newspaper the next day. Mess up, and all the world can see what a dope you are. That's embarrassing. Besides, your pay as a money manager is probably going to be tied to how well your portfolio performed over the course of the year either relative to the market as a whole or the portfolios managed by a group of your peers. No professional wants to be the last numbskull to sell out of a money-losing stock.

You, on the other hand, can be a numbskull and only your spouse will know. (This might be the time to point out that " . . . or for poorer" clause in your marital vows.) That gives you time to think. Time to consider whether an investment was a mistake or a wise move that simply needs more time to pan out.

In reality, few people make brilliant choices in the heat of the moment. The smartest thing to do when faced with a "catastrophe"— or a "hot stock"—is to take a deep breath and think for a moment.

What should you be thinking about? That's precisely what the rest of this book is all about. It will help you determine how different types of investments react in different markets—and how to choose specific investments in good times and bad. It will even explain when you ought to invest on your own and when you ought to consider hiring a professional to help. With that knowledge, you can weather any investment storm.

Better yet, you can do it calmly, rationally, and with an eye to what matters in life, which, incidentally, is not the size of your portfolio.

So, read. Learn. Enjoy. And then do me one favor: Vow to spend more time with your family and friends than you spend with your portfolio. I guarantee you, it's not going to matter if you have $10 million when you die, if you have no one you care about to leave it to.

Investing 101

Updated and Expanded

QUICK TAKE

What You'll LEARN

Everybody has little hang-ups that keep them from handling their money as wisely as they might like. In this chapter, you'll find problems that are common among investors:

- Saving too little—or not at all
- Getting greedy
- Being tax-wise and bottom-line foolish
- Emotional spending
- Matriarchal martyrdom
- Financial overdependence
- Running scared
- Competing with strangers
- Tinkering away your profit
- Forgetting what the money is for

What You'll DO

- Identify the personal problems that might be holding you back
- Identify potential solutions to help you get past financial roadblocks and begin investing wisely

How You'll USE This

By facing your money fears and foibles, you can separate fiction from reality. That allows you to put money in its proper perspective. Money is a tool to make your life calmer and more comfortable. This chapter gives you directions on how to use it without hurting yourself.

FIXING MONEY PROBLEMS  1

When I started writing about finance, the world according to Wall Street was promoting something called the "efficient markets theory." In a nutshell, this theory contends that the day-to-day price movements of stocks and bonds are ultimately rational—based on investors making informed and savvy choices about what to do with their cash at any given moment of the day. The idea was that we all went into the investment markets with a fist full of cash and all the accurate information we'd need. Then, our conversations would go something like this: "Hmm, that stock is a bargain at this price: Buy! Those bonds aren't yielding enough: Sell and redeploy our capital!" As the market moved to reflect the increasing demand on the savviest investments and the dearth of buyers for the less attractive investments, the prices would shift accordingly and investors would make new choices. Supply and demand are always in sync and investors are always rational.

The bulk of the world has now recognized this controversial theory to be largely irrelevant to individual investors.

It's not that people never make rational decisions about their money. They do—just not all the time and not even when taken as a group. Wall Street's favorite theory is now "behavioral finance." This theory explains why smart people often make dumb decisions about their money.

The great thing about this shift is that behavioral finance is something we all can relate to. We know instinctively—or from personal experience—that ignorance, fear, or greed can get in the way of making smart choices. Instead of decisions, we make excuses. Instead of making money, we make . . . well, a mess.

This book is going to tell you how to invest wisely. *Investing 101* is simple. It's straightforward. You'll get step-by-step instructions throughout. Anyone who reads and follows the directions will find investing easy to do. But if you let bad money habits overshadow your money smarts, your road to wealth will be long and bumpy.

How do you avoid that? Like anything else: You identify the problem and find a solution.

Here are some of the most common problems that face investors and simple ways to fix them. Many of these problems won't relate to you, so skip them, unless you simply want to gloat.

Certain investment roadblocks are universal and can be relevant for any investor. Other problems are more likely to strike women than men, or men than women. The following sections look at all three types.

# UNIVERSAL PROBLEMS

PROBLEM: Saving too little, or not at all.

"I would invest, but I just don't have the money," says the well-dressed twenty-five-year-old driving a BMW. "I'm going to start as soon as I get a raise."

Okay. That was a slight exaggeration. And it would be easier to save if you earned more money, but sometimes life is just not fair.

Now, be fair with yourself and answer honestly: When was the last time you bought lunch or dinner at a restaurant instead of going for the cheaper alternative of packing a sack lunch or making your own dinner? When was the last time you bought a suit, a high-tech gadget, or a pair of shoes that you knew you didn't need?

If you have a job that pays a decent wage—meaning anything that keeps you above subsistence level—you can afford to invest. Spend $2 less per day—the cost of one Starbucks coffee or one snack from the vending machines—and you've got $60 a month. That's enough to plop into an automatic investment plan with a mutual fund.

Still think it's a matter of poverty, not spending habits?

DID YOU KNOW?
Saving Habits and Salary Bumps

A number of studies have been done about whether individuals can afford to save, based on their income. They have found that aside from people at the polar ends of the income scale—the very rich and the very poor—the bulk of people in between think they could save, at least small amounts. Often, it's a matter of whether they do, rather than whether they can. Increases in salary often lead to incremental increases in spending rather than increases in savings. This suggests that saving is a matter of habit, not income. If you aren't saving now, you won't start when you get a raise.

SOLUTION: You need a budget.

A budget doesn't necessarily spell deprivation. In fact, a good budget is like a good diet. It feeds both your wants and needs in a healthy and sustainable way.

To put together a good budget—a real budget—you need to gather some records:

- Pull out your check register and bank statements.
- Collect your credit card bills.
- And find either your most recent tax return or your pay stubs.

You'll need these to remind yourself of your monthly, annual, and semiannual expenses—from rent or house payments to car insurance. The chart on the following pages will help you plot out what you're shelling out each month.

You thought you were going to make up a projected budget? People who try to make up budgets without looking at their actual expenses are kidding themselves. The amount that you think you're spending—or think you ought to be—is almost always less than what you actually spend. By writing down your actual purchases, you're going to uncover your own personal money pits—places where you're spending more money than you meant to. It might be dining out. It might be dry cleaning. It might be a shopping habit.

This isn't about fitting your expenses into smaller boxes. This is about figuring out where your money is going and determining whether that's where you want it to go. If it is, leave things alone. But if lots of little outlays are robbing you of long-term happiness by making it impossible to save for big goals—like a house or car or retirement— you might want to nip and tuck here or there. So, fill out the worksheet to find the flab in your financial life.

■ MONTHLY BUDGET

INCOME:

Wages: _____

Tips: _____

Interest: _____

Other: _____

EXPENSES:

Income taxes: _____

Employment taxes: _____

Health insurance: _____

401(k) contributions: _____

Mortgage/rent: _____

Property tax: _____

Homeowner's/renter's insurance: _____

Water: _____

Gas: _____

Electric: _____

Garbage: _____

Phone: _____

Newspapers/magazines: _____

Cable: _____

Repairs: _____

Housekeeper/gardener: _____

Groceries: _____

Clothing: _____

Car payments: _____

Auto insurance: _____

Auto repairs: _____

Public transit: _____

Credit card payments: _____

Student/personal loan payments: _____

Child care: _____

Meals out: _____

Entertainment: _____

Other: _____

You've done the worksheets, but still can't figure out where the money is going? You're underestimating some expense because you're paying more cash than attention. Do this: Start carrying a notebook around with you. Jot down every expense, from the $1 bagel to the $50 you spend filling up your car. Review your notebook after a month. Include the expenses in the budget and see if there's something you can trim to add to savings. Realize that if you cut just $3.35 per day, you've found $100 a month to save. Voilà.

PROBLEM: Getting greedy.

You bought a stock figuring that it was going to go to $50. Then lo and behold, it popped up to $65. Based on all of your market knowledge, this is an incredibly high price for this stock. Its price/earnings ratio (see Chapter 5) has never been this high, and you can't imagine why it might be now. And yet, if it went to $65, it could go to $70, right? Maybe you ought to hang on just a little longer and see.

The fact is, the stock could go higher. Or it could go much, much lower. Consider 1999, when the prices of technology stocks had soared into the stratosphere and market pundits were contending that the sky was the limit. "It's a new paradigm!" they shouted. It was hype. During the following three years, those stocks crashed and burned. A few have recovered. Many have not. People who were smart enough to sell when the prices were high made a killing. Those who got greedy got killed.

SOLUTION: Target price.

Every time you buy a stock, you should have a target—a price at which you would either sell the stock or reevaluate its prospects before you decide to leave it in your portfolio (see Chapter 6). Don't let emotion—regardless of whether that emotion is fear, greed, or hope—rule your actions.

Evaluate all your stocks once a year. Make reasonable decisions about whether each one is a buy, a hold, or a sell. If you realize that you wouldn't buy a stock today given its future prospects and that there are better opportunities out there, sell it. Live with the idea that you may never sell at the peak. That's okay, as long as you also don't sell at the nadir.

PROBLEM: Being tax-wise and bottom-line foolish.

> I hear it all the time: "Never pay off your house. Your mortgage interest is tax deductible!" I'm always tempted to respond, "Okay, humor me for a minute here and let's go through the math. If I pay $1 in mortgage interest, I'll get to deduct it, which will save me, say, thirty cents on my federal income tax return. Aren't I still out seventy cents?"

There are dozens of equally "tax-wise" investments being marketed in today's world. My favorite is the variable tax-deferred annuity. What these say they do is allow you to save additional money for retirement in investments that mimic stock mutual funds.

The money you invest in this type of annuity isn't tax deductible going in, but the investment gains are not taxed as returns and accumulate in the account. This allows you to trade all you want within the annuity and not immediately pay taxes on your gains. That's the selling point that continues to push variable annuity sales ever higher. Roughly $90.6 billion in variable annuities were purchased during the first half of 2007. Total assets in these accounts were nearly 1.5 trillion, according to LIMRA International Inc., an insurance research and consulting firm.

Annuities are able to offer this benefit because they're an insurance product. The insurance you get with an annuity generally is a guarantee that if the stock market crashes, which causes you to have a heart attack and die, your heirs are guaranteed to get at least as much as you originally invested in the annuity. That's not much of a guarantee, but you pay for it dearly. The typical mortality and expense ratio on an annuity is around 1 percent. In other words, if the investments you hold within the annuity yield 10 percent, you'll get 9 percent of that after the mortality expense is taken off the top. (To get a good read on the dollars-and-cents impact of that fee, read "The Real Cost of Fund Fees" in Chapter 8.)

But there's a second cost too. Ironically, it's a tax.

When you earn a profit on a long-term investment in a taxable account, you pay tax at preferential capital gains rates—usually 15 percent. However, money pulled out of a retirement account—and tax-deferred annuities fall into this category—is taxed at ordinary income tax rates, which can be as high as 35 percent. Even though you don't have to pay taxes right away on money earned in an annuity, when you do pay, the tax rate is so much higher that it almost always overwhelms the short-term benefit of the annuity.

SOLUTION: Do the math.

Figure out whether the tax benefit of an investment is worth the cost. All too often, it's not.

FOR WOMEN ESPECIALLY

By and large, women start investing later in life than men, set less money aside, and invest more conservatively. That has the unpleasant effect of leaving them poor in their old age. Some 80 percent of the elderly people living in poverty are women. So what's their excuse?

PROBLEM: Emotional spending.

Do you shop when you have a fight with your boss or your spouse? Do you find that you "need" to hit the mall whenever you're feeling down, as a way of boosting your spirits? Letting your psyche drive your spending is a common problem.

The bad news is your credit card balance is likely to rise faster than your spirits. As a result, you're sentencing yourself to a life of servitude—working harder or more hours to pay your debts, which makes you all the more depressed.

If you need to get rid of your boss or your spouse, stop spending and start saving. Having money in the bank creates financial independence, which can lead to emotional and physical independence if you want it to. But how do you reverse the emotional drag that you've previously shopped away?

SOLUTION: Find a healthier alternative.

Ideas:

- Take a walk.
- Go to the gym.
- Play catch with your kids.

- Pull out a board game.
- Ask a friend to come over for wine and whining.
- Volunteer—help build a house for Habitat for Humanity; take a foster child to lunch; feed the homeless.

The possibilities are endless. Better yet, these won't cost you much and will make you happier and healthier.

PROBLEM: Matriarchal martyrdom.

Some women are natural-born martyrs. "How can I save for myself when Johnny needs a new soccer uniform and we haven't even gotten close to funding Susie's college account?" they worry. Is that a gravy spot on your husband's shirt? He'd be happier and more successful at work if he had a better wardrobe—even if that meant there was no money left to fund your retirement account, right?

Certainly, it would be nice to think of yourself once in a while, you admit, but how can you when you're so busy being the family caregiver? After all, somebody has to take care of the rest of the family, and no one else has stepped up to the plate to do it. All of your worldly concerns are going to be put on the back burner until you take care of theirs—today, tomorrow, and forever. Right?

It's lovely to take good care of your loved ones, but realize that when you are strong physically and financially, you can solve a lot more problems for your kids than if you're weak. That's precisely why young parents need to balance their long-term financial needs with the pressing day-to-day expenses of managing a young family.

SOLUTION: Set some priorities.

Make your retirement account one of them. If you are working and have access to a company 401(k) plan, contribute to it. It is, hands down, the best way to save for your retirement needs. If you don't have a 401(k)—if you don't even have a paying job—set up an automatic savings account with a mutual fund (see Chapter 12). Even if all you're saving is $50 a month, you'll have started taking care of yourself and making yourself financially strong. You owe that to yourself and to your family.

But your kids are the ones giving you a hard time about money? They say that you owe them clothes, cars, and a college account? Ask them which one is going to agree to support you in your old age. Draw up a contract and have them sign it. "Since I (Johnny) decided that my Camaro was more important than my parents' retirement savings, I agree to always have a bedroom in my home where my parents can live. I promise to clean their room once a week, and cook their favorite dinners, just like they did for me. . . . " A notary might be advisable.

PROBLEM: Financial overdependence.

Why save and invest for yourself when there's always been someone willing to take care of you? First there was Dad. Then there was your husband. Both of them are kind and thoughtful and wonderful providers.

But what happens if they both predecease you? Women usually live longer than men.

Then there's that other uncomfortable fact of life: About half of marriages end in divorce. Are you prepared to take care of yourself if you're forced to because of death or divorce? Roughly 90 percent of women are going to need to take care of themselves financially at some point in their lives. Think about it.

SOLUTION: First steps.

Not everyone is familiar with the story of Cinder Edna, but it's one of my favorites. The tale, written by Ellen Jackson, goes like this: There are two girls living next-door to one another, both ill-treated by their stepfamilies. One is Cinderella. The other, Cinder Edna. When Cinderella is done with her myriad chores, she sits in the cinders, by the fire. When Cinder Edna finishes, she takes in odd jobs to earn extra money. When the ball comes around, Cinder Edna doesn't need a fairy godmother. She's got a dress on layaway and a bus pass. Guess who ends up the happiest?

We women need to do much the same. If you're reading this book, you're already taking the first step. Put a toe in the market by joining an investment club or starting a monthly investment program with a mutual fund. You can learn about mutual funds in Chapter 8. If you want to join an investment club, you can find information on the Web at www.better-investing.org. If you find investing too dull or too demanding, read Chapter 14, "The Lazy Investor's Portfolio Planner"— and follow the instructions.

PROBLEM: Running scared.

Multiple studies have shown that women invest far more conservatively than men do, preferring bonds and bank accounts to company stocks. They do this because they imagine that buying stocks is like gambling. They know stock prices can vary significantly over short periods of time, and they don't want to lose their hard-earned cash. This is an understandable, but a serious— and costly—misunderstanding about how markets work.

SOLUTION: Take reasonable risks.

Read Chapter 2 and concentrate on the section "Considering Rates of Return." It explains how taking reasonable risks can boost your investment returns and why being too cautious can leave you poor. Then divvy up your money based on goals—instructions are in Chapter 3. Put your short-term money in safe investments that let you sleep at night; and put your long-term money in stocks and mutual funds. Do your best not to peek at that portfolio too often—look once or twice a year. By not looking too often, you'll miss most of the market's volatility—the stuff that makes you nervous—and you'll get the portfolio growth that can make you rich.

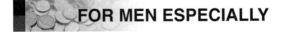 **FOR MEN ESPECIALLY**

Although men typically have more money than women do, they still make some surprising mistakes with it. Sometimes they invest too aggressively; sometimes they worry too much and second-guess their best judgment; sometimes they get so caught up in saving and investing that they forget what the money is for. By and large, it appears that the bulk of their problems stem from one thought: This is a game. I've got to win, either for the pure competition or for the spoils. Such thinking sours investment returns—often substantially. Though the following problems are mostly male afflictions, women sometimes fall victim to them as well.

PROBLEM: Competing with strangers.

You go to a cocktail party and start talking to some guy. He's wearing a nice suit, he's confident, and he starts telling you that he's making a killing in the stock market. "Yeah, I doubled my money on Google in three months," he brags. "Then I bought this little penny stock and whammo! It tripled in value!"

You stand there quietly, wondering why you've been doing it so wrong. Here you are investing in companies with track records, earnings, sales, and supposedly skilled managers, and what is your portfolio earning? A paltry 10 percent, you grouse. "What kind of loser am I? Why didn't I buy that penny stock?" you think. You begin to question your whole investment strategy. You need to be more like that guy . . . that cocktail-party guy.

You go home, and you buy some of that guy's stock. Maybe you sell some of your boring stocks and mutual funds. When you lose money on those new investments, you know that it's your fault. You're a loser—not a winner like that cocktail-party guy.

In the meantime, you've derailed a perfectly good portfolio.

SOLUTION: Match your goals to your investments.

Remember what your mother used to tell you: "If your friends all jumped off a bridge, would you follow them?" Don't be taken in by a big talker.

Naturally, what the cocktail-party guy didn't mention was that two weeks before he met you, he was downtrodden because his portfolio had declined in value by half, and he was wondering whether he'd have enough cash to make his mortgage. Why didn't he tell you about that? Well, it's not really cocktail-party chatter, is it?

You should know that anyone who makes a fortune overnight can also lose a fortune overnight. Risk and reward go hand in hand in the financial markets. Create a reasonable investment strategy by matching your goals to your investments. You can do that in Chapter 3.

PROBLEM: Tinkering away your profit.

You saw it on *Tool Time*. You do it in your portfolio. Here you have a perfectly functioning item, be it a lawn mower or a stock. But you know that if you just fiddle with it a little bit, you could make it better.

When you're dealing with tools, the worst thing that can happen is you'll have to replace them. When you're dealing with your portfolio, the stakes are considerably higher. But now that you can check your stocks on the Web—and trade for just a few bucks a pop—it's tough to leave well enough alone.

Tinkerers are particularly apt to sell stocks when they've got a bit of a profit. "Lock that in," they say. Naturally, if the stock keeps rising, they've missed out. Worse still, every time you sell a stock at a profit in a taxable account, you not only have to pay a trading fee, you also pay tax on the gain. If you held the stock for more than one year, that tax will be at capital gains rates, which max out at 15 percent; if you've held it for less than a year, the gain is taxed at your ordinary income tax rates, which are certain to be higher. Either way, to make up for the taxes you pay, you'll have to earn more than a 15 percent return on your next stock purchase just to break even. And few people pull that off.

SOLUTION: Once again, do the math.

Read Brad Barber and Terrance Odean's paper titled: "Boys Will Be Boys." You can find it on the Web at http://faculty.haas.berkeley.edu/odean/papers/gender/BoysWillBeBoys.pdf.

Odean is a professor at Berkeley's Haas School of Business. He's done loads of research about investor behavior. This study chronicles the differences in how men and women trade stocks. The short version: By studying the account data for over 35,000 households, Odean found that men trade 45 percent more often than women.

What does that do to the value of their portfolios? It depresses their returns by an average of 2.65 percentage points per year. What does that mean in dollars and cents? If you started with $100,000, your tinkering would have cost you roughly $250,000 over a twenty-year period.

This may be one of those moments that you really ought to listen to your wife.

Do the math. Sell when an investment no longer makes sense—when its prospects are poor. Don't sell just because you can.

PROBLEM: Forgetting what the money is for.

You invest every dime, often scrimping and saving to do it. And thanks to this superfrugality, you have a lot of money saved and invested. But it's not enough, you theorize. It's never enough. So you work extra hours; you skip vacations; you urge your spouse to do the same. All the while, your riches are growing bigger, and you are growing older.

Before you postpone one more vacation or miss one more baseball game, stop and consider what all this money is for. What are the things in life that you hold precious? Have you saved enough to buy those things? In fact, is your emphasis on saving robbing you of enjoying those things? Too many men work themselves into ulcers, heart attacks, or divorces in a quest to get something that they already had but were too busy working to notice.

SOLUTION: Slow down. Step back. Reevaluate.

Figure out how much money you realistically need for your personal goals and how close you are to accumulating that amount of money. (You can answer that by completing the worksheets in Chapter 3.) Once you have enough, relax. Enjoy it. To be sure, you can be more successful at work, if you spend every waking hour there. But do you really want your kids to only remember you through the Jaguar that they bought with the money you left them when you died?

Put your wife and kids on your calendar. If that costs you money, take comfort in the fact that if they love you, they might take care of you in your old age. If they don't, your wife will divorce you and take half of your assets; and your kids will end up fighting with your second wife for whatever is left after you're gone.

As your mother used to say, "Be careful what you wish for."

QUICK TAKE

What You'll LEARN

Risk and reward go hand in hand in the world of investing. All investments carry some sort of risk, but investing smartly and safely can lead to consistent returns over the long term with minimal risk. In this chapter, you'll learn about:

- Understanding Market Risks
- Considering Rates of Return
- Why a Bad Market Could Be Good for You
- How Much Investment Risk Can You Tolerate?

What You'll DO

- Review average returns for different types of investments—taking note of the number of money-losing years and just how bad the bloodletting can get
- Take the Risk Quiz
- Calculate your score to determine how much risk you can handle

How You'll USE This

Whether you invest on your own or you use a financial planner, you'll need to know just how much risk you can take and still sleep at night. The Risk Quiz will help you figure out where you stand on the risk spectrum—from a person who can take almost no risk to a thrill-seeker ready to gamble for a potential pot of gold.

Later in the book, you'll be asked to estimate a return when calculating how much you need to save for your long-term goals. The lower your risk tolerance, the lower the return you should use in those charts. (Risk and reward go hand in hand.)

And, if you decide you want advice, your risk quiz will help you explain to a financial planner what you're comfortable with.

Financial planners tell stories about people who hesitate to invest in the stock market because they fear risk. There are widows who fear that a stock crash could leave them destitute. There are young couples who pine for a new home but worry that an investment loss could kill their chances. And there are people who want to avoid the devastation their parents or grandparents experienced after the 1929 market crash.

Often, however, these fears are rooted in a misunderstanding of what risk is when it comes to the financial markets. Those who understand market risks—and properly evaluate their ability to tolerate them—can supercharge their investment portfolios by embracing a certain amount of uncertainty and getting rewarded for it.

UNDERSTANDING MARKET RISKS

James P. King, a financial planner from Walnut Creek, California, illustrates this point with a riddle: Consider two investments. With the first, you are guaranteed to lose money. Invest $1,000, and you'll lose $1,000. The other could allow you to cash out with an amount ranging from $0 to $5,000 on your $1,000 investment. Which is riskier?

Many individuals would say the riskier investment is the first, because their principal would be in greater jeopardy. But to financial professionals, the first investment is merely stupid—not risky— because it's a sure thing to lose.

In the financial world, risk translates to uncertainty. It's measured by "standard deviation from the norm"—in other words, it's measured by how much the returns swing up and down. Says King, "Most individuals measure risk as their chance of loss, but we measure risk by the variability of returns."

In a market that hangs its hat on the close correlation between risk and reward, that's an important distinction. Stocks are considered risky because their prices fluctuate, sometimes by a lot. In the stock market's worst year, the value of big-company shares fell 43.3 percent. In its best year, they rose 53.9 percent. But even as prices swing wildly, the odds are in your favor over the long haul.

Nothing illustrates this point better than charts compiled by Ibbotson Associates Inc. in Chicago that show the variability of returns—and total returns—from 1926 through 2006. The summary version: The returns on small-company stocks—which are even more volatile than big-company stocks—have varied by as much as 78 percent in a given decade, whereas the returns on Treasury bills have varied by less than 1 percent. But because the Treasury bill returns are a relative sure thing—there's very little deviation—the rewards are slim.

Consider this: If you had invested $1 in the U.S. stock market in 1926 and left it there until 2007, you would have suffered some sickening jolts, including the 1929 market crash, the 1987 minicrash, and the 2000–2002 bear market, along the way. In fact, big-company stocks lost value in twenty-three years out of eighty-one, according to Ibbotson. But you also would have enjoyed some years in which your wealth soared. In the end, your $1 would have grown to a stunning $3,077.33 (this doesn't include taxes and assumes dividend reinvestment).

If on the other hand you had invested that $1 in Treasury bills in 1926, you would have seen only one down year, and the loss would be too small to mention. In all eighty others, your return would have inched ahead. Still, because your average annual return would amount to a lackluster 3.7 percent, your $1 would have been worth just $19.29 at the end of 2006. If you factor in inflation and income taxes, T-bills begin to look a great deal like the first investment option in King's riddle. Indeed, on an inflation-adjusted basis, Treasury bills lost money more often than stocks.

In fact, every type of investment poses some type of risk. While so-called principal risk, or the chance of losing all or a portion of your initial investment, is the risk that most fledgling investors know about, even instruments that you would call supersafe pose some type of risk. Treasury bonds, for example, pose something called interest-rate risk. (When interest rates rise, the market value of older, relatively low-rate bonds falls.) Bank accounts, certificates of deposit, and Treasury bills pose inflation risk, which is the chance that the after-tax return on your investment won't keep pace with the rate of inflation. That means you lose buying power with every dollar you save.

Still, there's one reason that stocks tend to worry people more: You never know when the stock market is going to dive. "What if it falls right before I need to sell?" the risk-averse investor asks. The presumption is that your plans would be ruined, your finances devastated. However, the real answer to that question may surprise you. There are very few points in history when you would have been behind by investing in stocks, as long as you left your money invested for at least several years.

 CONSIDERING RATES OF RETURN

Consider this: The average annual return of big-company stocks has exceeded 10 percent over the past eighty-one years; the average annual return of medium-term government bonds was just 5.3 percent during that same period. So what would have happened if you had invested in stocks over a twenty-year period but then were unlucky enough to cash out the day that the market took a nosedive? Chances are you'd still be significantly better off than somebody who invested the same amount in bonds, taking home that relatively steady 5.3 percent return.

How much better off? If you invested $1,000 and earned 10 percent annually for ten years, you would have accumulated $6,727. If the market took a 30 percent loss before you had a chance to cash out, you'd lose $2,018 of that, taking home just $4,709. (If you suffered a 40 percent loss, you'd end up with $4,036.)

If you had invested the same amount in bonds or certificates of deposit and earned a 5.3 percent average annual return instead, you would have cashed out with $2,809 after twenty years—significantly less than even the postcrash value of your stock portfolio. In other words, because stocks have higher average returns, you can suffer some serious losses and still end up vastly ahead over the long run. It's important to note that overall market losses this steep—in the 30 percent and 40 percent range—are rare. There have been only two times in history when large-company stocks have lost that much of their value in a single year—once in 1931, and once in 1937. Outside of the Great Depression, the worst years for big-company stocks hit during the early 1970s, when stock prices dropped 14.66 percent in 1973 and then 26.47 percent in 1974. After that, prices came roaring back, with big-company stocks posting a 37.2 percent gain in 1975 and a 23.84 percent gain in 1976. The 2000–2002 bear market showed much the same pattern—losses of 9.15 percent in 2000, 11.95 percent in 2001, and 22.1 percent in 2002. Then came a 28.7 percent gain in 2003, followed by a 10.87 percent gain in 2004.

Indeed, when you have a long time horizon, the stock market begins to look downright stable. While there are twenty-three one-year periods when you would have posted a loss when investing in a broad basket of big-company U.S. stocks, there are only two ten-year periods that were equally bleak. Again, both occurred during the Great Depression.

But these statistics track the market as a whole—not individual stocks. If you buy individual shares, it's not unusual to suffer a 30 percent or 40 percent loss if you happen to buy shares in a company that falls on hard times. Naturally, if that company doesn't recover, neither would the value of your portfolio. That's why you should never invest your entire portfolio in one or two companies' shares. Instead, you diversify your holdings, buying shares in a number of different companies. Diversifying dramatically reduces your risk.

That said, there's only one time when you should not have a diversified basket of U.S. stocks in your portfolio. That's when you don't have time to let the market work for you. In any given year, you have about a one-in-four chance of taking a loss in the stock market. If you plan to invest for only a few years, stocks boil down to a gamble. This is not a wise place to invest your rent money.

But if your time horizon is five years, ten years, or more—as it is for virtually anyone who is investing for retirement—there is a very good chance that putting at least a portion of your money in stocks will boost the performance of your entire portfolio. As your mother used to say, "Nothing ventured, nothing gained." If you take a little risk, you just might gain a lot.

WHY A BAD MARKET COULD BE GOOD FOR YOU

A bad market has a way of demoralizing and derailing investors. That's because investors assume that whatever has happened lately is probably what's ahead, says Hugh Johnson, chief investment officer of First Albany Corp. in Albany, New York. So, when the market turns bad and stays bad for a while, investors tend to get out and stay out.

Huge mistake. If you're young and have lots of time before you need the money you've invested, a bad market could be just the ticket to ensure you a lifetime of wealth. Why? The technical term is "reversion to the mean."

That's statistical market-speak for the fact that over long periods of time, investors tend to get average returns. And, in the stock market, average is darned good. Average annual returns (as you can see from the chart on page 28) of small company stocks are 12.7 percent; big-company stocks post average annual returns of 10.7 percent. Over a twenty-year time frame, those averages would turn your $100,000 portfolio into a $1.1 million portfolio (in small-company stocks), or a $763,750 portfolio, if invested in big-company stocks.

But here's the deal. Even though those are the market's average returns, it's rare that an actual return will equal the average in any given year. Instead, stock prices bounce around wildly over short stretches—up 20 percent in one year; down 10 percent the next—to deliver those long-term geometric averages.

So what happens when the market is down one year, up just a nudge the next, and plummets in the third year—as it did at the beginning of this decade? Chances are, stock prices are going to surge at some point in the future, just to catch up to the average.

Consider what happened to someone who put $1,000 a month into the stock market starting in January of 1970—the most recent really rotten decade for U.S. stocks. Over that decade, because of several years of double-digit losses, this investor earned a paltry 5.9 percent compounded return.

But if he had the fortitude to stick with what appeared to be a stupid investment, he would have been richly rewarded. That's because stock prices zoomed forward over the next two decades to catch up to (and then exceed) their norms.

The average return in the 1980s was 17.55 percent, and it was 18.2 percent in the 1990s. The investor who stuck through 30 years, making consistent investments every month, would have ended up with $4.03 million.

What would happen if he earned the same returns but in a different order—the good returns early and the bad returns later? He'd end up with $3.08 million, or nearly $1 million less. The trick? Investors who start in bad years suffer when they've got the least at stake and reap a windfall after they've been able to build up a nest egg.

For a young investor, those figures are cause for optimism. The beginning of this decade looked remarkably like the 1970s. So, if you've been investing, and you're willing to be diligent and consistent about staying in the market, there's no reason to believe that you won't profit just like the investor in the previous example.

The flip side: You've got to know when to get out. That's not a market-timing comment. That's about life timing. When your time horizon shortens—such as when you get close to retirement—you need to lighten up on stocks. That's simply because you no longer have the time to ride through the market swings. And bad markets can last.

This doesn't mean you should sell every stitch of stocks in your portfolio when you quit the working world. It means that when you retire you should start putting between five and seven years of living expenses into investments that are more stable, such as medium-term government bonds, money market accounts, and certificates of deposit. That gives you the income to handle your life's needs and the time to wait out temporary market swings without giving yourself an ulcer.

"We tell people that they have to have a long horizon," says Roger Ibbotson, a professor at Yale School of Management and the founder of market research firm Ibbotson Associates. "If you are going to get jumpy every time there's a drop, you're going to feel whiplashed by the stock market."

HOW MUCH INVESTMENT RISK CAN YOU TOLERATE?

Want a graphic illustration of how much risk you can handle? Here's a quiz that brings up many of the issues that should affect your risk tolerance and your investment strategies.

In a nutshell, it will show you that you can take more risk in your investment portfolio when you have less risk in your life. Your age, your earnings capacity, and just how nervous you get when the value of your investments drops sharply also have an impact.

RISK QUIZ

HOW MUCH RISK CAN YOU TAKE?

1. My age is between:
   a. twenty and thirty-five.
   b. thirty-six and forty-five.
   c. forty-six and fifty-five.
   d. fifty-six and sixty-five.
   e. sixty-six and ninety-nine.

2. I have a stable job in a growing industry. I imagine I'll:
   a. continue to work for my present employer unless I get offered a higher-paying job, which is very likely in my industry.
   b. work for my present employer for the rest of my career, because I like it here and the company is growing enough to provide me with some opportunity for advancement.
   c. work here as long as I can, because I don't know what else I'd do.
   d. switch jobs soon. The boredom is killing me.
   e. get fired any day now. I've never been good at this work, and as time goes on, I get worse.

3. Over the next five to ten years, my salary and overall earnings will:
   a. probably grow significantly.
   b. most likely grow steadily—at least as fast as inflation.
   c. stay relatively stable.
   d. possibly decrease somewhat.
   e. decrease significantly.

4. I have a spouse who:
   a. loves me and earns enough to support us both.
   b. earns almost as much as I do and doesn't mind sharing it.
   c. earns a good living.
   d. works part-time.
   e. stays home with our children.

5. I (we) have always lived:
   a. on significantly less than we earn. That's allowed us to save 20 percent or more of our income each year.
   b. well within our means. We save close to 10 percent of our income.
   c. modestly, but we haven't been able to save much of what we earn.
   d. to the outer edges of our income, spending every dime and borrowing a few dimes here and there, too.
   e. on credit.

6. The following number of people rely on me for their financial welfare:
   a. zero.
   b. one.
   c. two.
   d. three.
   e. four or more.

7. The number of years remaining until I expect to retire is:
   a. twenty-five or more.
   b. fifteen to twenty-four.
   c. five to fourteen.
   d. less than five.
   e. none—I'm currently retired.

8. My net worth (the value of my assets minus my debts) is:
   a. more than $350,000.
   b. $150,001 to $350,000.
   c. $50,001 to $150,000.
   d. $15,001 to $50,000.
   e. less than $15,000.

9. The amount I have saved in nonretirement assets equals:
   a. more than two years' salary.
   b. one to two years' salary.
   c. seven months' to one year's salary.
   d. two to six months' salary.
   e. one month's salary or less.

10. I (we) have life insurance that:
    a. is more than adequate to take care of my family's financial needs if anything happens to my spouse or me.
    b. I believe would be adequate to cover my family's financial needs in the event that something happened to my spouse or me.
    c. would pay off the mortgage but would not provide much else.
    d. would help us survive for a year or two.
    e. is inadequate (or nonexistent).

11. I (we) have disability insurance that:
    a. is more than adequate to take care of my family's financial needs if either my spouse or I become disabled for any amount of time.
    b. is adequate as long as the disability is not particularly long-term. In other words, it will cover us as long as I'm not out of work for more than six months to a year.
    c. would tide us over for a while, but we'd have to cut back.
    d. would cover some but not all of our expenses, and not for any length of time.
    e. . . . Disability insurance?

12. I have health insurance that provides:
    a. great coverage for my family and me.
    b. adequate coverage for my family and me.
    c. catastrophic coverage, after I pay a significant deductible.
    d. good coverage only if I see certain doctors, in whom I have little faith.
    e. I don't have health insurance.

13. When I buy stock investments, I:
    a. contemplate what the money is for and feel comfortable leaving it alone until I need it for that specific goal. As a result, I may not look at the market value for months.
    b. analyze what I'm buying and why and usually feel capable of sticking with the program. But I have to know what the market is doing on a very regular—ideally daily—basis so I can reanalyze and consider whether I was wrong the first time.

    c. try to match my investments with my goals, but I'm never quite certain that I've got the mix just right.

    d. stick with them unless they start to decline in value. Then I get nervous and second-guess myself, which sometimes causes me to trade at all the wrong times.

    e. watch them like a hawk, because I don't want to lose any principal.

14. The majority of my financial goals are:

    a. very long-term—things that are at least fifteen to twenty years in the future.

    b. fairly long-term—things that are between ten and fifteen years in the future.

    c. mixed—I have some relatively short-term goals, like establishing an emergency fund; some medium-term goals, like buying a house; and some long-term goals, like retirement, which is decades from now.

    d. mostly short- to medium-term—my kids are in (or about to enroll in) college, and my retirement is looming on the not-too-distant horizon.

    e. very short-term—I'm in retirement, and my main goal is to have my current savings provide enough monthly income to live on.

15. My family and friends are:

    a. very supportive. They're the type of people who would let me move in with them if I happened to lose all of my money in a stock market reversal or a bad commodity trade.

    b. pretty supportive. They'd lend me money and—in a pinch—let me move back home if my finances crumbled due to some event that was outside of my control.

    c. supportive but not financially capable of helping a great deal.

    d. not supportive, but as long as I don't ask for anything, they leave me alone.

    e. a constant drain on my assets. They don't provide support, ever; they just ask for it.

■ SCORING

Give yourself five points for every (a) answer; four points for each (b); three points for each (c); two points for each (d); and one point for each (e).

Your score: _____

__ **65 to 75:** You probably have the money and the inclination to take lots of risks. High-risk investments include aggressive-growth stocks, start-up companies, commodities, junk bonds, international stocks, stock options, and investment real estate. However, be sure to diversify at least some of your portfolio into safer investments. You could regret your high risk tolerance if you lost everything.

__ **51 to 64:** You have an above-average tolerance for risk and probably enough time and income to cover some investment losses. Investors in this category are wise to mix high-risk and medium-risk options.

__ **36 to 50:** You have an average tolerance for risk but don't like to gamble. Make a point of dividing your assets by goal and then investing those assets in quality stocks, bonds, notes, and money market funds that address your needs while allowing you to sleep soundly at night. Since you're likely to have a wide range of goals— from beefing up an emergency fund to maximizing returns on a retirement account—expect that your assets will be mixed among high-, low-, and medium-risk options.

__ **21 to 35:** You have below-average tolerance for risk, either because of your age or because of your income and family circumstances. Comfortable investments for you would probably include your home, high-quality bonds, government-backed securities, and federally insured savings accounts. But make sure you keep at least some of your retirement savings in stocks. After all, even if you're retired or near retirement, you're probably not near death. That means at least part of your retirement dollars are long-term investments. Keeping a portion of your long-term investments in stocks should allow that portion of your portfolio to grow as fast as (or faster than) inflation over time. That allows you to maintain long-term buying power.

__ **15 to 20:** You have virtually no tolerance for risk. Look for investments that have government backing, such as bank and thrift certificates of deposit, Treasury bills, bonds, and notes. As you learn more about investing—or as your life circumstances change for the better—check your risk tolerance again. You may find that a good grounding in investment education will boost your comfort with taking some investment risks, which should help improve your long-term financial health.

■ ### The Bare Facts About the Variability of Investment Returns

Just how much do stock returns vary in a given year? Just how likely are you to lose principal from one year to the next? Just how bad could that loss be? Here are a few of the key statistics that tell you how different types of investments have fared over the eighty-one-year period tracked by Ibbotson Associates. The chart shows the investment class, the average return, the worst return, and the number of negative-return years, divided by the total number of years tracked, to give you an idea of your chance of loss in any given year.

Asset Class	Average Annual Return	Lowest Annual Return	Number of Negative Years	Chance of Loss
U.S. small-company stocks	12.7%	−58.01%	24/81	30%
U.S. large-company stocks	10.4%	−43.34%	23/81	28%
Long-term corporate bonds	5.9%	−8.09%	17/81	21%
30-year Treasury bonds	5.4%	−9.18%	21/81	26%
Intermediate T-bonds/ notes	5.3%	−5.14%	8/81	10%
30-day Treasury bills	3.7%	−0.02%	2/81	2%
International stocks*	11.6%	−23.19%	10/37	27%

As measured by the MSCI EAFE (Morgan Stanley Capital International Europe, Australasia, Far East) Index, which has tracked the prices of international stocks since 1970.

DID YOU KNOW?
Diversification

A little later in this book, we're going to talk about the cost and benefits of diversification—spreading around your assets among different types of investments. But since we're on the topic of returns, here's a little preview.

By divvying up your assets among a variety of different types of investments, you reduce the violent swings in your portfolio. The idea is that when one type of investment is up, another might be down. Put them together and you have a little less return, but a lot more stability.

Ibbotson Associates, a Chicago-based research firm, illustrates the point with the average annual returns of a portfolio mixed with just big company stocks and long-term government bonds.

If you mix a portfolio with 70 percent stocks and 30 percent bonds, you reduce the number of money-losing years to twenty out of eighty-one, instead of twenty-three. You also dramatically reduce the severity of your losses. Instead of losing as much as 43.34 percent of your portfolio value, this diversified portfolio's worst year registered a 32.31 percent loss.

Better yet, there were fewer long stretches where you would have ended up behind when you diversified. With a portfolio of all stocks, there were ten five-year periods in which you would have suffered an average loss over the entire stretch of time. With a portfolio of 70 percent stocks and 30 percent bonds, there would have been only five times in history (or at least the eighty-one years that Ibbotson has tracked so far) in which you would have posted an average loss over the entire stretch. And the worst loss, again, was less severe—31 percent versus 12.47 percent—for the all-stock portfolio.

The downside of diversification: The average return over time is also lower. According to Ibbotson, the mixed portfolio produces a 9.3 percent average return versus a 10.4 percent average return for the all-stock portfolio. Still, giving up 1.1 percent of your average return may be a small price to pay for peace of mind and for having the amount of money you need when you need it.

QUICK TAKE

What You'll LEARN

Investing wisely is about having the money that you need when you need it. You can do that by putting your investments into categories, based on what the investments can do for you. You'll learn about:

- Allocating Assets Based on Goals
- Identifying Investment Categories
- Identifying Financial Goals

What You'll DO

- Identify the types of emergencies you might suffer
- Calculate the amount of money you might need for those emergencies
- Identify your other personal goals—from saving for retirement to cobbling together a college fund
- Figure out what sort of nest egg your current savings will generate in the future, based on the amount of time you have until you need the money and the investment return you expect to earn
- Calculate how much you should save each month now to fund future goals

How You'll USE This

This is the first step in allocating assets among different types of investments. You'll take what you learned and use it to put the right amount of money in each investment and investment category—stocks, bonds, mutual funds, bank accounts, real estate investment trusts (REITs), international securities, and others.

John has been investing for about five years—long enough to know that a bull market is a market in which stock prices are climbing strongly and a bear market is one in which they're languishing. The only trouble is, he's never quite sure whether he's got the bull by the horns or is about to be mauled by the bear. With his life savings riding on the answer, he says that he approaches each day with nail-biting nervousness.

"Every time the market climbs, I'm wondering whether I should sell to lock in my profits. When it drops, I wonder whether I should sell to cut my losses," he says. "Most of the time, I don't actually do anything—other than worry about it."

Anecdotal evidence indicates that John, a broker who asked not to be named for fear of losing all his clients, isn't alone. Investing makes many people nervous, because they know that their future financial health can hinge on the choices they make. And there are a huge variety of highly complicated options confronting investors every day.

However, investing doesn't have to be difficult or nerve-racking. In fact, wise investing is simple, once you understand a few key facts.

First and foremost is this: The goal of this game is not to accumulate more money than God. It is not about getting a 50 percent or 40 percent or even 20 percent investment return. It is not about bragging at cocktail parties. It is this and only this: having the amount of money you need when you need it.

Make this your mantra. If you ever wonder about whether you are investing wisely, ask yourself this question: "Will I have the amount of money that I need when I need it with my present investment strategy?" If the answer is yes, you're doing it right. If the answer is no, you need to change something. It is that simple.

ALLOCATING ASSETS BASED ON GOALS

So how do you make sure that you have the money you need when you need it? You start by putting your assets in appropriate investment categories, based on your goals. In market-speak, this process is called asset allocation. Pundits make this process sound complex—as if there's some secret formula to doing it right that they know and you don't. But, in reality, it's a simple process.

IDENTIFYING INVESTMENT CATEGORIES

Asset allocation begins with categorizing investments into five basic types. These categories are based on what the investment does for you rather than what the investment is. By categorizing in this fashion, you can easily allocate your assets into broad investment groups.

1. Investments that safeguard your principal
2. Investments that provide you with income
3. Investments that promise strong growth of your principal
4. Investments that protect you from the ravages of inflation
5. Investments that allow you to speculate

If you are like most people, you will need investments in the first three of these five categories. If inflation makes you nervous, you may choose to invest in the fourth. But unless you are very young or very rich, you should skip investments in the fifth category simply because investments that allow you to speculate are more like gambling than investing. If (or when) you have enough money that you can take a pot of cash and roll the dice—knowing that you've got just as good a chance of losing it all as you do of doubling your money overnight—then you can invest in that last category. Until then, stick to the first four.

Why do you want investments in at least the first three of these categories? Mainly because nearly everyone has a financial goal that is best addressed by one of these three investment types. For instance, every one of us would be wise to keep some money safe to handle life's curves—that's anything from unexpected medical expenses or car repairs to the loss of a job.

Income investments are perfect for two things: to fund short- and mid-range goals and to provide extra income to handle daily living expenses. The people who can most benefit from income investments can be anyone from a retiree to a young family intent on buying something big in the near future, such as a house or a car.

Anyone who hopes to retire someday needs some investments that promise strong growth of the principal investment. Growth investments tend to grow substantially faster than the rate of inflation. Therefore, they increase your buying power over time. Increase your buying power enough and you can finance massive goals, like the urge to quit your job and live off your savings in comfort for forty years or so.

Who needs inflation-protecting investments? Mainly people who worry that their buying power will be whittled away to nothing because the dollar will lose all of its value, stocks will be rendered worthless, and people will be forced to barter with commodities, like gold and grain, because they'll be the only things with value. The biggest proponents of having a large portion of your assets in inflation-protecting investments are people who also have stored gold, guns, and canned goods in their bomb shelters. In reality, inflation has averaged just about 3 percent per year since 1926. You should be able to earn significantly more than that on your invested cash.

Still, although it is easy to make light of the "end is near" crowd, there have been times in history when protecting yourself from high inflation was a remarkably good idea—the 1970s, for example. Even though most experts don't advise that you keep a lot of your investment assets in inflation-protection-type securities, there is one investment that does a great job protecting you from inflation and provides other comforts as well. And there's one relatively new and liquid security that addresses inflation concerns, without the need for a bomb shelter. You'll learn about them in Chapter 4.

In fact, the only hard part about asset allocation is deciding how much money to put in each type of investment. Frankly, that's not tricky or complex, it's simply time-consuming. Why? To do it right, you have to consider precisely what you are saving for and how much you need in order to reach each goal. Once you do that, your assets practically allocate themselves.

IDENTIFYING FINANCIAL GOALS

So now it's time to think about what you want in life and just what your goals and dreams are going to cost you. To help, the rest of this chapter talks about seven common goals—having emergency money, saving for a car, buying a house, paying for college, creating a "freedom" fund, saving for retirement, and generating savings that will produce income to live on.

You may have other goals, but chances are they're similar enough to at least one of these that you can use the discussion and worksheets provided with each of these goals to help you figure out the right amount to save. The end of each section will discuss what types of investments best suit that goal and will direct you to the part of this book that gives more information about those types of investments.

RUNNING THE NUMBERS

Goal: Emergency Money

Prepare to get depressed. To appropriately estimate your need for emergency cash, you need to mull a variety of worst-case scenarios— all of the things that you are not financially prepared to handle, whether that's the loss of a job or the loss of a spouse. Then you need to consider what other resources you could tap to tide you over.

The reason you have to consider your other resources in the same breath as your disasters is a simple one. Emergency money needs to be kept in very safe investments that pose little risk to your principal— things like bank accounts, money market mutual funds, and short-term Treasury bills. However, as you'll learn in the next chapter, this type of investment also produces very little return. Normally, in fact, the yields are so slim with super-safe investments that the after-tax return on your money is unlikely to keep pace with inflation. That means you lose buying power over time.

Does that mean you shouldn't have an emergency fund? Not at all. If you are likely to suffer some type of emergency and have no better way to deal with it, an emergency fund is invaluable. You just don't want to keep more money in emergency savings than absolutely necessary.

To dedicate the right amount to emergency savings, you must handicap your risks and quantify the potential cost. To clarify, you need to consider the type of emergency that you're most likely to suffer. Then, figure, as closely as you can, just how much money you'd need to muddle through it.

Like what, you ask?

Disaster Central: Delineating Potential Emergencies

• **Car repairs.** If you're just starting out in life, your biggest risk may be the junker in your driveway. (You know that if you lost your job, Mom and Dad would let you move back in. While that's not ideal, it's better than living on the street. But if your car breaks down—again—you'll have to repair it, and quick, or you'll lose your job and end up living with Mom and Dad.) How much do you need to have in emergency savings to fix the car? The best way to figure it is to consider four things:

1. What has it cost to repair the car in the past?
2. What would it cost to put a down payment on a new car if the current repair cost is way more than you're willing to spend?
3. Do you have borrowing power—an unused line of credit or credit card that could be tapped to cover the bill if necessary (keeping in mind that you'd then have to work hard to pay it off so you wouldn't end up paying stunning amounts in interest)?
4. How averse are you to riding the bus? The seriously bus-averse are likely to need more—somewhere between $500 to $1,000—to deal with car repairs, whereas those with reliable cars and/or bus passes may dedicate significantly less to this goal.

How much do you need? Make your best guess: $_____

• **Home repairs.** You fell in love with that 1914 bungalow. The chipped paint and broken windows ensured that you got it for a price that you could afford—although just barely. But then the water heater blew. It was fix it, take cold showers, or start wearing very strong deodorant. Now from the noise that's coming from the furnace, you're thinking that'll go next. How much emergency money you ought to set aside for this repair hinges on the answers to the following questions: How many blankets do I have? Is the furnace in only slightly worse shape than the roof? How do I feel about camping?

It's worth mentioning that if you have a newer house that's in decent shape, home repairs aren't generally emergencies, they're planned events. But if the previous story describes you, you'll need to do a little shopping at your local hardware store or Home Depot to get a read on how much you'll need. The result:

$_____

• **Short-term disability.** Do you have insurance that would pay you monthly income if you were unable to work for an extended period because of some disabling injury or illness? Most people who pay into the Social Security system through payroll taxes do. However, Social Security disability covers just long-term problems—those that last one year or more. (If you're a high-income wage earner, it's likely to replace only a small fraction of your wages.) The best way to deal with the risk of a short-term disability is to insure against it, preferably through a policy offered through your employee benefit plan at work. However, if your disability insurance has a waiting period—or if the monthly payment would be so low that it wouldn't cover your day-to-day fixed expenses—you might want to save a little extra money to fill the gaps.

How much? To answer, you'd be wise to consider your personal risk of disability. If you are in construction and a broken leg would put you out of work, your risks are much higher than if you're like me, a writer, who could be in a full-body cast and still be able to dictate a story. Additionally, your need for emergency money will be affected by just how much sick leave your employer provides. If your employer allows an indefinite amount of sick leave, your need for an emergency fund to handle short-term disability evaporates completely. On the other hand, if you don't get any sick leave and you're in a relatively high-risk profession, you might want at least a month's wages in the bank.

$_____

• **Job loss.** For most adults, losing a job is the biggest potential emergency that isn't covered by life, health, or disability insurance. It is also the primary reason why some financial planners suggest having six months' worth of wages in emergency savings. However, as we've already discussed, keeping a big hoard of cash in low-yielding investments might not be the best thing to do for your long-term financial health—unless, of course, your risk of job loss is high and the potential repercussions of that job loss are great. For instance, you work in an industry (or for a company) that's undergoing major change. Layoffs are rampant. You are the only wage earner in your household, and your monthly expenses are so close to your monthly income that even a short period of unemployment would send your household into a tailspin. If that's you, load up on emergency savings. (As a practical matter, though, you might want to keep a portion of your emergency money in slightly longer-term, but safe, investments such as certificates of deposit. These lock your money up for a few months, but pay a little more than simple savings accounts that allow you to pull your money out at any time. And, as long as you keep the maturities relatively short—five or six months—they'll provide the same safety net. You'd just drain other savings first in the event of a job loss; take the CD money out last.) On the other hand, if you have a working spouse, don't spend all of your income, work in a relatively stable job in an industry that's growing, and have the reputation and skills to find other work quickly, your need for emergency savings may be relatively minimal.

$_____

• **Death of a spouse.** The death of a wage-earning spouse is not only a tragedy, it's a financial emergency. However, it is not one that an emergency savings account can be adequately prepared for. That's simply because the gap between what you as the surviving spouse would be able to earn and what you'd need to save is likely to be far too great, particularly if you have young children. (Indeed, even if your stay-at-home spouse dies, you are likely to face serious economic consequences. Consider adding the cost of hiring a full-time baby-sitter, cook, and housekeeper to your monthly budget, and then give your stay-at-home spouse a grateful kiss.)

For this risk, you need life insurance. To determine how much, consider what would happen if you or your spouse died. How much of an annual gap would there be between what you need and what you earn? How many years would you need to fill that gap? Calculate those figures, and then go to the Internet (or a life insurance agent) to buy a policy big enough to fill the gap.

It is worth mentioning that term life insurance prices are exceptionally cheap, if you are young and healthy. A thirty-something parent who doesn't smoke or have chronic ailments can easily pick up a $1 million, twenty-year level-premium term life insurance policy for less than $600 annually—less if you're a woman. Some Web-based shopping services you might consult: 20yearterm.com, intelliquote.com, accuquote.com, termfinder.com, and reliaquote.com. There's just one thing to beware of: insurance agents who try to talk you into a more expensive policy that has more bells and whistles. ("This one will return your premium at the end of the policy term!" "This one will build up a cash value that you can borrow against, if you ever need to!") You don't need bells and whistles. You need protection from an emergency. All those bells and whistles will cost you a small fortune, and that money is better invested elsewhere.

$_____

• **Serious illness.** Years ago, if you had a medical ailment, it was usually covered by your employee health insurance plan. Today, those plans often leave significant gaps in coverage. In fact, many companies are moving to high-deductible plans, where you would need to pay the first $1,000 to $5,000 of your medical bills. If you have a significant deductible, or coverage that doesn't pay for prescriptions or root canals, you might want to save to cover those gaps.

$_____

• **Total emergency fund needed.** Before you simply add all the numbers in the previous paragraphs (plus a bit more for unmentioned emergencies that you may not anticipate), remember that no one (except the biblical Job) is likely to suffer every emergency imaginable back-to-back or at the same time. Put aside an amount that's sufficient to handle your biggest emergency. Once that crisis is over, vow to quickly replenish the emergency savings.

$_____

For appropriate investments for your emergency money, see "Investing for Safety" in Chapter 4.

Goal: Saving for a Car

Of all financial goals, figuring out how much you need to save for a car—and how to invest that money—is among the easiest. That's because you already have a clear idea of the type of car you want. You know—or easily can find out—roughly how much it costs. In addition, you can fairly accurately predict when you want to make your purchase. (Of course, the reality of how much you've got saved could cause you to change the purchase date or model of the car.)

You also know just how precious this goal is to you, so you can make some reasonable determinations about how much investment risk you're willing to take in the pursuit of that goal. If, for example, you wouldn't fall into a deep depression if your Porsche purchase had to be delayed because the stock market had a bad stretch, you could gamble a bit and put part—or even all—of your auto-purchase money into domestic stocks.

On the other hand, if you are trying to buy a new Honda because your old one is nearly worn out and you're worried about your ability to get safely to and from work, you'd be wise to invest more conservatively. You'd want to put your money in high-grade fixed-income investments that would mature at the point that you wanted to make your purchase. (If you prefer to invest through mutual funds, a medium-term bond fund that has a fairly stable net asset value would do the trick.)

The only other issue is how you want to pay for the car: Will you buy it outright with cash, lease it, or put some money down and finance the rest? Your answer will determine just how much you need to save. How much do you figure?

$_____

Now, assuming that you need to save that money over time, we'll need to do a little math to determine just how much you need to save each month to reach your goal. You've written the amount that you think you'll need. Do you have current savings? If so, log the amount you've already got on the following line and multiply that number by the appropriate multiplier in the chart below. The appropriate multiplier is the one that corresponds to the amount of time you have to reach your goal and the interest rate you believe you'll earn on your money in the meantime. You'll notice there are only four interest rates listed, ranging from 3 percent to 6 percent. In a normal market, this is the best you can expect to do on relatively short-term savings (anything from one to five years). If you earn more than this, celebrate. It means you can buy the car sooner or with a bigger down payment or get more extras. (A note of advice—the less time you have until the purchase, the lower your likely rate of return.)

Your current savings:

$_____ × _____ = $_____

(amount I have) (multiplier) (future value of my savings)

TIME TO GOAL	ESTIMATED RATE OF RETURN			
	3%	4%	5%	6%
1 year	1.03	1.04	1.05	1.06
2 years	1.062	1.083	1.105	1.127
3 years	1.094	1.127	1.161	1.197
4 years	1.127	1.173	1.221	1.270
5 years	1.162	1.221	1.283	1.349

Now subtract the amount you need from the amount you have. This is the gap that you'll need to fill with additional monthly savings. Gap:

$_____

How much will that cost you each month? Since this is a relatively short-term goal, the interest you'll earn on your monthly savings is not likely to amount to much. As a result, you can save the fancy math and go for something simple: Divide your number by the number of months you have to go. In other words, if you figure you'll need $1,000 more than you've got and you want to buy the car in two years, divide $1,000 by 24 months. You must save $41.67 per month to reach your goal. Your result:

$_____

Appropriate investments for auto-purchase money can range from very low risk to relatively high risk. Low-risk investments, such as those mentioned in Chapter 4 in the section "Investing for Safety," are appropriate if you need the car very soon and you can't stand the idea of delaying the purchase because you took a loss on your investments. You can choose moderate-risk investments, including short- to medium-term bonds, bond funds, and stock mutual funds, if you have a little more time and a market loss won't devastate you.

If the car is a luxury and you can handle delaying the purchase, you can invest in growth investments, including stock mutual funds or even individual stocks. If you're lucky, these investments could return significantly more than you planned, leaving you with a bigger down payment or a better car. If you're not lucky, you may have to go for the Lumina rather than the Lexus. If this is your biggest problem in life, count yourself lucky.

Goal: Buying a House

The process of figuring out how much you ought to save for a house and how you ought to invest that money is very similar to the process you go through when saving for a car. You simply need to consider what kind of house you want and what it costs.

If you want to buy with a traditional 20 percent down payment—which will net you the lowest interest rate—you multiply the cost of the house by 20 percent. That's the amount that you need to save. You can't possibly save that much before you buy? If the market's right and your credit is good, you can probably get a loan with a low down payment. But you'll end up paying a somewhat higher rate of interest if you do. However, even in the best of circumstances, you'll need somewhere between 3 percent and 5 percent of the purchase price in cash to handle a down payment and closing costs. Keep in mind that home prices can rise over time too, so make sure your estimate gives you a little wiggle room. Enter the estimated down payment amount for your home:

$_____

Where is that money going to come from? Two sources: the money you already have saved and invested, and the additional savings you'll set aside each month. To figure out how much you need to save monthly, you first need to know roughly what your current savings will be worth in the future. To do that, multiply your current savings by the appropriate figure in the following chart. The less time you have before you want to buy, the more conservative you need to be about the rate of return you're likely to earn on your money.

Your current savings:

$_____ × _____ = $_____
                  (multiplier)   *(future value of my savings)*

■ Goal: House (Future Value of Savings)

TIME TO GOAL	RATE OF RETURN							
	3%	4%	5%	6%	7%	8%	9%	10%
1 year	1.03	1.04	1.05	1.06	1.07	1.08	1.09	1.10
2 years	1.062	1.083	1.105	1.127	1.150	1.173	1.196	1.220
3 years	1.094	1.127	1.161	1.197	1.233	1.270	1.309	1.348
4 years	1.127	1.173	1.221	1.270	1.322	1.376	1.431	1.489
5 years	1.162	1.221	1.283	1.349	1.418	1.490	1.566	1.645
6 years	1.196	1.271	1.349	1.432	1.520	1.613	1.712	1.818
7 years	1.233	1.322	1.418	1.520	1.630	1.747	1.873	2.007
8 years	1.271	1.376	1.490	1.614	1.748	1.892	2.049	2.218
9 years	1.309	1.432	1.567	1.714	1.874	2.049	2.241	2.450
10 years	1.349	1.491	1.647	1.819	2.010	2.220	2.451	2.707

Now subtract what you'll have from the amount you want. The result is the amount you need to save between now and then.

$_____

How much do you need to save each month to accumulate that amount? Assuming that your home purchase is more than a few years away, you'll want to figure in the impact of investment returns on your monthly savings to come up with a fairly accurate estimate. (It's only "fairly accurate" because you're often guessing on the investment return. Frankly, you're probably guessing a bit about the time you have before you buy, too. Realize that these are educated guesses that ought to get you close to your goal. In the end, you might have a bit more or a bit less than you planned.)

$_____ × _____ = $_____

(amount you want) (multiplier) (additional monthly savings needed)

■ Goal: House (Additional Savings Needed)

TIME TO GOAL	RATE OF RETURN							
	3%	4%	5%	6%	7%	8%	9%	10%
3 years	.0266	.0262	.0258	.0254	.0250	.0247	.0243	.0239
4 years	.0196	.0192	.0188	.0184	.0181	.0177	.0174	.0170
5 years	.0155	.0151	.0147	.0143	.0140	.0136	.0133	.0129
6 years	.0127	.0123	.0119	.0116	.0112	.0109	.0105	.0102
7 years	.0107	.0103	.0100	.0096	.0092	.0089	.0086	.0083
8 years	.0092	.0088	.0085	.0081	.0078	.0075	.0071	.0068
9 years	.0081	.0077	.0073	.0070	.0067	.0063	.0060	.0057
10 years	.0071	.0068	.0064	.0061	.0058	.0055	.0052	.0049

To find the right investment mix for your home savings, you need to go through virtually the same thought process as the person who wants to buy a car does. Consider whether this is a necessity or a luxury. How devastating will it be if the home purchase is delayed, or if you have to buy a little less house than you planned?

You'd be wise to invest in a mixture of income and growth investments. That will keep some of your principal relatively safe while giving you a chance at getting your nest egg to grow faster than the rate of inflation—a virtual must if you ever want to get in that home. Since your goal is relatively short term, you would be wise to stick with mutual funds rather than trying to pick individual stocks for the growth portion of your portfolio. Mutual funds can provide you with much greater diversification of your assets, which usually smooths out the big bumps in market value.

Goal: Paying for College

There's only one problem with figuring out how much money your kids are going to need for college: your kids. The darned youngsters just aren't born with labels reading "Destined for Harvard" or "Community College, Here I Come!" Naturally, the difference between paying for Harvard and paying for a community college amounts to a fortune. In fact, most middle-income parents could probably pay for community colleges—and even state universities—as they go, since many of those schools cost about the same per semester as it costs to send the kids to summer camp. The cost of Harvard? Brace yourself: Tuition alone was nearly $35,000 in the 2007–2008 academic year. The all-inclusive cost, with room and board and books: roughly $50,000.

Unfortunately, the best time to save is when the children are tiny (that allows compound interest to work and makes the job of saving enough significantly easier on you). But when they're young, you have no idea what school you're saving for, so you aren't going to know whether you are saving too much or not enough. What do you do? You guess.

If you went to an Ivy League school and thought it was the best thing on the planet, you might want to save for Ivy League tuition to give your child that option. To get an idea of what that will cost, go to the College Board's website at www.collegeboard.com or buy the annual *College Cost & Financial Aid* handbook, which gives advice on financial aid and spells out the cost of tuition, room, board, and books at thousands of U.S. colleges and universities. College cost inflation rates have been running about 6 percent per year. To calculate the full amount you'll need to save, you should factor that in.

If, on the other hand, you paid for your own education and thought that the corresponding independence was worth its weight in gold, your education savings goals may be significantly more modest. Obviously, if you expect your children to pay a significant portion of the cost, you'll need to save less than you would if you wanted to finance their education yourself. In any event, you need to pick a number. Weigh the factors you consider important and decide how much assistance you plan to give each child. Then use the following chart and worksheet to figure out just how much you need to save each month to have that amount in the future. If you have more than one child, add the numbers to determine how much to put in the college account each month to finance education for the whole family. A quick note: Unless you are very well-heeled, save this money in your name, not in your children's names—or save it in a so-called 529 plan. (You can learn all about 529 plans in Chapter 12.) That will give your children a better chance of qualifying for student aid later, and it will allow you to keep control of the cash—just in case Junior turns out to be irresponsible and wants to go to Europe (or the Ferrari dealer) rather than to school.

■ Goal: College (Future Value of Savings)

	RATE OF RETURN							
TIME TO GOAL	3%	4%	5%	6%	7%	8%	9%	10%
1 year	1.03	1.04	1.05	1.06	1.07	1.08	1.09	1.10
2 years	1.06	1.08	1.10	1.13	1.15	1.17	1.20	1.22
3 years	1.09	1.13	1.16	1.20	1.23	1.27	1.31	1.35
4 years	1.13	1.17	1.22	1.27	1.32	1.38	1.43	1.49
5 years	1.16	1.22	1.28	1.35	1.42	1.49	1.57	1.64
6 years	1.19	1.27	1.35	1.43	1.52	1.61	1.71	1.81
7 years	1.23	1.32	1.42	1.52	1.63	1.75	1.87	2.01
8 years	1.27	1.38	1.49	1.61	1.75	1.89	2.05	2.22
9 years	1.31	1.43	1.57	1.71	1.87	2.05	2.24	2.45
10 years	1.35	1.49	1.65	1.82	2.01	2.22	2.45	2.71
11 years	1.38	1.54	1.71	1.90	2.10	2.33	2.58	2.85
12 years	1.43	1.60	1.80	2.01	2.25	2.52	2.81	3.14
13 years	1.47	1.67	1.89	2.13	2.41	2.72	3.07	3.45
14 years	1.51	1.73	1.98	2.26	2.58	2.94	3.34	3.80
15 years	1.56	1.80	2.08	2.40	2.76	3.17	3.64	4.18
16 years	1.60	1.87	2.18	2.54	2.95	3.43	3.97	4.59
17 years	1.65	1.95	2.29	2.69	3.16	3.70	4.33	5.05

If you already have money set aside for college, use the preceding worksheet to determine what your current savings will be worth in the future. You can subtract the result from your savings goal before using the second worksheet, which will tell you how much you need to save each month from now until your kids graduate high school to have the amount you want available when they need it.

Your current savings:

$_____ × _____ = $_____
            (multiplier)   *(future value of my savings)*

Subtract the result from the total dollar amount you want to have for each child. That's the amount you need to save between now and then. You'll use this goal figure in the college cost worksheet on page 48.

How much do you need to save each month to accumulate the right amount? Assuming the kids' schooling is more than a few years away, you'll need to account for investment returns. That's always a guesstimate. But understand that if your kids are young, the guess about investment return could have a big impact on how much you save. The higher your anticipated investment return, the less you need to save each month. But, if you guess unrealistically, your savings won't amount to anything close to what you've calculated.

Making an educated guess about investment returns is tough, but you should figure that the more conservative you are (look back at the results of your risk quiz), the lower your investment return is likely to be. In addition, if you are saving for toddlers, you can expect a better return—in the range of 7 or 8 percent—than if you're investing for teens. If you have teenagers, figure on a 6 percent return or less. You may earn more, of course, but you could also earn less. When guessing, it's best to guess conservatively and be happily surprised than the other way around.

Appropriate investments for your kids' college savings depend on how long they have before enrolling. If you're saving for a teenager, be relatively conservative. You can put some money in stocks and other growth investments such as balanced mutual funds, but not a lot. Most of your savings should go in short- and medium-term income

■ Goal: College (Additional Savings Needed)

TIME TO GOAL	RATE OF RETURN							
	3%	4%	5%	6%	7%	8%	9%	10%
3 years	.0266	.0262	.0258	.0254	.0250	.0247	.0243	.0239
4 years	.0196	.0192	.0188	.0184	.0181	.0177	.0174	.0170
5 years	.0155	.0151	.0147	.0143	.0140	.0136	.0133	.0129
6 years	.0127	.0123	.0119	.0116	.0112	.0109	.0105	.0102
7 years	.0107	.0103	.0100	.0096	.0092	.0089	.0086	.0083
8 years	.0092	.0088	.0085	.0081	.0078	.0075	.0071	.0068
9 years	.0081	.0077	.0073	.0070	.0067	.0063	.0060	.0057
10 years	.0071	.0068	.0064	.0061	.0058	.0055	.0052	.0049
11 years	.0064	.0060	.0057	.0054	.0050	.0047	.0045	.0042
12 years	.0058	.0054	.0051	.0048	.0044	.0041	.0039	.0036
13 years	.0052	.0049	.0046	.0042	.0039	.0037	.0034	.0031
14 years	.0048	.0044	.0041	.0038	.0035	.0032	.0030	.0027
15 years	.0044	.0041	.0037	.0034	.0031	.0029	.0026	.0024
16 years	.0041	.0037	.0034	.0031	.0028	.0026	.0023	.0021
17 years	.0038	.0034	.0031	.0028	.0026	.0023	.0021	.0019

investments that will mature when your child is ready to enroll. If you save through a 529 plan, the money manager is likely to suggest an age-appropriate portfolio that's very conservatively invested. On the other hand, if you're saving for a toddler, you can be aggressive. Put the bulk of your savings in stocks and very little (if any) in fixed-income investments.

If you have several children—some in high school and some in diapers—you'll want a broad mix of investments, so you'll have some money in relatively stable investments to ensure the funds are there for the high schooler and some money in stocks to help the baby.

■ College Cost Calculator

I want to give _____ for college: $_____
       (child's name)   *(dollar amount)*

Number of years before this child is old enough to enroll: _____

$_____ x _____ = $_____
(amount you want)   *(multiplier from chart)*   *(monthly savings required)*

I want to give _____ for college: $_____
       (child's name)   *(dollar amount)*

Number of years before this child is old enough to enroll: _____

$_____ x _____ = $_____
(amount you want)   *(multiplier from chart)*   *(monthly savings required)*

I want to give _____ for college: $_____
       (child's name)   *(dollar amount)*

Number of years before this child is old enough to enroll: _____

$_____ x _____ = $_____
(amount you want)   *(multiplier from chart)*   *(monthly savings required)*

I want to give _____ for college: $_____
       (child's name)   *(dollar amount)*

Number of years before this child is old enough to enroll: _____

$_____ x _____ = $_____
(amount you want)   *(multiplier from chart)*   *(monthly savings required)*

Total amount of monthly savings needed

= $_____
       (sum of monthly savings for all children)

48

Goal: Freedom and Options

Let's say you're young. You don't have kids. You are happy in your apartment. You don't need a fancy car. You could save money, but why? Here's a thought: Buy yourself future freedom. Think about your future life and what you, as a person, hold dear. Do you want, for example, the ability to stay home and raise kids (assuming, of course, that you'll one day have them)? Would you like to know that if you someday work for a complete jerk, you could quit and survive for a while without an income? Do you imagine that you may want to retire early? Or take summerlong vacations with the partner of your dreams (someday, after you meet him or her, naturally)?

If so, you're in a great spot. You can save today for goals you may have at some point in the future. How diligently you save now should depend on the likelihood of these future goals. For instance, if you know you love kids and you'd want to spend at least a few years raising them at home, save diligently. You have nothing to lose and great freedom to gain. Because it is virtually impossible to put a dollar amount on a goal that doesn't yet exist, you shouldn't torture yourself trying to figure the right amount to save and invest each month. Instead, figure out an amount you can afford to save. Have that amount automatically deducted from your paycheck or checking account. Invest it aggressively—after all, you have plenty of time to wait out market swings, since you haven't even figured out what the money is for yet. And then, aside from an annual investment checkup (something you need to do with all your investments), forget about it. One day you'll wake up and realize this money you've got gives you options that your friends don't have. That's a nice feeling.

When investing this money, go for broke. Read Chapter 5 on picking individual stocks and think about international investing (Chapter 11) as well. If you're not wild about picking and choosing individual stocks or simply don't have the time to do it, check out Chapter 8 on mutual funds.

Goal: Retirement

Trying to figure out the right amount to save for retirement is tricky. That's simply because before you can possibly know how much you need to save for retirement, you need to know how much you're going to spend in retirement. That means you have to draw up an estimated retirement budget. How? By looking at today's budget and imagining how life will change when you're no longer working.

Will your house be paid off by then? If so, deduct the cost of the mortgage, but not the cost of repairs. Do you plan to golf every day? If so, add in the cost of greens fees. If you're saving diligently each month, you can also scratch that amount from the budget. Retirement is the spending phase of your life. Then there are a few things that are impossible to figure, such as how much you're going to spend on medicine. Figure that you'll buy some health insurance, and leave yourself a little cushion—just in case.

When you're done, you'll have come up with an estimated amount that you expect to spend each month in retirement. We're going to adjust it for inflation by multiplying it by the appropriate number in the following chart. You'll note there's only one inflation rate given. That's because inflation has averaged slightly over 3 percent over the past eighty-one years. Since this is a long-term question, long-term averages are reasonable numbers to use.

$_____ × _____ = $_____
(monthly budget) *(multiplier)*   *(inflation-adjusted budget)*

■ Goal: Retirement (Inflation-Adjusted Budget)

Time to Goal	3% Average Annual Inflation Rate
5 years	1.159
10 years	1.344
15 years	1.558
20 years	1.806
25 years	2.094
30 years	2.427
35 years	2.814
40 years	3.262

Now that you have an inflation-adjusted number, you need to realize that your retirement income is likely to come from three sources: your savings, a company pension (if you have one), and

Social Security. If you qualify for Social Security but don't know how much monthly income to expect from it, call the agency and request an Earnings and Benefit Statement. (The agency can be reached at 800-772-1213, or you can request a statement online at www.ssa.gov.) The agency should send you a statement automatically each year. Realize that the farther you are from retirement age, the less accurate this statement will be. But it's a start.

If you also qualify for a defined benefit plan at work—that's the type that pays monthly benefits for life—call your company and get an estimate of what to expect there, too. You can subtract both of those monthly amounts from the amount that you need before you figure out how much you must save.

It's worth mentioning that both the Social Security and pension projections will change each year, as you rack up raises and additional earnings years in the calculation. Because retirement is such an important goal, it's smart to redo this calculation every few years. You don't need to obsess about it. But the occasional checkup is wise.

Your final step is to determine how much your current retirement savings will generate in monthly income. You can use the multipliers in the following chart to come up with a good guesstimate.

$_____ \times _____ = \$_____$

(current savings)   (multiplier)   (future value of your savings)

■ Goal: Retirement (Future Value of Savings)

TIME TO GOAL	ESTIMATED RATE OF RETURN							
	5%	6%	7%	8%	9%	10%	11%	12%
5 years	1.28	1.35	1.42	1.49	1.57	1.64	1.73	1.82
10 years	1.65	1.82	2.01	2.22	2.45	2.71	2.99	3.30
15 years	2.11	2.45	2.85	3.31	3.84	4.45	5.17	5.99
20 years	2.71	3.31	4.04	4.93	6.01	7.32	8.93	10.89
25 years	3.48	4.46	5.72	7.34	9.41	12.06	15.45	19.79
30 years	4.47	6.02	8.12	10.94	14.73	19.84	26.71	35.95
35 years	5.73	8.12	11.51	16.29	23.06	32.64	46.18	65.31
40 years	7.35	10.96	16.31	24.27	36.11	53.70	79.83	118.65

Now, just to be safe, multiply that figure by 5 percent to determine just how much annual income your nest egg will throw off without your dipping into the principal. Enter the result here:

$_____

Is this less or more than what you figure you'd still need after accounting for your company pension and Social Security? If it's more, you've done enough. You can save more to boost your retirement lifestyle (or to handle any future contingencies that you may not have imagined today), or you can relax. If it's less, you need to save more.

Determining how much more is a two-step process. First, multiply the amount of your monthly shortfall—that's what you expect to need minus what you'll have from your current savings, company pension, and Social Security—by 207. (The result is the nest egg you'd need to generate that amount of cash annually, assuming a 6 percent rate of return.) Result:

$_____

Now multiply that number by the appropriate multiplier from the chart below—the one that most closely corresponds to the number of years you have until retirement and the rate of return you expect to earn on your money.

$_____ × _____ = $_____
(your savings gap)   (multiplier)   (required monthly savings)

■ Goal: Retirement (Required Monthly Savings)

	ESTIMATED RATE OF RETURN							
TIME TO GOAL	5%	6%	7%	8%	9%	10%	11%	12%
5 years	.0147	.0143	.0140	.0136	.0133	.0129	.0126	.0122
10 years	.0064	.0061	.0058	.0055	.0052	.0049	.0046	.0043
15 years	.0037	.0034	.0031	.0029	.0026	.0024	.0022	.0020
20 years	.0024	.0022	.0019	.0017	.0015	.0013	.0011	.0010

Even if you are almost ready to retire, you should keep your retirement money in moderate-to-higher risk investments. Why? They have the most growth over time, and your retirement is likely to be long. Given rising longevity and the large number of people who hope to retire relatively early—say between fifty-five and sixty years old—the typical American can expect to live for twenty to forty years after leaving the workaday world. That means your retirement dollars are invested for a long haul, even if you're close to retiring.

The typical rule of thumb for how much of your retirement money you should invest in stocks versus bonds is this: Subtract your age from 100. The result is the percentage of your retirement assets that ought to be in stocks. But it should never be more than 80 percent or less than 20 percent—or so says the rule of thumb. You can better determine what percentages you're comfortable with by reading about risk in Chapter 2.

Goal: Regular Income

Chances are if you're looking for regular income from your savings, you've passed the accumulation phase of your life and are in the spending phase. In other words, you're probably retired and living on your savings. You don't need to calculate an amount to save. You need good ideas about which investments will deliver a decent amount of regular income from your nest egg. The appropriate investments for you are listed primarily in the "Investing for Income" section of Chapter 4 and in Chapter 7 on investing in bonds. However, be sure to put a portion of your money in stocks, too. That helps diversify your holdings, which both increases the stability of your portfolio and provides some potential for growth.

What's the right portion? Remember the rule of thumb (subtract your age from 100) and put the result in stocks. In other words, if you're 60, you'd still hold 40 percent of your portfolio in stocks. If you're 70, you'd drop the stock holdings to 30 percent of your overall investments. Of course, a rule of thumb is for the average Jane or Joe. If you've got more than enough assets and don't mind taking a few risks, goosing that percentage up a bit won't hurt you. On the other hand, if your risk quiz (Chapter 2) told you that you'd have trouble sleeping at night with more than a tiny amount of risk in your portfolio, edge those numbers down. There's no "right" investment mix in this world. What you're looking for is a comfortable mix for you.

QUICK TAKE

What You'll LEARN

The investing world is full of choices, each with different risks and rewards. Risks vary even among choices within a single investment category—and you're generally rewarded for taking a little more risk. By spreading your investments among different asset categories, you can cut the swings in your investment portfolio—both up and down. This chapter describes:

- Investing for Safety
- Investing for Income
- Investing for Growth
- Investments That Protect You from Inflation
- Speculation
- Investments to Avoid

What You'll DO

- Evaluate the risks and rewards of each type of investment to find options that suit your personality, as well as your portfolio
- Match the money you allocated to fund specific goals to a handful of investments that would do the job

How You'll USE This

You'll make your investment search more manageable by narrowing your choices to the relative few that suit you best. As your assets increase and you become more comfortable with managing your portfolio, you can use this chapter as your personal investment smorgasbord. Return and choose again.

G reta thought she was following sound financial practice by spreading her investments among more than a dozen mutual funds. She reasoned that her portfolio would be diversified enough to reduce the risk of loss. But when the value of small-company stocks plunged one summer, so did Greta's entire portfolio. It turned out that most of her mutual funds were invested in small-company stocks. The moral of this story: Having a lot of investments does not necessarily make your portfolio diversified. What matters is whether you have a lot of different *types* of investments.

It is important to look at the structure of your portfolio and the types of companies that are in it. If you are buying all pharmaceutical stocks or all technology stocks or all international stocks—or, for that matter, all stocks—you are not diversifying, no matter how many different company or mutual fund shares you buy.

The purpose of diversification is to protect your overall portfolio from major shocks. Because different types of investments tend to move at different times—one investment may be moving up in value when another is moving down—having a variety of investments lends stability to a portfolio.

Diversification, however, can also reduce your overall return, as does any strategy that reduces risk. (But you already know that, because you read Chapter 2.) Consider this: A portfolio of big-company stocks gained about 10.4 percent annually on average since 1926, whereas a portfolio that is half stocks and half government bonds returned 8.4 percent. In terms of total wealth over a long time, that difference is substantial. Invest $10,000 at 8.4 percent and leave it alone for thirty years, and you'll have $112,429. Invest the same amount at 10.4 percent, and you'll have much more: $194,568, to be exact.

So the real trick to diversification is doing just enough to allow yourself to sleep—and meet near-term goals—without doing so much that you rob yourself of generous long-term returns.

How do you do it? If you have read Chapter 3 and followed the instructions, you've already taken the first step, which is to divide your investments by goal. That allows you to allocate your assets based on how long you have before you need that specific pile of cash—and how you'd react if the pile was a bit bigger or smaller than you'd planned. That determination immediately leads you toward different investment categories, because the nature of certain investments makes them best suited for specific purposes. As you go along, you'll see more clearly why.

Your second step is to diversify your holdings within each of your asset categories. So, for instance, you've already figured out that you need X amount of money for retirement and that the bulk of that money ought to be invested in the growth investment category. However, you now realize there is a wide array of different growth investments to choose from. You've got to pick one, two, or several to diversify your portfolio within that asset group. That should prevent your entire retirement fund from evaporating before you spend it.

If you have dedicated a lot of money to a specific category, you'll want to choose several investments within it or invest through a mutual fund, which will do that for you. If your pot of cash in a particular category is small, you can make do with just one or two investments per category.

What are your choices?

 ## INVESTING FOR SAFETY

The primary characteristic of supersafe investments—called *cash and cash equivalents* by those in the know on Wall Street—is that they have some type of government backing that protects the principal. They're highly liquid, which means you can get your hands on your money fairly quickly and easily. That makes all of these investments ideal places to put your emergency money.

The downside: Because there is so little risk, there's virtually no return. Once you factor in inflation and income taxes, you can expect to actually lose buying power over time in each of these investments. As a result, you want to be careful not to put more money in safe, low-yielding investments than absolutely necessary.

If you completed the "Goal: Emergency Money" section in Chapter 3 and came out with a big number to be invested in this category—an

DIVERSIFICATION

amount exceeding three to six months' wages—you might want to recheck your figures while reminding yourself that you're saving for fairly likely emergencies only. Remember, too, that unused borrowing power on your credit cards can be used just like an emergency fund. If you've got credit cards that you're not using, you can use them to pay for your auto repairs and even medical bills, if you're in a pinch. Naturally, you'll want to pay off the credit cards as quickly as possible after your emergency has passed—credit card debt is expensive. But they can provide you with a little extra leeway.

Here are your choices when you're investing for safety:

Bank Deposits

Whether your money is in a checking account, passbook savings account, money market account, or short-term certificate of deposit, deposits in your local bank or savings and loan have the dual advantage of being available at nearly a moment's notice and being federally insured up to $100,000.

What will this money earn? It depends on the type of account and market conditions when you're depositing. However, **checking accounts** typically pay just 1 percent to 3 percent, depending on your balance. On the bright side, banks normally waive your monthly checking account fees if you maintain a minimum balance—usually anywhere from $500 to $1,500. That can save you anywhere from $3 to $10 a month. Since you need a checking account to pay your bills, maintaining that minimum balance gives you some cushion and saves you a fee, which isn't half bad.

Passbook savings accounts frequently earn no more than your checking account, and they're half as useful. On occasion they'll pay 1 percent or 2 percent more than the checking account, but once you consider the fact that they don't (usually) land you free checking, that's no big bargain. But every bank is a little different, so check to see if your bank aggregates all your balances when determining whether to waive your checking account fees. If it does, and the passbook account pays more, certainly take advantage of it.

Money market accounts at banks are almost the same as passbook savings, except the bank gives you a checkbook to go with the account. But chances are the bank won't let you write lots of small checks on the account without some sort of penalty.

Certificates of deposit, more commonly called **CDs**, are deposit contracts between you and the bank. You agree to deposit your money for a set period of time; the bank agrees to pay you a set rate of interest over that same time period. If you pull your money out before the time is up, you get penalized. (Usually the bank takes away all or part of the interest you earned.) The rate on your CD varies with the duration and size of the deposit. Short-term CDs usually pay less than long-term CDs. Big depositors are offered better rates than small depositors are.

A short-term CD—a time deposit of six months or less—is a great place to put money for predictable short-term goals. For instance, if you need to have $500 or $1,000 saved to pay your next insurance premium or your real estate taxes, you can plunk that money into a CD. Since you know when those payments are due, you can choose a CD that matures at just the right time. By the same token, because you've locked your money up for a set period (taken a little risk), the bank is likely to pay you a bit more than it would pay on a passbook savings or money market account.

It's also worth noting that, if you have a fair amount of money or are a particularly good bank customer, the advertised CD rates may not apply to you. You can usually get a higher rate, particularly if neighboring banks are offering more for the same deposit. But you have to ask for it. The difference between the advertised rate and the better rate you could negotiate may be only a matter of 0.10 or 0.20 percentage points. But, if your deposit is substantial, that can add up. All it requires of you is the few extra seconds it takes to ask.

DID YOU KNOW?
Being a Good Bank Customer

What does it mean to be a "good bank customer"? Generally speaking, banks give you favorable treatment if you have several different types of accounts, such as a mortgage, a credit card, and a savings account, and you handle them responsibly. That means you don't bounce checks, and you pay your credit card and mortgage bills on time. Being a good bank customer, incidentally, can win you more than preferential CD rates. In the unlikely event that you do have a late payment or a bounced check, for instance, the bank will often waive the fee.

One caution: Bank deposits and CDs are only safe to the degree that they're federally insured. The Federal Deposit Insurance Corp. (FDIC) offers the backing of the U.S. government on just $100,000 per person, per bank. There are ways to title accounts to get additional insurance. However, hundreds of millions of dollars in excess funds are lost in bank failures every year because people deposit more than $100,000, without going through the trouble of ensuring that all the money is federally insured. If you are going to deposit more than $100,000 in any one bank, make sure you read the FDIC's brochure on deposit insurance and follow the instructions carefully. You can find it at www.fdic.gov.

Money Market Mutual Funds

Money market mutual funds are offered by mutual fund companies (see Chapter 8) rather than banks. While they are considered very safe, because they invest in short-term government and corporate securities and bank deposits, they do not guarantee your principal value. As a result, they pay somewhat higher average rates of return—usually about 2 or 3 percentage points more than a bank money market account (which does offer a guarantee of your principal value). Usually you have the ability to write checks against these accounts, but the mutual fund company may limit the number of checks you can write each year. So, generally speaking, these accounts cannot be used to pay your monthly bills. However, they can be used, like CDs, to hold money for big near-term obligations, such as insurance and tax payments.

Unless your fund manager is doing something fancy (and probably inadvisable), you should expect these funds to pay roughly the same amount as you'd get if you invested in a mixture of short-term Treasury securities (see below) and bank deposits. If your fund is paying considerably more, carefully read the prospectus (see Chapter 8). Particularly concentrate on the section in the prospectus labeled "risks." If you are getting a higher return, you are taking a bigger risk. There's no way around it. That's okay as long as you know what the risks are and you're prepared to handle them.

Short-Term Treasury Securities

Every week the U.S. government borrows money by issuing short-term IOUs that pay set rates of interest. These IOUs are called Treasury bills (T-bills), and they are held by literally millions of investors all around the globe.

Treasury bills technically don't pay interest. Instead, they're sold at a discount to their face value. In other words, a $10,000 fifty-two-week bill may sell for $9,500. At maturity, the buyer gets back the $10,000 face value—$500 more than was paid—which generates an effective yield of 5.26 percent.

You can buy Treasury bills that mature—or pay off—in thirteen weeks, twenty-six weeks, or fifty-two weeks. They are sold in minimum denominations of $10,000. If you have more than $10,000 to invest, you can buy additional bills in multiples of $1,000.

Treasury bills can be purchased through a broker or directly from the Treasury. If you buy them from a broker, you will pay a commission that simply reduces the rate of return that you'll earn on each T-bill. If you buy them from the Treasury, you don't pay a commission, but you'll have to set up an account with the Treasury department to get started. If you're connected to the Internet, this shouldn't be too difficult. Go to www.treasurydirect.gov.

Treasuries, like bank deposits, are backed by the full faith and credit of the U.S. government. That makes them very safe and secure. However, if you try to sell one before it matures, you might get slightly less than its face value. Treasury yields vary based on interest rates at the time they're sold. Their average return since 1926 has been 3.7 percent, according to Ibbotson Associates, a Chicago-based market research and consulting firm.

 INVESTING FOR INCOME

At some point in your life—perhaps after you retire, perhaps sooner—you'll want at least a portion of your investments to generate income. That income can be used to supplement your wages, Social Security benefits, or pension, making your life more comfortable. Even before you want investment income to live on, however, you might want to include some income-oriented investments in your portfolio to handle shorter-term and medium-term goals that are important to you—things like buying a house or car or paying your teenager's college tuition. There are numerous investments that can provide that kind of income, including bank certificates of deposit, bonds, and dividend-paying stocks.

Didn't we talk about CDs in the "safety" investing category? And aren't stocks listed under "growth investing"? Yes. But the CDs and stocks mentioned here are significantly different from those discussed above. That's because the CDs purchased for income are the longer-term variety, which pay higher rates of interest in exchange for your promise to leave your principal alone for a significant time, such as a year or more. If you break your promise, you'll pay for it—sometimes dearly.

Meanwhile, although many growth stocks pay dividends, those dividends usually account for just a tiny fraction of the total return on a growth stock investment. On the other hand, some "mature" companies have reached a point where they are unlikely to grow quickly, if at all. At that stage, instead of plowing profits back into the business to help it grow, these companies pay out a large portion of their profits to investors in the form of quarterly cash dividends. The stocks of these companies are considered "income" stocks. Many of these same companies also issue so-called preferred stocks, which can sometimes bear a greater resemblance to bonds than to stocks.

Certificates of Deposit

Certificates of deposit are bank deposits, like any other. They're insured by the federal government to $100,000, which means you can't lose any principal—and usually can't lose any of the promised interest—unless you pull your money out of the bank before the end of the contracted period. (Or unless the principal and interest you have in one institution exceeds $100,000 and the bank fails.)

If you pull your money out early, you are likely to face an early withdrawal penalty that can amount to six months of interest payments or more. If your savings have not generated enough interest to pay the penalty, the bank has the right to take the penalty out of your principal.

How much would the early withdrawal penalty be on your CD? It varies based on the maturity and the bank. On a six-month CD, it's common to be charged one month's interest. On a five-year CD, the penalty can be between six months' and one year's worth of interest. If there's any chance that you'll need your funds before the end of the contracted period, ask your banker about the early withdrawal penalties and under what circumstances these penalties can be waived.

Treasury Notes

Treasury notes are a lot like Treasury bills—they're issued and backed by the U.S. government. That government backing means that Uncle Sam promises to pay back the principal and interest on your note, as long as you hold the note to maturity.

The difference between Treasury notes and Treasury bills is how long they take to mature, or pay back your principal. Whereas Treasury bills are short-term investments, with maturities of one year or less, Treasury notes can be purchased with two-year, three-year, five-year, or ten-year maturities. The government pays back your principal on the maturity date, and it generally also sends you interest payments at regular intervals during the years that you hold the note.

However, Treasury notes are often sold before maturity. If you sell the note before maturity, you could make money or lose money on the sale. Generally speaking, when interest rates fall, the market value of old high-interest notes rises (because you have an investment that guarantees a higher rate of return than the market currently offers). Conversely, when market interest rates rise, the value of old, relatively low-interest notes falls.

Treasury notes are sold in denominations of $1,000 or more. They can be purchased directly from the government through the Treasury's noncompetitive bidding process at www.treasurydirect.gov, or they can be purchased through brokers. Under normal circumstances, Treasury notes pay higher interest rates than Treasury bills.

Treasury Bonds

These are just like Treasury notes, but they're issued with even longer maturities. You can buy Treasury bonds that mature thirty or forty years from the date they are issued. Again, as long as you hold the bonds to maturity, the U.S. government promises to pay back your principal, plus interest at a set rate. Similarly, if you sell before maturity, the amount of money you make or lose is based on the prevailing interest rates and market conditions at the time of the sale.

It's important to note that when interest rates climb or fall, the value of Treasury bonds varies even more than the value of Treasury notes (discussed in the previous section). That's simply because your money is locked up at a set interest rate for a longer period of time, which makes Treasury bonds more volatile than the shorter-term Treasury notes and far more volatile than the very short-term Treasury bills.

However, since volatility is a type of risk, and you usually get rewarded for taking increased risks in the financial markets, Treasury bonds typically pay more—often 1 or 2 percentage points more—than ten-year Treasury notes. (You'll find more on bonds in Chapter 7.)

Ginnie Maes

These are the best known of a variety of so-called mortgage-backed securities. What's a mortgage-backed security? It's a loan that's pooled together with a bunch of other loans and then turned into a security through the magic of investment banking.

Let's look at an example to explain how mortgage-backed securities work: John and Jane Doe buy a house and finance it with a $100,000, 9 percent fixed-rate loan. Their bank then sells the Does' mortgage to a third party. It may be to another bank or financial institution, but usually it is to one of several quasi-governmental agencies such as the Government National Mortgage Association (Ginnie Mae), the Federal National Mortgage Association (Fannie Mae), or the Federal Home Loan Mortgage Corp. (Freddie Mac).

Despite their cutesy names, Ginnie, Freddie, and Fannie are major corporations with some U.S. government backing. They take the Does' mortgage and put it into a pool of similar mortgages that pay like amounts of interest and are expected to pay off at the same time. They then sell interests in this pool of mortgages to investors. What investors get when they buy a Ginnie Mae, for instance, is a bond that pays somewhat less than what the Does are paying on their loan. (If the Does pay 9 percent, for example, the investors may get 8 percent; the 1 percent difference is eaten up in fees and charges.) Because Ginnie, Fannie, and Freddie are government backed, these organizations must make up for any losses if the Does stop paying on their loan.

There's only one problem with the securities sold by Ginnie, Freddie, and Fannie: the Does. John and Jane may never default on their loan, but when interest rates fall, they are going to refinance their mortgage to get a lower rate. So instead of getting comparatively high rates of interest for thirty years, investors in mortgage-backed securities are likely to get back only their principal. In market-speak, that's called prepayment risk. If rates rise, the Does will hang on to their mortgage, and investors will be stuck with comparatively low-yielding securities for thirty years. That's called interest-rate risk.

Brokers who sell Ginnies should explain these risks to investors who buy them.

CMOs

Collateralized mortgage obligations, or CMOs, started life as mortgage-backed securities. But then some smart investment bankers thought about the problem with the Does. They knew they couldn't change the Does' behavior, but they could find ways to "restructure" the average mortgage-backed security to shift around some of the prepayment risk and interest-rate risk.

How? They took the Does' mortgage (and thousands of other mortgages like it) and sliced it into pieces. Each piece included an element of the original mortgage. For instance, one slice might give investors the right to half of the interest payments made by the Does, plus the first repayment of principal. The next piece might give the investor the right to the second repayment of principal, plus another half of the interest. A final piece might be structured like a zero-coupon bond, where the investor doesn't get anything until the bond matures, at which time he's repaid an amount that works out to what he paid for the bond plus some. (In reality, CMOs are usually cut into more slices than that, but you get the idea.)

Of course, investors who buy the first type of CMO have the greatest prepayment risk, and investors in the final category have the greatest interest-rate risk. Investment bankers assess the risks of each slice (or *tranche*, as they like to say on Wall Street), and they price the securities with that in mind. Thus, some CMOs—which usually sell in minimum denominations ranging from $1,000 to $25,000—sell for less than their face value, others sell for more.

Corporate Bonds

Some companies finance growth by selling debt—IOUs—to investors. These formal IOUs are called bonds, and in many ways, they're like the bonds issued by the U.S. Treasury. They have stated interest rates and maturity dates, and they're sold through brokers.

However, because individual companies are presumably less financially secure than the U.S. government, which can exercise its taxing authority if it ever runs short of cash, corporations pay higher rates of interest than the U.S. Treasury pays on bonds with similar maturity dates.

The less financially sound the corporation, the higher the interest rate. You're taking a bigger risk that such a company will default and fail to pay back your principal and interest, so you get a higher return. When the bonds are especially high risk and high yield, they're called junk bonds.

Conversely, bonds issued by healthy companies—or backed by bond insurance—pay comparatively less interest but pose far less default risk to investors. High-quality bonds are frequently termed investment quality, triple-A, double-A, or simply A-rated bonds.

Properly chosen, this type of bond can increase the yield on the income-producing portion of your investment portfolio while only modestly increasing the risks.

Municipal Bonds

Issued by state and local governments and some government agencies, municipal bonds pay relatively low interest rates, but the interest you earn is usually federal and state tax free. That can make these bonds attractive to investors who are in high tax brackets and who would otherwise have to pay a large portion of their interest earnings to Uncle Sam (and, perhaps, to Aunt California or Aunt New York).

Like corporate bonds, municipal bonds are graded. Some are good quality, some poor. Some are backed by private insurance companies that promise to pay bondholders the principal and interest that's due if the issuer fails to pay. By and large, the safer your municipal bond, the less interest you get.

REITs

Real Estate Investment Trusts, or REITs, are publicly traded investment companies that pour their cash into shopping centers, medical buildings, and mortgages on commercial properties. They resemble closed-end mutual funds (see Chapter 8). After they are launched through a public offering, their shares usually trade on major U.S. stock exchanges and are sold through stockbrokers. The shares can sell at a discount or a premium to the company's net asset value.

On the bright side, REITs distribute more than 90 percent of their taxable earnings to investors each year. These earnings come from two sources: rents on the real estate owned by the REIT and capital gains from selling real estate. Consequently, as an investor, you are exposed to two risks: a rotten real estate market, where property values decline; and/or a rotten rental market, where there is more rental space than renters.

As a practical matter, it's tough to find a REIT that isn't going to suffer from one of these risks eventually. That's simply because the moment a rental real estate market gets hot—a lot of prospective tenants move in—developers rush to meet the demand by creating more office space. Rental markets go through regular shortage/glut cycles. The result: In good years, a REIT's taxable earnings can be substantial—anywhere from 8 percent to around 20 percent. In bad years, REITs can lose equal amounts and pay virtually nothing to investors.

Indeed, even in good markets, you have to be very careful about what REIT you buy. Some have been plagued by questionable insider deals that have drastically increased management costs, reduced share value, and eliminated dividend payouts to investors.

Still, REITs are worth considering for a couple of reasons. First, even in bad years, REITs can often generate generous yields. For instance, North American REITs lost 22.7 percent of their value in 1998, but produced a 5 percent yield. In 1999, REIT prices fell another 11.3 percent, while generating a 6.89 percent yield. In other words, while the market may beat the stocks up because they're worried about the health of the real estate market, a good REIT is still going to be collecting rents and passing on a portion of those rents to investors. For someone looking for income, they're pretty consistent payers.

Second, REITs rarely move in tandem with stocks. When REIT shares were getting killed in the late 1990s, for example, domestic stock prices were soaring. When the stock market tanked in 2000, REIT prices soared. And that pattern of moving in opposite directions is more the norm than the exception, which makes REITs a good tool. Devoting 10 percent to 20 percent of your portfolio to REITs can make the whole portfolio a bit more stable.

You can learn more about the specifics of investing in REITS in Chapter 10.

Preferred Stocks

This investment class is used to describe stocks in the true sense of the word. However, in 1993, most of these securities were restructured for tax reasons. (The reasons are complex and mostly boring, but the bottom line is that issuers can get a tax deduction for paying interest but not for paying dividends, so they restructured preferred stocks to resemble bonds rather than dividend-paying stocks.) Technically how "trust preferreds" work is this: A company sells long-term bonds to a trust, which then issues preferred shares that pass on the bond interest to investors.

Since the new preferreds are geared to individual investors, they are sold in bite-sized denominations. They generally are sold at $25 per share at initial issue. Most are listed on the New York Stock Exchange, so they can be bought and sold freely.

Their value, like the value of the underlying bonds, is affected by interest rates. When rates rise, the value of preferred shares can fall sharply. When rates fall, the value of preferred shares rises, but fairly modestly.

Why do you get less on the upside than the down? Because the bonds that back preferred shares generally have thirty- to forty-year maturities. But they also have so-called call dates at five- or ten-year intervals. In other words, the issuer can choose to buy back your debt by paying par value—$25—for your shares on the call date. The issuer is not obligated to buy back or redeem your shares. It simply has the right to do so. As a result, issuers redeem preferred shares on the call date when interest rates have fallen since the time of issue. That allows them to refinance their debt at lower rates of interest. That means you don't get to lock in that preferential interest rate for very long.

On the other hand, if interest rates are rising, the issuers are not going to redeem their bonds. You are saddled with a relatively low-yielding investment for the duration—unless you want to sell your shares on the open market. And if you do, you should expect to sell for less than the $25 face value. On the bright side, preferred stocks tend to pay interest a little more frequently than bonds. Bonds usually pay interest every six months; preferred stocks normally pay interest every three months.

Because of the higher prepayment and interest-rate risk that you take when buying preferreds, you also should expect a somewhat higher yield than you'd get on an ordinary bond. Typically, preferreds pay about 1.5 to 2 percentage points more than comparable Treasury bonds and 0.25 to 0.5 percentage points more than comparable corporate bonds.

Income Stocks

What kind of company would accept growth prospects that are so lackluster that the company simply gives most of its income away to shareholders? Traditionally, utilities.

Utility companies are regulated and often restricted to doing business in a set geographic area. They sell a commodity—such as water, electric power, or gas—that is not likely to see a big upsurge or drop in demand. (Your need and desire for water is dictated by thirst and landscaping. Unless there's dramatic growth in a community— lots of thirsty people move there and plant lawns—the community's demand for water doesn't change much from year to year. And a community's growth is limited by the available amount of real estate.) So when a utility completes its expansion—has the majority of its power plants built and its infrastructure solid—it traditionally becomes a cash cow for investors. This has changed in recent years, as an increasing number of utility companies have sought new methods to create energy and new sources to provide water.

However, now, a host of mutual fund managers have devoted their time to finding investments with strong dividend yields. The reason: Tax laws have changed, making dividends a very attractive source of revenue.

Specifically, "qualified dividends" received between January of 2003 and December of 2008 are taxed at capital gains rates, rather than ordinary income tax rates. For many investors, that's a 20 percentage point savings. When you look at dividend yields on an after-tax basis, you will see an also-ran yield turn into something stellar.

What's a dividend yield? It's a ratio that indicates how much money the company pays out in annual dividends compared to what you originally paid for the stock. Let's say, for example, that you bought one hundred shares of a company for $10 a share, and that company pays dividends of $.15 per share each quarter, or $.60 per share each year. Your $1,000 investment pays $60 annually. That's a 6 percent dividend yield, because $60 divided by $1,000 is 0.06, or 6 percent.

The benefit of income stocks is that you get current income and you get the chance to participate in the company's stock price appreciation, if the company happens to have a good year that's reflected in its stock price.

The downside of dividend stocks: You also participate in the company's stock price depreciation, if the company has had an unusually bad year. Worse still, there's no law requiring a company to continue paying regular cash dividends. If the company decides it can no longer afford to pay you that $60 annually, it can unilaterally announce that the dividends will stop, and there's little, if anything, you can do about it. That can hammer the stock price. So investors suffer something of a double whammy—less income and less appreciation—all at the same time.

On the bright side, you don't have to pick good, consistent dividend stocks on your own. There are dozens of mutual fund companies that specialize in the category, and some are excellent at picking stocks that pay good yields, while delivering good growth prospects. Both Vanguard Group Inc. and T. Rowe Price Group Inc. have excellent choices, recommended by fund research firm Morningstar Inc.

Closed-End Funds

Closed-end funds are investment pools that buy a large variety of securities and provide each shareholder with a pro-rata stake in the entire investment pool, much like the far more prevalent "open-end" mutual fund. (You'll learn more about both types of funds in Chapter 8.) What makes closed-end funds unique is that these funds do not take money from investors after an initial public offering. Instead, their shares are traded on a major exchange, such as the New York Stock Exchange, much like a stock.

When you buy or sell shares of stock or closed-end funds, you are paying another investor for their stake. The cash flow of the closed-end fund (or the company) generally is not affected by the day-to-day trading.

With an open-end mutual fund, on the other hand, investors buy shares directly from the fund company and sell them back to the fund company. That can make the pool of cash available to invest ebb and flow based on market conditions.

Because closed-end funds don't need to worry about investors selling out, they can invest 100 percent of their cash, says Anne Kritzmire, managing director of closed-end funds at Nuveen Investments LLC in Chicago. The funds can also borrow against their portfolio to invest even more than the amount they've got in the bank. For a manager investing money to generate income, that can be a significant advantage, Kritzmire says. Closed-end funds aimed at providing income typically pay dividends ranging from 6 percent to 9 percent per year, she adds.

The downside is leverage. Borrowing to buy securities—which is common among income funds in this category—magnifies returns, both good and bad. So, if the fund makes the wrong bet, its value can sink fast.

Immediate Annuities

Some savvy retirees get the urge to run for the hills when a salesperson says the word *annuity*. That's understandable considering that the says of so-called deferred variable annuities to seniors has been a source of controversy, sparking lawsuits and drawing the ire of regulators. But another type of annuity, known as an immediate annuity, can provide significant benefits to risk-averse retirees who want their savings to generate income—and who want to make sure that they don't outlive the savings.

An immediate annuity provides regularly scheduled payments for a specified period of time. (State lotteries often purchase them to pay off big winners over twenty- or thirty-year periods.) Retirees, who need a reliable source of income, can deposit a lump sum in a fixed-rate immediate annuity and receive a regular check for life.

For example, a husband and wife, both 65, could deposit $100,000 in an immediate annuity with a joint-survivor option and get a $650 to $700 monthly payment, guaranteed for life. (The payment difference hinges on both the company that's selling the annuity and market interest rates.) However, once they both die, the payments stop and there is no residual value to pay to heirs. With an immediate annuity, you are essentially buying a pension—payments for life. If you die young, you get a pretty lousy return. But if you live far beyond the average life expectancy, you essentially reap a windfall.

The disadvantage? The average return—based on living to an average life expectancy—is relatively modest, usually 3 percent to 6 percent per year. Savvy investors often can earn more investing on their own in a diversified mix of other fixed-income investments, albeit with considerably more risk.

You thought the return was 6.5 percent to 7 percent? No. With an annuity, the payments you receive are partially a payment *on* your money and partially a payment *of* your money. A portion of your principal is returned to you with each payment. But the insurance component of this product guarantees that the payments will keep coming, even if the principal you paid in has theoretically all been paid out.

Another disadvantage is that inflation can slowly erode the purchasing power of the fixed monthly payments. That can make immediate annuities a good choice for a portion of your retirement savings, but a poor choice for all of your retirement income.

 INVESTING FOR GROWTH

If there's something big that you want—from a comfortable retirement to a mansion on the beach—and you can't afford it today, you need to save and make your money work for you. When you have lots of time, the best way to do that is to invest for growth.

There are two main investments in this category: domestic stocks and international stocks. Both are volatile, which is another way of saying they're likely to experience wide swings in value. However, over long periods of time, there's good reason to believe stocks also will appreciate dramatically faster than any other type of asset. That makes it easier to attain your long-term goals.

Here's the rundown on how domestic and international stock markets work, as well as their risks and rewards.

Domestic Stocks

When you buy a share of stock, you are buying a piece of the issuing company. Admittedly, it's probably a small piece, but that share you purchased gives you the right to participate in the company's wealth (or fiscal decline) and vote on matters of some importance—directors, company auditors, and some shifts in corporate policy.

In some cases, you are also entitled to dividends—payments of cash or stock to shareholders. Some companies also provide their shareholders with perquisites, such as tickets to the company's theme parks or discounts on its merchandise.

Because companies tend to grow and prosper over time—and because a share of stock allows you to participate in the prosperity—stock prices, in the aggregate, tend to appreciate over long periods of time. Individually, however, some companies prosper; others fail. If you buy a share in a loser, you could lose all, or a significant portion, of your initial investment. In other words, when you invest in stocks, you risk losing your initial investment, but because you are taking a bigger risk, you get the opportunity to earn far bigger rewards.

How big a reward? The research company Ibbotson Associates has tracked the performance of U.S. stocks from 1926 to the present. That period includes the Great Depression, World War II, the Vietnam War, the Kennedy assassination, the dismantling of the Iron Curtain, Reaganomics, the dot-com bubble, and the September 11th terrorist attacks.

In other words, it is a fairly diverse period that has had its share of ups and downs, just like any period in history. During that time, the average annual return on small-company U.S. stocks was about 12.7 percent. The average annual return on big-company stocks was 10.4 percent. Over the same period, inflation rose 3.0 percent per year, and the return on U.S. Treasury bills was 3.7 percent.

To put it another way: If you had a diversified portfolio of large-company stocks during that period, the value of your investment portfolio rose 7.4 percentage points faster than the rate of inflation. For every $100 you put in the market, you hiked your buying power by $7.40 each year. At the end of twenty years, your real (inflation-adjusted) buying power increased fourfold, to $417 from $100, without any additional payments from you.

Although investing is as much an art as a science, it's reasonable to expect that future investment returns will mirror historic returns over long periods. In other words, it's reasonable to assume that stocks will continue to appreciate faster than the rate of inflation and other types of traditional investments.

The downside: It is also reasonable to assume that stocks could repeat their short-term historic performance over shorter periods, too. And that's been far less illustrious than the long-term performance. To be specific: The market crash of 1929 so depressed stock prices that investors who put $100 in the market saw the value of their securities fall to less than $20 at the market's nadir in 1932. It took roughly eight years before securities prices rose back to ground zero, where $100 invested in 1929 was worth $100 again. And then the market took another sickening slide, from which it didn't recover until after World War II had ended. From start to finish, it was a full fifteen years of pain for stock market investors.

The market also took a sharp, decade-long dive in 1969. And it experienced short-term "crashes" in 1987, 1989, and 1990 and a far longer-term crash in 2000.

But the stock market's performance in 1995 was enough to make an investor beam. Stock values as measured by the Standard and Poor's 500 Index were up more than 37 percent. The next several years were almost as impressive. Big-company stocks posted a 23 percent gain in 1996, a 33 percent gain in 1997, a 28 percent gain in 1998, and a 21 percent gain in 1999.

Incidentally, although investors in small companies have done better than investors in large companies over the long haul (average annual returns of 12.7 percent versus 10.4 percent, respectively), at various points in time, small-company stocks do worse than big-company stocks. They fall farther and faster, and they stay depressed longer.

These heady climbs and sickening slumps are called volatility. When an investment is as volatile as the stock market, it is unwise to invest unless you have a fairly long time horizon that allows you to wait out the price swings and go for the long-term price appreciation.

How long is a "fairly long" time horizon? That depends on you and why you are investing. Let's say you want to buy a house in five years, and you're trying to determine where to invest the down-payment money. The stock market would be a good place for all or part of that money if you wouldn't be crushed if your home-buying plans had to be put off because of a market slump that depressed the value of your investment portfolio and thus reduced the amount you had saved for the down payment. What if you would be crushed if you couldn't buy the home as planned? Then put the down-payment money in bonds that mature (or pay back their principal) at the time when you want to use the money.

Stocks are also ideal to have in your retirement portfolio. The younger and farther from retirement you are, the more stocks you can handle. And they're a good choice for college funds for young children. However, if you are investing in individual stocks rather than mutual funds, you must diversify your portfolio by buying stocks in several different companies that do business in several different industries. That ensures that your net worth won't crash if one industry, whether it's oil, technology, or retailing, hits a slump. Experts suggest you own shares in at least eight to ten different companies. Ideally, those companies should be operating in substantially different industries.

Foreign Stocks

Just as U.S. companies issue ownership interests in the form of stock, so do foreign companies. The risks and rewards of foreign stock markets are similar to those of the U.S. stock market, but they frequently are magnified. There are a variety of reasons why, including political instability in some countries and the fact that many foreign markets are smaller and more thinly traded than the U.S. market. That tends to make them subject to wider price swings, both up and down.

In addition, U.S. investors who buy foreign equities face something called currency risk. Here's why. When you buy stock in a foreign country, you buy the shares with that country's currency. When you sell them, you get paid in that country's currency, too. Before you can spend the proceeds in the United States, you have to convert the foreign currency into U.S. dollars at the going exchange rate. And exchange rates vary day to day based on the relative strength of any given country's balance sheet and the interest rates that country is paying on government securities (the equivalent of Treasury bills). If currency values in the foreign land have risen since you purchased your foreign stocks, you win when you exchange the currency. If they fall, however, you lose.

In some cases, the currency swings can be more significant to your total return than the actual appreciation or depreciation of the particular stocks you purchased (see Chapter 11). On the bright side, there are years when a foreign country's stock market can nearly double in value. And if currency swings are working in your favor at the same time, your returns can be stunning.

Equity Mutual Funds

Mutual funds are investment companies that pool the money of many investors and buy securities in bulk. The securities that a fund buys are determined by the fund's investment objectives. These investment objectives are spelled out in the prospectus and by the fund manager, who makes the investment decisions.

So-called equity funds—also known as growth or aggressive growth funds—buy stock in U.S. companies. When you buy a share in an equity fund, you're actually buying an interest in all of the different stocks held by that fund. That gives you the benefit of broad diversification, which reduces the risk that your investment portfolio will be savaged by a single bad stock. In essence, if you buy the right mutual fund, you may not need to diversify the stock portion of your portfolio further. One fund could do it all.

There are lots of other benefits and tricks to buying mutual funds. However, since an entire chapter is devoted to investing in them (Chapter 8), let it suffice to say that investing in equity mutual funds is an alternative to investing in individual stocks. It is a particularly good alternative for those who don't want to spend a lot of time picking individual investments or for those who are starting out and don't have a lot of money.

Global/International Mutual Funds

Just as buying shares in a domestic equity mutual fund is similar to buying domestic stocks, buying shares in global and international mutual funds is similar to buying shares in foreign stocks.

The big benefit of buying foreign stocks through a fund is that global mutual funds not only spread your money among numerous stocks, they also can spread the investments among numerous countries. That reduces currency risk, too. Moreover, because of language barriers and steep trading costs involved in buying and selling individual foreign shares, global and international mutual funds may well be the smartest way to get a little international flavor in your portfolio. That area will be discussed more in Chapter 11.

INVESTMENTS THAT PROTECT YOU FROM INFLATION

For some people, the goal of investing is not so much getting ahead as it is not falling behind. Because inflation marches forward each and every year, the fear is that you will fall behind if your investments don't rise as quickly as the cost of buying necessary goods and services.

There is also a group of investors who fear that the U.S. dollar could become worthless someday. At that point, the only way to buy things you need would be to trade "hard assets," such as precious metals and gems, or barter something you have, like food, for something they have, like shelter. (Personally, I figure if things get this bad, your investment portfolio will be the least of your worries, but . . .)

Three types of investments are widely considered inflation hedges: precious metals, real estate, and a relatively new type of Treasury bonds called real-return bonds.

Precious Metals

If you talk to a gold bug, he'll tell you that gold—the bellwether of precious-metal investments—holds its value over time. An ounce of gold would buy you a suit of clothes in the days of Henry VIII, and it will still buy you a suit of clothes today.

What gold bugs won't tell you is that while inflation has risen 3.1 percent per year since 1925, the value of gold—which became publicly traded in the United States in the late 1970s—fell from about $800 per ounce in 1980 to less than $300 in the late 1990s. In early 2008, it was trading near the $800 range, which means that over a twenty-seven-year period, you got no return at all. Meanwhile, inflation has eroded the buying power that $800 will get you. In other words, whereas it would buy you a marvelous suit and plenty of accessories in 1980, it would buy you a merely adequate suit and, perhaps, an inexpensive pair of socks in 2008.

There are other disadvantages to buying gold, too. Namely, if you buy gold bullion or coins, you have to store them somewhere—like in a bank safe deposit box. And a safe deposit box is likely to cost you $40 to $60 a year. In addition, gold doesn't pay dividends and it doesn't pay interest. It just sits there. In a box. In the bank. In the dark.

Certainly, you can buy gold (or silver or platinum) coins for their beauty. Some are miniature objects of art. But that's less investing than it is purchasing. To be sure, the coins may some day be worth more, but if you bought them for their beauty, you are no more likely to sell them when they appreciate than you are to sell the paintings off your walls. Gold bars, meanwhile, are as attractive as, well, bricks. It's tough to justify buying bullion as an investment with a reasonable argument that doesn't include some kind of doomsday scenario.

However, there have been times when you could make a small fortune merely by speculating in the gold market by buying shares in gold-mining companies. When inflation fears are high, for example, the value of gold tends to rise. When per-ounce prices rise a nudge, the value of gold-mining shares often soars. If you are quick on your feet—or on the phone, calling your broker—you can make a tidy sum. But this is less protecting yourself from inflation than it is speculating—rolling the dice and hoping you'll hit seven.

Residential Real Estate

Residential real estate—in other words, your home—can provide a real hedge against inflation no matter what happens to the price of your house in the future. How so? By buying a home that you can live in, you eliminate the need to pay rent. That protects you from possible rental rate increases that could come down the road. You also get some tax benefits when you buy residential real estate, so your actual out-of-pocket cost, or after-tax cost, may be less than the sum of your down payment and total monthly payments. (Mortgage-interest expenses are tax deductible.)

In addition, if you finance your house with a thirty-year, fixed-rate mortgage, you have ensured that your second-largest household expense (after income taxes) will not budge. Indeed, your personal inflation rate will actually drop at the end of thirty years, because you will have paid off the loan. Then you will be sitting on an asset of substantial value that you can sell, if need be, or simply live in for the rest of your life.

Can you analyze your home as an investment, like you analyze stocks or bonds? Not really. National statistics tracking the price of residential real estate are dubious because they track only sales prices without attempting to determine the size and quality of the residences sold in any given period. (In fact, while the "average" home sales price has risen, so has the average square footage and the average number of bathrooms.) However, real estate prices do appear to rise over long periods of time, seemingly somewhat faster than the rate of inflation.

House prices don't rise in lockstep with inflation. In fact, when inflation is high, real estate prices are likely to fall (because when inflation is high, interest rates go up, and when interest rates go up, so do mortgage rates, which means people can't afford as much). But later, home prices catch up by taking dramatic leaps in value when inflation and interest rates drop.

If you're a subscriber to the doomsday theory—the idea that inflation will be so high that U.S. currency will become worthless and we'll be driven to barter to survive—you should remember that you can't eat gold, but you can grow vegetables in your backyard.

Real-Return Bonds

Real-return bonds, also known as inflation-adjusted bonds, were developed in 1997, with the idea that investors might want an inflation hedge that really did move in lockstep with inflation. These new bonds are pegged to the Consumer Price Index (CPI), the main measuring stick of inflation in the United States. They pay a current return, and once a year the bond's principal value is adjusted to reflect hikes in the index. Your future interest payments are then based on the boosted principal value. For example, let's say you bought a $1,000 bond. You earned $35, or 3.5 percent, on it. At the end of the year, the CPI indicates that inflation rose 4 percent that year. The principal value of your bond rises to $1,040. The following year, your interest payments will rise to reflect a 3.5 percent return on a $1,040 principal value. The catch: If your bonds are not in a tax-favored retirement account, both the interest and the inflation adjustment are taxable. So you pay income tax on both the interest and the $40 boost to your principal value, even though you didn't receive the $40 in cash.

Some bond experts are big fans of real-return bonds. The biggest buyers of them to date have been institutions, including mutual funds.

So if you are interested in addressing inflation directly but you don't want to buy the bonds yourself, look for so-called income funds that include them in their portfolios.

"I" Savings Bonds

The Treasury department also offers a U.S. savings bond that pegs its interest returns to inflation. Known as Series I bonds, or "I bonds" for short, these savings bonds derive their return from two things: a fixed interest rate, which remains the same for the life of the bond; and a variable rate, which adjusts for inflation every six months.

The return on the bond is equal to the fixed rate, plus the inflation adjustment. Like other savings bonds, however, the yields on these tend to be fairly paltry. But that's mainly because inflation has been low. If inflation becomes a threat, they could prove worthwhile. Like many other Treasury products, they're easy to buy and sell through the Treasury's website at www.treasurydirect.gov.

 ## SPECULATION

There are a wide number of speculative investments that range from limited partnerships to commodities contracts to derivative securities. And there are trading strategies, such as buying and selling "puts" and "calls" (stock options), that can occasionally supercharge—or decimate—the value of your investment portfolio.

Unless you are both wealthy and highly sophisticated about investing, you should avoid this type of speculation. Not only is there a good chance that you will lose all or a significant part of your money, in some cases you can actually lose more than you originally invested.

Since this book is for beginning investors, speculative investments are not covered in detail, with one exception: viatical settlements. Why make the exception? Because viatical settlements are being heavily marketed to unsophisticated investors as a "safe" and/or "guaranteed" investment that pays double-digit returns. This is a lie. Viatical settlements are highly speculative investments. Worse still, in the past several years, the industry has become pockmarked with swindlers. To thoroughly understand the risk requires some background both on the industry and on how these investments work.

Viatical Settlements

These so-called investment vehicles are insurance policies that are sold to investors, who get paid off when the person whose life is insured dies. Barry Fisher, an attorney in Century City, California, dubs them "death futures." Ghoulish, you say? Absolutely, although the industry started for a very practical (and sympathetic) reason: AIDS, or acquired immune deficiency syndrome. In the beginning of the U.S. AIDS crisis, when the disease was a mystery and there was nothing to treat it, AIDS patients—primarily young, gay men—were getting horribly ill. Seemingly inexplicably, they would be hit with one ailment after the next, causing them to call in sick time and again. So they lost their jobs. They ran through their savings. They found themselves dying and destitute.

Yet many of them had life insurance. In fact, roughly 75 percent of Americans have life insurance, because big companies commonly provide a certain amount of life insurance as a company-paid employee benefit. And if you have had a policy for some time, it generally cannot be canceled unless you fail to pay the premium. For many of these young men, this was a horrible irony. They had no dependents—no children who relied on them for financial support—so they really had no need for life insurance for the traditional reason of protecting a spouse and children from the financial disaster that the death of a breadwinner can bring. The policyholders could desperately use the cash from that death benefit, but they had to die to get it.

Viatical settlements sprang up to address this need. Terminally ill AIDS patients could sell their policies to an "investor." That investor would be paid back when the policyholder died. Investors would make a return on the policy by buying it at a discount to its death benefit. In other words, a $100,000 policy might be purchased for $70,000. The AIDS patient would get the cash today; the investor would get a $30,000 profit when the policyholder died.

However, medical advances have helped many AIDS patients live much longer than expected. Meanwhile, con artists have jumped into the viatical settlement market, selling policies on fictitious patients. For a variety of reasons, it's often difficult for investors to differentiate a valid viatical settlement from a fraud.

Worse still, securities regulators who normally attempt to protect investors from investment scams have been unsuccessful in their attempts to regulate viatical settlements. Part of the problem is that they're a hybrid—part insurance, part investment. No one knows who has jurisdiction.

If you're still tempted, check out a book called *Viatical Settlements: An Investor's Guide*, by Gloria Grening Wolk, or visit Wolk's website at www.viatical-expert.net.

The latest twist in the viatical settlement industry is something called "senior settlements." These are death futures on old people. Sometimes, healthy old people.

And the salesmen take this one the opposite way: If you happen to be in your 70s and in good health, an insurance agent might urge you to buy a huge—$1 million to $10 million—policy on your life. Theoretically, you would hold that policy for two years (that's how long insurance companies have in which to "contest" the validity of the contract) and then sell it for a fraction of the face value, likely to a company that invests in life policies and promises to keep the insurance current and collect on the policy when you die.

What do you get? It will depend on your age and health, but if you have a $10 million policy, you might be able to get $1 million for it in the secondary market. In exchange, you would have had to pay the premiums on that policy for the first couple of years, so you'd net out only about $800,000.

Great deal? Sure, if it doesn't bother you that some stranger is going to make a fortune when you die—particularly if you die unexpectedly early. Personally, I'd prefer to limit the number of people who would profit from my untimely death to people who love me and would miss me enough not to want the money in a hurry.

 **INVESTMENTS TO AVOID**

Commodities Futures

The commodities markets were formed to battle something that economic texts called "the farm problem." In a nutshell, the farm problem was anticipating future supply and demand. Farmers had to plant their crops a year (or in the case of certain crops, such as coffee, avocados, oranges, and apples, many years) before bringing these products to market. With such a long lead time, it was difficult to know whether the market price for their goods would be sufficient to cover their costs. Often it wasn't, which led to scores of farm bankruptcies.

The commodities market aims to solve this problem by preselling shipments of farm products, from cattle to pigs, corn to coffee. Typically the way you do this is to set up a commodity trading account with your friendly neighborhood broker. The broker will set up a margin account for you as part of the deal. Then, let's say you want to buy a $100,000 coffee-bean contract. The brokerage will typically let you put down just 5 percent to 10 percent of that purchase price in cash. The rest is effectively borrowed.

Naturally, you don't want $100,000 worth of coffee beans (unless you have a coffee factory somewhere to process and sell it later, or unless you're really, really thirsty), so you plan to resell the contract before the coffee actually comes to market. If coffee prices rise, you can make a killing because you've paid just, say, $5,000 to purchase a $100,000 contract. If that $100,000 contract rises 10 percent in value, you earn $10,000 on your $5,000 investment—a 200 percent return on your money. But if coffee prices fall, you can be subject to a margin call. That means you'll have to kick more money into the account. In this unhappy scenario, you could lose several times more than your original investment. If you're not a farmer, a coffee manufacturer, or a person who can handle serious investment losses, this is not a good place to play.

Limited Partnerships

Limited partnerships became popular in the early 1980s partly as a result of favorable tax legislation that allowed these partnerships to pass tax losses through to wealthy investors. The partnerships of the early 1980s owned real estate, oil and gas deposits, windmills, and a variety of other speculative and often money-losing ventures. When the tax laws changed in 1986, barring limited partners from claiming tax losses that often exceeded their cash investments, limited partnerships went belly-up in droves.

You can still buy limited partnerships today. They continue to invest in speculative ventures, such as oil and gas, windmills, and low-income housing. For some investors, the low-income-housing partnerships still provide substantial tax breaks. However, the risks come on a variety of fronts. One of the most noteworthy is that the general partner usually has control over what is purchased with the partnership's money and how much is paid in fees to everyone from brokers to the general partner himself. If you have a bad general partner who charges excessive fees, you can have a bad investment even if the partnership's underlying assets are great. There is very little a limited partner can do to stop abuses by a general partner.

"Naked" Options

Investors can buy or sell options, which are rights to buy or sell a particular security at a set price in the future. There are conservative ways to use stock options, but going "naked"—trading options on stock you don't own—is a good way to lose whatever amount you've invested and occasionally more.

By and large, what you're doing is guessing about the direction of a stock and betting that it will hit a certain mark by a particular point in time. If it does, you make money. If it doesn't, you lose it.

Let's say, for example, you buy an option to buy one hundred shares of XYZ Corp. at $100 on April 15, 2001. Because XYZ currently sells for $90 per share, your option is cheap—say, $3 per share, or $300 for the contract to buy those one hundred shares. If XYZ's stock soars to $150 in the interim, the fact that your option gives you the right to buy those shares at $50 per share under the market price makes that option very valuable indeed. You make a killing of $47 per share, or $4,700 on your $300 investment.

But what happens if XYZ posts poor quarterly profits and declines in value to $80 or languishes at $90? Your option becomes worthless. If the stock price remains low until after your strike date of April 15, the option expires. You lost whatever amount you spent to buy this option in the first place. The even more frustrating thing is you may have called the direction of the stock correctly. XYZ may hit $100 or even $150 in the future. But because options expire on a particular date, you not only have to be right about the stock, you also have to be right about the timing. That's tough.

Conversely, you can sell a so-called naked put. What does that mean? Let's say you think XYZ is a bad company that's selling at a high price. You figure its stock price is going to decline. So you sell another investor the right to buy XYZ shares from you at $100 in the future. The other investor, who thinks XYZ is great and is going to appreciate, pays you $3 a share (or $300) for that right.

Now, let's say you were wrong. XYZ posts terrific profits. Its stock price soars to $150. You must buy the shares at $150 to sell to the option holder at $100. You lose $47 a share—the $150 you paid for each share that you sold at $100, minus the $3 per share you got for the option. Ouch.

Other Investments You Don't Understand

They can crop up on a regular basis. Somebody talks to you about foreign currency markets, derivative securities, insurance premium finance schemes, strips, or any one of dozens of other investments that you find befuddling. The salesman tells you what a great deal they are, but you can't figure out why this investment pays so much more than the traditional investments you're familiar with. Let that be the red flag that tells you to stay away.

There are two reasons you don't want to invest in things you don't understand:

1. You won't know when to sell, since you really didn't understand why you were buying in the first place.
2. You have no idea whether you've got a legitimate investment or a scam, because you don't understand the investment well enough to ask the right questions to find out.

It's one thing to lose money in a legitimate investment for which you understood the risks. It's quite another to lose money in an investment scam or in an investment that posed risks you were not prepared to handle.

Con artists prey on people who don't want to admit they're confused. They'll tell you that you'll earn a 20 percent annual return. They'll tell you that all of your friends are investing and you'll be left out if you don't. They'll tell you that this is a one-time offer. If you don't decide now, you'll miss it. They'll tell you your profits are guaranteed.

If you have the sense to ask why they don't just borrow money from the bank to finance this "opportunity," since the profits are guaranteed, they'll counter with "Bankers don't understand this investment." Make your life simple and decide that if a bank's going to turn down a "guaranteed opportunity," you can, too.

Remember your mantra: Will this investment allow you to have the amount of money you need, when you need it? With the investments just mentioned, there is no way to know. So skip them.

If you are wealthy beyond your wildest dreams one day, and then you decide you want to play in the commodities or foreign currency markets, more power to you. Until then, stick with risks you understand and plain-vanilla investments whose returns you can predict.

QUICK TAKE

What You'll LEARN

This chapter describes:

- Fundamental Indicators of Value
- How to Read a Financial Statement
- Ferreting Out the Right Numbers in Financial Reports
- Corporate Governance
- Finding Financial Data on the Web
- Manic Markets

What You'll DO

- Apply math and logic to investment decisions
- Look up financial information on the Web
- Create a target list of individual companies worth buying, if not now, later

How You'll USE This

Letting emotions drive your stock picking is a ticket to buying high and selling low. You can take at least some of the emotion out of stock evaluation by using the information and tools in this chapter. That might help you see the difference between a good company and a good buy.

PICKING INDIVIDUAL STOCKS | 5

Billionaire investor Warren Buffett looks for value when he buys stocks. Peter Lynch, the investment guru who once headed Fidelity Investments' giant Magellan stock fund, seeks companies with strong growth prospects. Both have been wildly successful, showing that stock-picking success can be achieved from different angles. Indeed, there is no one right way to pick stocks.

Knowing the basics of stock picking is a fundamental skill that all serious investors need to have. One relatively basic method, variations of which are used by many professionals, is to combine the growth and value strategies prescribed by Buffett and Lynch. Look for steadily growing companies that are selling at reasonable prices.

FUNDAMENTAL INDICATORS OF VALUE

Exciting and volatile markets warrant a dull approach to investing—an approach that involves asking a lot of questions about the company's fundamental business, and then doing a little mathematical analysis. So how do you do it?

Although there are no hard-and-fast rules, many professional investors screen companies based on a number of factors, including growth in sales and earnings, cash flow, and net profits. They also look at how profits compare with total assets—a ratio better known as return on assets.

These figures are important because the future value of a company's shares is likely to hinge on its ability to grow and prosper. Growth in sales and earnings is a mathematical reading of demand for a company's products and services. Meanwhile, a company that's earning a substantial amount on assets—some experts require more than a 1 percent return on assets for a financial services concern and more than 8 percent for nonfinancial businesses—has proved it knows how to deploy its resources in effective ways.

In terms of cash flow, look for whether the company is generating more cash from operations than it is spending. That tells you if the company is earning enough on its business to finance future growth without resorting to borrowing or issuing more stock—either of which can prove detrimental to existing shareholders.

Finally, try to determine whether the company has a product or provides a service that's unique and difficult to copy. If it does, it's likely the company will remain a market leader for a longer period of time. What products are hard to copy or unique? There is a wide variety, but they would include products that require formulas that are under patent protection for long periods, those that require unique technical skills, or those that require a great deal of capital to produce— such as cars and airplanes, for example.

If the company makes it through that gauntlet, its stock is analyzed to determine whether the price is cheap or dear. Often that analysis hinges on the price-to-earnings (P/E) ratio, which is a measure of how the company's stock price compares to its per-share earnings. A company that earns $2 per share annually and sells for $20, for example, would have a P/E ratio of 10. This company's stock price is equivalent to ten times its annual earnings per share.

When looking at this ratio, what investors must keep in mind is that there is not one P/E ratio that is right for all companies. Instead, each company has a normal P/E range. When the company's stock price breaks out of that range, it's time to ask why. If the company's stock price is higher than normal compared with earnings, it can be an indication that its stock price is too high. Or it can indicate that the company is primed for unusually fast growth. Likewise, when a company's P/E is low, it can mean either that bad times are setting in or that the company's stock price is a bargain.

The rule of thumb for considering the price of growth stocks that have broken out of their normal P/E ratio is this: The stock is still a good buy if the P/E is at or below the annual growth rate of the company's earnings. In other words, a stock that normally sold for fifteen times earnings might be a legitimate bargain when selling for twenty times earnings if its profits were growing by 20 percent or 25 percent per year.

Where do you find this average price-to-earnings range and a professional reading on the question of whether the stock is overpriced or cheap? There are numerous sources, but one of the most valuable— and easiest to find—is the *Value Line Investment Survey*. Value Line Inc. publishes detailed analyses of about 1,700 publicly traded stocks and ranks them for "timeliness" and volatility. These rankings are updated each week and are available in most major public libraries.

(Many institutional investors subscribe to the *Value Line Investment Survey*, but the subscription cost—$598 annually for the print survey and $538 annually for the electronic version—is high for a small investor.)

For investors who prefer small-company stocks, Value Line also offers a second book, its expanded survey, the Small and Mid-Cap Edition, which looks at 1,800 companies that are too small to get into its regular investment survey.

Stocks that receive rankings of 1 and 2 are those that Value Line thinks will end up on the top of the heap over the next six to twelve months. Value Line reports also give a history of each company's P/E and rate its cash flow and growth. The reports don't replace getting an annual report directly from a company, but they can certainly help investors narrow the search for a good stock. The company can also brag about one of the few consistent track records in the investment world. Over the past forty years, the company's top picks have beaten the performance of the overall market by a ratio of about 20 to 1.

Still, you need to be cautious about narrowing your stock choices based on Value Line's timeliness rankings: Sometimes the top-ranked companies are all clustered in just a few industries. If you aim to diversify properly—a requisite for anyone who wants to reduce his or her risks—you have to keep an eye on the industry groups you're choosing and make sure you choose stocks in many different industries. Moreover, the Value Line track record assumes that investors are shifting their assets annually, which is not a strategy that most individual investors should employ—particularly when they're trading in taxable accounts. Nonetheless, the firm provides all the data investors need to make sage investment choices.

Once you've chosen a stable of stocks to buy, all you need to do is keep an eye on your selections to make sure that these stocks remain worth owning. Doing that periodic analysis will help you determine when you ought to sell—and when it's time to buy more shares in the companies you like the best. There's more on that in Chapter 6.

 ## HOW TO READ A FINANCIAL STATEMENT

You need to take three steps when you are picking individual stocks for the long term. The first step is figuring out which industries will benefit from long-term trends, such as the globalization of the financial markets, the aging of the population, and the revolution in technology. The industries you expect to do better than others are ideal places to invest your money. The second step is finding a few—or a few dozen—specific companies in those industries that you want to consider more closely. The third step is the trickiest. That's when you've got to examine each company's finances to cull the likely winners from the losers.

Sound daunting? It's not as bad as it might appear, because most companies will provide you with all of the information you need. You simply need to ask for the appropriate reports and learn which numbers are the most telling.

What You Need

To start the process, get a copy of the company's annual report to shareholders and its 10-K filing. You can generally get these by simply requesting them from the company's investor relations office. You can also read, download, or print this information off the Web. However, if you get the data off the Internet, make sure you are looking at the full financial statement rather than a summary version that might leave out important facts.

The full financial reports are available at the SEC's website at www.sec.gov. To navigate that site, look in the directory under "Filings and Forms"; click on "Search for Company Filings." That will bring up a list of options. Scroll down to "Historical EDGAR Archives." Click that to get a search box in which you can plug in the company name and the form you want. If you want to take a look at Google's 10-K, for example, just type in *Google* and *10-K*. If you want to look at several years' worth of annual reports, adjust the start date next to the search box. The system holds electronic records going back to 1994.

The annual report and 10-K are similar documents. Both show how the company has done during the previous year and on a longer-term basis. However, you need both because the annual report doesn't always reveal certain sticky financial details, and the 10-K doesn't give you much of the personality of the company and its management.

Yes, companies have personalities, which generally reflect the nature of the company's chief executive officer. Knowing this per-sonality—whether aggressive, innovative, egotistical, or traditional—can help you predict what the company might do in the future.

Generally, you can start by looking at the annual report. It's prettier—usually including photographs and graphics—and generally easier to read than the 10-K. However, if you find that it doesn't have several years of financial information and lots of detail, toss it aside and look at the 10-K instead.

The Securities and Exchange Commission requires the 10-K to be the more complete document. It includes detailed descriptions of the business, allowances for losses, and contracts for significant transactions. If the company has outstanding lawsuits or tax debts that could have a significant impact on the company's business, it would also be noted in the 10-K.

Where to Start

Flip to the middle of the annual report, where you'll find a five- or ten-year comparison of "selected financial data." This chart shows year-to-year sales, operating income, net income, earnings per share, and balance sheet data that include how much the company holds in assets, liabilities, and working capital.

Your first move is to start making comparisons. Divide the current-year revenue, or sales, by the previous-year revenue and subtract 1 from the result. That gives you the year-to-year growth in sales, which tells you whether the company's products are gaining acceptance. (If the company sold $565 million this year and $522 million last, for instance, you'd divide 565 by 522 to get 1.08. That translates to an 8 percent growth rate.)

Then do the same thing with the operating income, which is income before taxes and unusual one-time expenses or profits, called "extraordinary items," the per-share net income, and the working capital. (Working capital is essentially the amount of money the company has on hand to finance its growth.) Repeat the process with the figures in the long-term comparison so you can come up with a trend line.

Also compare how much long-term debt, or liability, the company has versus its shareholders' equity and assets. Again, what you want to do is establish a pattern that tells you whether the company is paying off its debts or borrowing more than ever and whether its borrowing is within a normal range.

A few pages before or after this financial data chart, you'll find the "Statement of Cash Flow," which tells you how much money is coming in and how much is being spent. Another chart, which might be dubbed "Results of Operations" or "Consolidated Statement of Operations," notes where some of the money is being spent. For instance, is it going to research and development or general and administrative expenses? Is the company spending its money the same way it has in the past, or has something changed?

After you've looked at all these numbers, you're likely to have questions. If everything has been rosy, you'll want to know if this trend can continue. If the company has started to borrow heavily, you'll want to know whether that's because it's in a major growth phase that could cause it to become more profitable than ever or because the company is disastrously short of cash. If some expense or revenue item has jumped out of its normal range, you'll want to know why simply so you can determine whether that's a positive or negative sign.

To find the answers to these questions, flip to the front of the report. There you'll see two things—a letter to shareholders, which is written by the chairman, chief executive, or president, followed by the "Management's Discussion and Analysis of Financial Condition and Operating Results," which in industry jargon is called the MD&A.

In the MD&A, management explains what's happened to the company and the industry as a whole over the past year. It also discusses where the company thinks things are going and how it is responding to changes in its industry. Any balance sheet item that gave you pause should be mentioned here. If it's not, consider it a warning sign.

Last Step

The final thing you need to search for is something called the "footnotes" to the financial statement. In footnotes, the company explains its accounting and any significant estimates it has made, provides a description of the company's pension and employee benefit plans, and includes any other major assumption that was required to come up with the numbers you see in the annual report. In some cases, footnotes are only shown in the 10-K, so if you don't see them in the annual report, it's time to flip through this document.

Why do you need the footnotes? They often reveal pivotal details about the company's business. For instance, if the company derives 60 percent of its business from one customer—and that customer is going belly-up—it would be listed here. If the company patents are expiring and its future financial health relies on no one noticing, they'd put it in the footnotes. If there are significant legal actions pending, you should also expect to see a brief description of what they're about—and the types of risks they pose.

If there's nothing of significance in the footnotes, it's a good sign. If there's something there, but its significance isn't clear, you simply want to apply a reasonable-person standard to the information you see. If something seems off-kilter, you may want to investigate further, either by finding out how similar companies handle the same issue or by looking for analysts' reports.

FERRETING OUT THE RIGHT NUMBERS IN FINANCIAL REPORTS

How do you decide if a stock is worth buying? There are no hard and fast rules, but the following worksheet should help. The approach is based on the notion that the growth of a stock's price is a reflection of the company's growth in sales and earnings over time. However, to determine whether a stock is a buy from an investment standpoint, you need to ask a few questions. Then you need to do a little math to decide whether the price is reasonable.

Is It a Buy?

1. Does the cash produced by the company's operations cover its cost of doing business? You'll find the answer on the cash flow page of the company's annual report or 10-K. If the cash produced from operations is insufficient to cover operating expenses, the company is likely to have to borrow or issue more stock. Either could prove detrimental to existing shareholders.

    _____yes _____no

2. Has the company established a record of solid earnings growth? Can you see a pattern of rising earnings when looking at year-to-year comparisons in the company's 10-K or financial statement?

    _____yes _____no

3. Is there growing demand for the company's products?

    _____yes _____no

4. Does the company produce a product or service that's difficult to duplicate? In other words, does it have technology or a particular expertise that will allow it to maintain a leading position in the industry for a long time?

_____yes _____no

5. Is the company's return on assets (ROA) 8 percent or more if it's a nonfinancial company or 1 percent or more for a bank, savings and loan, or insurer? (Companies normally publish an ROA in their financial statements. However, if it is not there, you can calculate it by dividing the company's total—not per share—earnings by total assets.) If the ROA is lower than these amounts, is it improving?

_____yes _____no

If you answered "yes" to all of those questions, you know you're looking at a good company. Now the question is whether its stock is selling at a reasonable price.

To figure that, do the calculations below:

Current market price $_____

Annual earnings per share $_____

Price-to-earnings (P/E) ratio

(divide price by earnings per share) _____

Historical P/E* _____

Anticipated growth in earnings* _____%

Historical growth rate* _____%

*You can find these figures in the Value Line Investment Survey. This book, which has an annual subscription cost of $598, is available in most public libraries.

After completing the worksheet, compare today's P/E ratio to what it has been historically. If it's higher than normal, look at how today's earnings growth compares with the company's historic growth rate. If the growth rate is the same or lower than it has been in the past but the stock's P/E is higher, the stock's price is probably too expensive.

If the earnings growth rate is higher than normal, the stock can support a higher P/E multiple. The rule of thumb is that the stock's P/E can be as high as its expected growth rate. In other words, if a company is growing 30 percent per year, a 30 P/E wouldn't be too high. But do realize that as companies get bigger, double-digit growth rates become harder to sustain. A small company can sometimes double its sales and earnings for several years running. But once that company jumps from $10 million in sales to $100 million in sales, it's likely that its growth rate is going to taper off. When the company is at $1 billion in sales, it's likely to taper off dramatically. After all, increasing earnings by $10 million is a challenge, but increasing earnings by $1 billion in a single year is a miracle.

CORPORATE GOVERNANCE

Picking great stocks is not all about the numbers. It's also about the people who create them. Over the past decade there's been an increasing awareness that corporate structures that impose appropriate checks and balances on company managers can result in better returns for shareholders. The system by which a company operates is called "corporate governance." It's getting increasing scrutiny today partly because of a host of corporate scandals, which range from accounting blowups that brought down the likes of Enron Corp. to stock option backdating scandals that caused hundreds of companies to undergo securities investigations and caused dozens of companies to restate past-year earnings and jettison managers. But governance is also gaining importance because of the numbers.

There's a growing library of research that says good governance makes a better investment. For instance, a study by Institutional Shareholder Services (ISS), an organization that helps advise big shareholders, found that companies that had appropriate checks and balances—primarily an active, independent, and experienced board of directors—consistently deliver better and more stable returns to shareholders.

Why? Think of corporations as miniature countries. Some are run like democracies, where shareholder representatives—the members of the board—are responsive to their constituents and are unafraid to challenge managers. The board is consulted before major decisions are made and, sometimes, the board will form a committee to study a particularly significant move. Members of the board are usually top executives with expertise in pivotal areas, from law and accounting to marketing and sales. A company manager consulting with his board is something like a U.S. president consulting Congress. He may not always get the answers he likes, but the topic is likely to be thoroughly aired, giving reasonable people the opportunity to object or support a particular point of view.

Other companies are run like dictatorships, where one individual, usually the chief executive officer, makes the decisions and gets his ideas and initiatives rubber-stamped by the board. The dictatorship model may work for a time, particularly if the dictator is smart and benevolent. But everybody makes mistakes on occasion. And a board that's asleep or beholden to management won't stop a dictatorial CEO when he's about to embark on a course that's risky, or costly, or not in the best interest of all shareholders. That can prove devastating to long-term returns.

How much of a difference does good governance make? The ISS study found that the best-governed companies paid dividend yields that were more than four times higher than for companies with poor governance practices. They were more profitable, based on return on investment, return on equity, return on assets, and net profits. Well-governed companies also had better price/earnings ratios. According to the study, companies with the best governance practices sold for amounts ranging from 15.7 to 20.1 times earnings, while companies with poor practices sold for 10.2 to 14.9 times earnings. In dollars and cents, that means that a well-governed company that earns $2 a share is likely to sell for around $30 to $40, while a poorly governed company would sell for around $20 to $29.

How do you know whether a company has good or bad governance? You can buy a rating from a research firm called The Corporate Library (www.thecorporatelibrary.com), which grades companies on an A–F scale. Their reports can be costly, however. The individual reports cost $495 each. So, if you just want a quick read, you can employ the do-it-yourself approach by pulling one more financial report called the "proxy statement." This is also available at the SEC website. However, when searching for a proxy statement on the SEC site, call it a "14a." That's the form number for this document. (If you wanted to see the proxy for Countrywide Financial Corp., for example, you'd go to the historical EDGAR archives and type: "Countrywide and 14a" [without the quotes] in the search bar.)

The proxy statement includes several things: a notice of the company's annual meeting of shareholders; a listing of the members of the board of directors, including biographies; charts indicating how much stock company managers and directors, as well as other significant shareholders, own; and a series of charts showing the pay of the five most highly compensated officers of the company.

What are the warning signs of bad governance?

- The chairman of the board is also the company's chief executive officer.
- The bulk of the board is made up of people who work for the company or have close financial or personal ties to managers. (If a director is the wife of the company's accountant, she would not be considered an independent party because her husband is likely to derive a significant portion of their income from that firm.) How would you know about these relationships? Securities regulators demand that companies disclose at least some of them under a section in the proxy that's usually labeled "certain relationships and transactions." In the Countrywide proxy, for example, this section reveals that one director worked for a company that provided a significant amount of investment banking business for Countrywide; that several other directors and executive officers had children, brothers, or sisters who were also employed by the company in high-paying positions; and that the company made numerous loans to the members of its board. Until federal law barred the practice, these loans were made at preferential rates.
- The company has multiple "shareholder resolutions." When shareholders petition a company to officially change its practices, these petitions show up in proxy statements to be submitted for a vote. Although a well-governed company may occasionally draw such resolutions, these resolutions are relatively rare at companies that score As on The Corporate Library governance scale. Companies that have multiple resolutions, and particularly resolutions involving pay, directors, and provisions that discourage takeovers, are often governance nightmares.
- Executives receive excessive pay. Excessive, of course, is a relative term. But the median compensation of a Fortune 500 company CEO is currently about $10 million in cash and

stock. Those running smaller companies, predictably, earn less on average. Consider it a warning sign if a company's CEO earns significantly more than that or earns the bulk of his pay in salary, rather than pay that's related to performance. (It's worth noting that tax authorities penalize companies that pay executives more than $1 million in non-performance-related pay. If the company exceeds that threshold, it's likely to be noted in the proxy under "compensation practices.")

- Executives receive massive perks. The executive compensation table will also show a listing of "other" pay. Securities regulators now require companies to spell out what "other" includes. Most often, it's the cost of letting the CEO use the company jet to take his family on vacation, or what the company pays to provide its top dogs with security systems, company cars or chauffeurs, country club memberships, and financial planning services. Governance experts rightly note that people who are earning millions of dollars annually can afford to pay for their own country club memberships. And they argue that these perks are of dubious value to the companies that provide them. They also give a glimpse of just how regally top officers are treated. As a shareholder, you don't want your CEO to consider himself a king.

What if a company has great numbers, but bad governance? Think twice. Just like countries run by benevolent dictators, a dictatorial CEO can do well—sometimes for a long stretch of time. But the chance of a blowup is also significant. These companies may still warrant buying, but investors are taking more risk when they do.

 ## FINDING FINANCIAL DATA ON THE WEB

Years ago, it was tough to get the timely information you needed to invest wisely on your own. In the early 1970s, for example, the pinnacle of technology was the Dow Jones news wire, which tapped out one-line notes about per-share profits and losses when companies released their earnings. It took weeks before earnings were translated into analysts' reports, which were then mailed to investors.

If individual investors wanted to find a market price for a stock, they had to call their brokers or hang out in a brokerage office, where they could watch the "ticker"—an electronic message board that reported trades a few minutes after they happened. When clients wanted to buy or sell stock, they called their brokers, too, and they expected each trade to cost from $100 to $500 in commissions. A few days or a week later, they would get a written statement that showed how much they had paid—or gotten—for their stock.

These days, investors can get earnings releases in real time and real detail the moment trades are completed. Want a current market price? You can have it with a few keystrokes. To trade, all you need is a computer, an account, a modem, and, of course, some cash. Those costly trading commissions of yesteryear have shrunk to $4 to $30, depending on the discount broker. (You can certainly find brokers who charge more, but you're no longer forced to pay a fortune for each trade, so why would you?) And the trade is often completed and confirmed before you even sign off.

Experts say that this rapid and vast access to financial information makes the playing field more level, because individual investors can see market information as quickly as the pros. But it can be a challenge to navigate through the dozens of financial sites to find one or two that provide all the information you need.

Where do you go online to get company information and do research? Dozens of sites offer everything from companies' annual reports to detailed technical analyses of individual stocks. Some sites allow you to register and then track your portfolio on a minute-by-minute basis. If you use an online broker, the firm you use is likely to offer a "watch list" service, where you can plug in the names of the companies you want to watch regularly and get their stock quotes every time you sign on.

However, if you just need information—such as stock prices, ticker symbols, financial statements, and information about what managers are doing with their stock—a good option is to simply set up a personal home page at Yahoo!.

To do this, simply go to Yahoo.com and click on "My Yahoo!". Near the top of the page, it will ask if you want to sign in or if you're "new here." From there, the site will ask you to register by filling in your name, email address, and a few other details. When that stage is done, a new page loads. At the top of that page, you are asked if you want to personalize the page, adding information on a variety of topics, from entertainment to business. Yes, again. Click again on "Personalize This Page" to bring up a prompt to "Add Modules." The topic would be money, and "stocks and investing." This allows you to create as extensive a list of stocks to watch as you'd like. They'll appear—with their current market prices and change—every time you sign on to your home page. If a stock has had significant movement, you can click on the ticker in your chart to pull up details and recent news.

Not fond of the home page concept? You can get the same information by going to http://finance.yahoo.com. Feed in ticker symbols—the market abbreviations that are used when buying and selling stocks and mutual funds through an exchange—to get a quote. If you don't know the ticker symbol, just type the company name. If you have a full company name and you've spelled it correctly, you'll get the symbol. If you've typed a partial name and there are several possibilities, you'll get a list. Scroll down the list and click on the company you want.

Let's say you want to know about IBM. You type IBM into the "Get Quotes" search bar and find out that its symbol is conveniently also its name. The next screen gives you a detailed look at IBM's daily trading activity, including the number of shares that changed hands that day; the normal trading volume; the fifty-two-week high and low; the company's earnings per share, P/E ratio, dividends, and dividend yield; and a chart that can be modified to show short- or long-term trend lines.

If you had done this on May 13, 1999, for example, you would have seen that IBM's stock had soared $20, closing at an all-time high of $246 on twice the normal trading volume—a hint that something was up. Scrolling down you'll see a list of recent headlines. At the time, you would have read that IBM Chairman Louis Gerstner had said there was pent-up demand for the company's products because of rising acceptance of the Web. Gerstner wasn't usually so positive, so the market reacted strongly.

But let's say you wanted to know more. What were the company's most recent earnings? Are company executives buying or selling IBM stock? What do securities analysts think of IBM? It's all there, with just a few more keystrokes.

Click on "Analyst Opinion." This gives you analysts' ratings that rank the company on a scale of 1 to 5, with 1 recommending a "strong buy" and 5 meaning "strong sell." In a series of tables, this screen shows how many analysts are recommending the stock as a strong buy, a buy, a hold, and a sell. Analysts rarely say "sell," so anything neutral is considered relatively negative.

1. strong buy
2. moderate buy
3. hold
4. moderate sell
5. strong sell

Click the "Back" arrow at the top of your screen to return to the IBM chart, where there's another option called "Profile." This takes you to a page that includes a brief company description, the names of top executives, and if you scroll down a bit, a link to "Key Statistics." That link will provide you a variety of information, such as pertinent earnings and cash flow data, company news, insider trades, and what other investors are saying about the company on the message board.

Under "News & Info" is a message board where a host of people— many of whom know less about IBM than you and/or your local video store clerk do—tout or trash the company's stock. Consider this the electronic equivalent of cocktail-party chatter. If you feel curious, read it. But when you're considering an investment, ignore it unless you can tell who is posting the comments and you have reason to believe that they are reliable sources. In most instances, the people who post messages are anonymous. For all you know, they're company insiders, short-sellers (who profit when stock prices drop), or your local video store clerk. Besides, you already know the company's news, as well as the stock price, the trend, and the analysts' views of IBM. You don't need the gossip.

The insider-trading history can give you a hint of how well company executives like the stock. However, because many executives receive discounted shares as part of their compensation packages, you should expect there to be more insider sales than open-market purchases.

The insider-trading chart shows how the shares were bought—in other words, whether they were acquired via employee stock options or on the open market—and sold. Many analysts see open-market purchases as the most positive insider move. The insider trading screen can also be useful in tracking how many shares top officers continue to hold and whether, over time, they're adding to their holdings or divesting themselves of stock.

For in-depth earnings data, click on "SEC Filings." There you can read everything from the company's latest annual and quarterly reports to its proxy statement, which details how officers are paid and what outside business relationships the company has with its directors.

MANIC MARKETS

In the first edition of this book, written in 1999, a section was dedicated to explaining technology stocks. At the time, technology stocks were defying all market standards on fundamental value—often selling for hundreds of times their earnings, if they had earnings at all. Unlike most of what was published at the time, this book did not recommend buying tech stocks. Instead, it explained market manias—moments in time when logic is thrown to the wind and stock prices rise or fall much farther and faster than numbers and reason would say they should.

While the Internet mania of 1999 has faded, it still provides an important lesson that investors need to heed when the next mania—and no one knows precisely what that will be or when it will strike—rolls around.

Net Mania

"Dot-com" stocks had risen so far so fast by late 1999 that many experts said we had entered a mania, a moment when market math temporarily goes out the window. They sagely predicted that when sanity returned, valuations would plummet, laying waste to the millions of unsophisticated investors who bought Net stocks without questioning their true worth.

"The Internet is two different things," said Michael Murphy, editor of the *California Technology Stock Letter* and author of *Every Investor's Guide to High-Tech Stocks & Mutual Funds* back in 1999. "In the real world, it is a fundamental paradigm shift in how we do business. In the financial world, it's a bubble."

Murphy's argument has proven all too true. However, investors who want to use the Internet mania as a model to avoid future investment mistakes must understand that there were plenty of respected experts singing the opposite tune.

Another contingent of market professionals believed that Net companies were so fundamentally different from businesses that rely on bricks and mortar—buildings, branch offices, and retail outlets— that their high stock valuations were reasonable. Even Internet naysayers said the rush to buy was not completely irrational. While past market manias saw investors snapping up tulips at irrational prices in seventeenth-century Holland, for example, underlying the Net fever was a belief that the Internet will change the world. Tulips have no long-term economic value, but the Net transcends time and space and makes it easier to reach customers, communicate, and transact business. Prices may have been steep, but some companies would eventually prosper and make their investors rich.

How expensive were Net stocks? Most stocks sell for ten to thirty times their current year per-share earnings. In market-speak, that's their price/earnings multiple. At the height of the mania, many Net stocks fetched hundreds of times—sometimes even thousands of times—their projected earnings.

"Is a 90 multiple—or a 300 multiple—for America Online too much? No," said Alexander C. Cheung, who managed the Monument Internet Fund at the time. Citing Amazon's zooming sales growth, Cheung said, "Amazon.com is only a five-year-old company. Can we use the same methodology to measure Amazon as Barnes & Noble or Wal-Mart? No."

Yet experts agreed that plenty of Internet stocks would not survive. Cheung, for example, figured that at least half of the Internet highfliers of 1998 and 1999 would be bankrupt in five to ten years. Which companies would fall and which would prosper was nearly impossible to say.

The debate surrounding Amazon.com Inc., the Internet-based retailer, crystallized the arguments on both sides. While the company's sales were soaring in 1999, so were its losses. The company had lost an astounding $1.2 billion since it was founded in 1994. Still, investors poured in money. During 1999, Amazon.com's stock price soared from about $20 to an all-time high of about $113.

Why were investors so eager to buy this stock when other companies were more profitable? As Cheung put it, "You have to look at the business model, not just the business."

The Dot-Com Business Model

Amazon had roughly 10 million customers in early 2000. That was a big increase from a year earlier but still just a fraction of the roughly 125 million users of the Internet. And, of course, the number of Web users was expected to continue growing at a blistering pace.

If Amazon's growth mirrored that of the Web, it would have 25 million customers by 2002 and sales of $2 billion, Cheung projected. But Amazon didn't plan to grow merely at the same pace as the Web. One reason the company lost so much money is that it aimed to be a "killer retailer"—such a recognized name that when people think books, they click on Amazon. The company was spending a small fortune on advertising, acquisitions, and customer service to gain a loyal following. Meanwhile, the company was expanding its offerings in an effort to leverage its name and infrastructure into more sales. If the strategy worked, Amazon would become wildly profitable.

"When you cross that line, earnings could increase exponentially," Cheung said. "With a normal retailer, the profit margin is 2 percent to 4 percent of sales. But if you can do it without the brick and mortar, you can expect 5 percent to 6 percent."

Others questioned whether Amazon would ever see a profit. Virtually anyone with a computer, some programming expertise, and a connection with publishers can compete for book buyers, noted Alan F. Skrainka, chief market strategist with Edward Jones in St. Louis. Thus, the easiest way to gain market share when you're selling a commodity, such as books, CDs, or even stock trades, is to cut prices. That's good for consumers but rotten for profits, and ultimately it's bad for shareholders, he said.

"The Internet may soon be known as the great destroyer of profit margins," said Skrainka. "Companies that compete on price alone will not be able to earn a return for shareholders in the virtual marketplace."

Newsletter editor Murphy agreed. He expected other established booksellers that had already broken into the Web, including Barnes & Noble, and some that promised to hit the Web soon to erode Amazon's market share. Because the Web makes reaching consumers so simple, publishers might sell their books directly, he said. "A company like Amazon is probably never going to make any money," Murphy said. "I think they might as well change their name to Amazon.org." (*Org* is the Web designation for nonprofit groups.)

Both arguments have proved partially true.

Amazon has become a killer retailer. The company, which had $147 million in sales in 1997, boasted $10.7 *billion* in sales in 2006, producing a $190 million net profit. But the company's stock price, which closed over $85 a share in November of 1999, plunged to $25 a year later. By mid-2001, Amazon was selling for a tiny fraction of its previous market value—roughly $6 a share. It's taken eight years for Amazon's stock price to rise to its 1999 levels. And some analysts believe its current stock price still isn't supported by earnings, which boosts the chance that its market value will tank again.

 ## WHY I LOVE COSTCO

First, a disclaimer: I no longer buy individual stocks. That's because my day job is as a business reporter for the *Los Angeles Times*. A couple of years ago, when Tribune Co. took over the Times Mirror Co., the company updated and tightened its stock-ownership guidelines for business reporters in a way that made it difficult for me to buy company shares without spending a great deal of time considering possible conflicts of interest. Instead of spending additional hours researching whether I could buy the companies I wanted to own, I opted for the simple approach: I bought (and continue to buy) index mutual funds. (This is the same strategy I'll recommend in Chapter 14, which explains how lazy investors can put together a simple, all-weather portfolio.)

Nonetheless, I occasionally long to buy shares in an individual company. In the interest of illustrating how a reasonable person might bring all the things you learned together to evaluate an individual company, I'll tell you what intrigues me about Costco Wholesale Corp.

First, like most investors, my list of potential companies to invest in is based on things that I know, either from news or experience. I know a lot about Costco because I shop there.

Costco is a warehouse club store, selling everything from groceries to furniture. It competes with grocery stores, as well as the likes of Wal-Mart and Target. But if you walk into a store, you'll quickly realize it's little like those competitors. The stores are massive. The merchandise is on the shelves above the stock that's being sold. Items are sold in bulk, but there's little variety—and absolutely no junk.

The company offers a wide variety of merchandise, but it chooses just a handful of quality products in each category and that's all it sells. That gives it negotiating power with sellers. It's going to carry, maybe, six types of cold cereal instead of six dozen. So everybody who buys cereal at Costco is going to be buying Honey Bunches of Oats, Frosted Mini-Wheats, or Raisin Bran, for example. If you happen to make one of those brands, you're going to sell a ton of your product if Costco chooses to carry it, so you'll give it an exceptional volume discount.

But, because the company carefully screens its products for quality, buyers also trust it. If you want the best steaks, you buy them at Costco. Need a good wine? Costco again. Good tennis shoes, socks, a quality down pillow? How about a nice leather chair? Office supplies, bouquets of flowers, cell phones, and refrigerators. They're all there, and the company stands behind them with a terrific return policy, so you don't have to worry about getting a faux bargain on inferior merchandise.

This has fueled tremendous growth over the past decade. However, Costco is now the nation's fourth largest retailer and the eighth largest retailer in the world. At that size, growth begins to slow. Where sales jumped 13 percent from 2005 to 2006, they grew just 7 percent in 2007, to $63.1 billion.

Net profits were flat in 2007, but that's mainly because the company recognized a series of one-time charges. Without those one-time items, profits would have risen 14 percent, according to the company's chief financial officer, Richard Galanti. Notably, the company started as an old-fashioned retailer, but its Web business is growing by leaps and bounds, from $76 million in sales in 2001 to $1.24 billion in sales in 2007.

On the corporate governance front, it helps to compare Costco to other retailers.

Here's one simple comparison: When worker contracts were up for renewal three years ago, Safeway endured a lengthy and costly strike. Why? Chief Executive Steven Burd said the industry's profit margins were too narrow to pay union wages. Thousands of shoppers abandoned Safeway stores to avoid picket lines. Many ended up at Costco, where there are no strikes because the company's workers were earning an average of $40,000 annually, plus benefits, which wasn't half bad in 2004.

Workers at Safeway might also note that whereas Safeway was unwilling to share profits with the checkers and clerks in the company's supermarkets, the company hasn't been anywhere near as stingy with its executives. Burd earned $7 million in 2006, according to the company's proxy statement.

James Sinegal, chief executive of Costco, takes the opposite approach. As far as CEOs of Fortune 500 companies go, he's lamentably underpaid. He earned $454,629 in 2006. As a shareholder, you can think of it this way: With the $6.5 million Sinegal didn't pay himself (compared with Safeway), Costco can hire 163 workers to staff its warehouses.

A few other warm and fuzzies about Costco's management: When asked to speak at a conference of business reporters, Sinegal arrived wearing a Kirkland shirt. Kirkland is Costco's signature brand. Sinegal mentioned that it was good quality and a great price—exactly what the company is about.

When the stock option scandal broke—revealing that hundreds of U.S. companies cheated when granting executive stock rights in order to give executives an unfair advantage over common shareholders—Costco instigated an internal investigation to find out if it had the proper controls to ensure that didn't happen at the Issaquah, Washington–based company. It didn't. A couple of its option grants were sloppy enough that the company couldn't determine whether there was cheating, Sinegal said in a statement to shareholders.

While the company found no sign of fraud, a couple of executives may have profited by as much as $200,000. Sinegal apologized to shareholders; the company took a hit to earnings to recognize the potential income tax cost to employees of the gaffe; and it instituted internal controls to ensure that it wouldn't happen again.

Naturally, it would be better if it never happened at all. But if it did, this is how you'd want an ethical company to respond.

So, buy the stock, right? Not so fast. You want to make sure you get as good a bargain on Costco stock as you get on its steaks. And, when this was being written, you weren't. That's because the company's shares had experienced a significant run-up, so Costco was selling for roughly 27 times trailing earnings and 19 times projected earnings. Both multiples are high for a retailer, and both exceed the company's growth in sales and net profits.

What do you do? If you like the company but don't like the price, you put it on a watch list and keep your eye out for dips, when the company's shares might sell for a price that's a better bargain.

QUICK TAKE

What You'll LEARN

This chapter describes:

- Keeping an Eye on the Financials
- What About Stock Price Movement?
- Tax Implications of Selling at a Profit
- Calculating the Break-Even Sales Price

What You'll DO

- Check your investments quarterly to ensure profits, revenue, and cash flow remain on track
- Sell investments when they're no longer living up to expectations
- Calculate an after-tax break-even point if you want to sell stocks in less than a year

How You'll USE This

Most of the time, periodic analysis should tell you to hold tight to your position. On occasion, however, you'll determine that you made an investing gaffe and bail out. If you decide to sell out early, this chapter can help you know how much to put aside to pay your year-end tax bill.

TOUGH SELL

M any of the nation's top investors have one common credo: Buy good companies and hold them long-term. Billionaire investor Warren Buffett goes a step further. He suggests you buy good companies and hold them "forever."

But everyone makes an occasional mistake. Knowing when to cut and run can be as important as knowing what to buy. Still, even professional investors acknowledge that determining when to sell is tough, for reasons both psychological (it's hard to admit you've erred) and practical (you must keep a close eye on your portfolio).

However, determining when—or whether—you should sell is easier if you spend some time each quarter keeping up with your investments and occasionally subjecting them to the detailed analysis that you conducted when determining which stocks to buy.

KEEPING AN EYE ON THE FINANCIALS

To track your investments with a minimum of time and effort, make a point of looking at the quarterly statements you receive. Publicly held companies send out statements every three months that show how their sales and earnings have fared over the period compared with the preceding three months and the year-ago quarter. The statement also includes a message from the chief executive or chairman that briefly describes the factors that contributed to the quarter's results.

Wise investors take a look at just a few key elements, such as profit, strategies, and extraordinary items. On the profit side, investors want to look at year-to-year comparisons of net earnings. Year-to-year earnings comparisons are usually better than quarter-to-quarter comparisons, because many companies are subject to cyclical swings. A retailer, for example, is likely to post a higher profit in the final quarter of the year—Christmas season—than the following quarter. Consequently, to accurately gauge this company's growth, you must compare fourth quarter with fourth quarter, first quarter with first.

When making the comparisons, ask this: Are net earnings growing as you expected when you purchased the stock? If they're not—no matter whether the earnings are much higher or much lower—you need to ask why.

For instance, has a one-time event, such as the sale of a profitable subsidiary, boosted near-term profits to the detriment of long-term results? Or has the company simply found more efficient ways to operate, which are likely to make it even richer over the long term? The answer to that question determines whether you should consider selling now or whether you should consider buying more shares.

If earnings have been disappointing, the analysis is the same. Are earnings down because the company is retooling to accommodate strong growth? Or is it because demand is slack or competition is stiff?

The answers to those questions are likely to be found in the chairman's message right at the beginning of the report. If the numbers you've reviewed—and that message—leave you with continued positive feelings about the company's prospects, hang tight. Consider yourself a budding Buffett and keep a firm grip on your shares.

WHAT ABOUT STOCK PRICE MOVEMENT?

But shouldn't you check the stock price before you decide to hold? Even if the company's fundamentals are sound, doesn't it make sense to sell when the stock price has risen a set amount? If the stock price has risen far past the point where you think reason dictates price, maybe. Otherwise, probably not.

If you sell to lock in a profit and the stock is not held in an individual retirement account or another tax-favored retirement plan, you've also locked in a taxable gain. In addition, you'll pay trading costs to sell and purchase new shares. Ultimately, your next investment must be substantially better than the first, once you account for the tax and trading costs. Consequently, many seasoned investors advise that you ignore the day-to-day price movements as long as you are convinced of the stock's fundamental value.

Of course, there are always exceptions, such as those "hot" stocks selling in "hot" industries. On occasion, the value of a high-flying stock will get so out of whack that reasonable investors would have to conclude that it makes some sense to take their profits and invest their money elsewhere. Still, for those who were lucky enough to enjoy that type of appreciation in a very short time, it still may make sense to hold on for a few extra months. Why? You need to hold a stock for more than a year to qualify for long-term capital gains tax rates on the profit. Those capital gains rates can sometimes save you so much versus paying tax at your ordinary income tax rate that you can suffer a fairly substantial loss on the stock and still come out better off for waiting.

Otherwise, look at the stock price only when the company's earnings are troubling and the chairman's message gives you further pause. At that point, you use the current market price to calculate the firm's price-to-earnings ratio. You then evaluate its future prospects for growth by consulting the *Value Line Investment Survey*.

As described in Chapter 5, the price/earnings (P/E) ratio can be calculated by simply dividing the current market price by the annualized earnings per share. If the resulting figure is less than the five-year projected earnings growth rate in *Value Line*, it may be best to hang on.

If, however, the P/E is higher than the projected growth rate, it's a signal that the stock price could decline. Naturally, you can hang on and hope for a recovery. But before you do, ask "Is my money better invested elsewhere?" and the corollary question, "Would I buy this stock today?"

It makes sense to hold on to a lackluster performer only if you think your prospects with other investments aren't any better. Holding on because you've suffered a loss and want to "get even" before selling only serves to put you farther behind, investment professionals say.

Consider Mary, who bought one hundred shares of XYZ Co. at $10 each but then saw the per-share price drop to $7, leaving her with a $300 loss. She decides to hang on, waiting for a recovery. Five years later, the share price does climb back to $10. But Mary shouldn't consider that breaking even.

If she had sold five years earlier and reinvested $650 (the stock's $700 value, minus a $50 trading fee—there is no tax when you have no profit) in another company that appreciated 10 percent annually, she would have had $1,069.45. Had Mary's initial investment been $100,000 instead of $1,000, the $69.45 she'd forgone would amount to $6,945. In other words, the more you have invested, the more it hurts to stick with a loser.

TAX IMPLICATIONS OF SELLING AT A PROFIT

You understand that you ought to sell your losers, but what about those winners? Every once in a while an investor strikes it big in a big hurry.

Consider those who invested in Qualcomm Inc. stock at the beginning of 1999, when the company was selling for $28 per share. By late November, the stock price had soared to a stunning $372. Meanwhile, analysts who had touted Qualcomm's stock when it was selling for 40 times earnings were considerably less enthusiastic about the company's appreciation potential when the stock started selling for 290 times current-year profits.

Yet if an investor was holding the shares in a taxable account at the end of 1999 and had owned the stock for less than a year, he'd be wise to do a little math before selling. Why? If you sell stocks that you've owned for less than a full twelve months, you pay federal tax at your ordinary income tax rate rather than the lower capital gains rate. Even for somebody in a fairly modest tax bracket, that difference can amount to thousands of dollars. But what if the stock's price drops before your one-year anniversary? You may still be better off if you wait. Indeed, a middle-income investor could suffer about a 10 percent loss on his or her shares and still end up better off, after tax, by waiting for the lower capital gains rate.

To illustrate, consider two hypothetical investors: John Average, who is in the 28 percent federal tax bracket, and Gina Gotrocks, who pays 35 percent of her income in federal tax. They each bought one hundred shares of Qualcomm stock in January 1999, when it was selling for $28 a share. But by Thanksgiving, Qualcomm was selling for a stunning $372, leaving these investors with taxable gains of $344 per share.

If John sold at Thanksgiving, he'd pay tax at his ordinary income tax rate, which would cost him $9,632 in federal tax. If he waited until January, and Qualcomm's stock managed to maintain its value, he would pay tax at capital gains rates, which currently top out at 15 percent. That would cost him just $5,160, or $4,472 less than if he paid income taxes on the gain.

But what if the stock price fell in the interim? John could actually suffer a $48 per share decline in the value of his Qualcomm stock and still end up ahead, after tax, thanks to the lower capital gains rates. No kidding. If he sold at Thanksgiving, he would cash out with $37,200. But after paying the $9,632 in federal income tax, he pockets just $27,568. On the other hand, if he waited and the stock dropped to $324 in the interim, he would pay $4,440 in federal tax and walk away with $27,960—$392 more—after tax.

What about Gina? She'd have to lose more than $80 per share on the stock—in other words, Qualcomm's stock price would have to drop from Thanksgiving's $372 to $292—before she'd be better off selling then, rather than waiting for the lower capital gains rate. If she sold at Thanksgiving, she'd pay $12,040 in federal tax—that's 35 percent of her $34,400 gain—and go home with $25,160 after tax. If she sold at $292 the following February, she'd pay just $3,945 in federal capital gains taxes and go home with $25,161.

Incidentally, Qualcomm's case also illustrates another reason to hang on. In late December the company's stock split four-for-one. By March 2000 the company's shares were selling for the equivalent of $525 on a presplit basis. John and Gina were well rewarded for a few months of waiting.

Shortly after that, though, the tech stock bubble burst and Qualcomm fell from its insanely lofty highs. A year later, Qualcomm was selling for about one-fifth of its previous market value. It remains, incidentally, a great company with good products, strong earnings, and excellent growth. When it's selling for a reasonable multiple of earnings, it's a great stock too. But, when the market gets too enthused about the company—or the industry—investors are wise to do what our hypothetical investors did and figure out a good time to sell.

CALCULATING THE BREAK-EVEN SALES PRICE

Let's say you have a huge winner in your portfolio—a company whose stock price has soared fast and furiously and now you're considering a sale, even though you haven't owned the stock for a full year. Do you hold it a little longer and bite your nails wondering whether its price will drop again? Or do you sell now and take the tax hit, paying tax at vastly higher ordinary tax rates versus the bargain capital gains rates that you get for investments you've held longer? It may be easier to weigh this decision if you know where your break-even point is. That's the point where the tax cost of selling today meets the risk of losing a portion of your gains.

How do you figure it? To calculate it correctly requires high-school algebra that most investors have long since forgotten. However, for the nostalgic, here is how to calculate the break-even sales price: Take the net after-tax sales proceeds (assuming you're paying tax at ordinary income tax rates) and subtract the product of the long-term capital gains rate and your tax basis in the stock; then divide that number by one minus the long-term capital gains rate.

You followed that, right?

Never fear, you can come up with a fairly accurate guesstimate by simply comparing the tax you'd pay on each share at ordinary income tax rates to the tax at long-term capital gains rates—assuming that the stock price stays steady. With Gina, for example, you know that she'd pay roughly $120 in federal tax on every share that she sold at $372 in November. (The sales price of $372 minus the $28 she paid equals $344; multiply that by 35 percent to get $120.40, which I rounded off to $120.) If she waits until February to get the lower 15 percent rate, she pays just $51.60 per share in tax. The $68 difference tells you she can easily suffer a $68 per share loss on Qualcomm's price without suffering any after-tax loss to her pocketbook.

Of course, this method understates the real impact. (In reality, if you wait and get less for your shares, you have a lower profit, and that means you pay even less in tax.) But it's a far cry simpler for those who prefer a back-of-the-envelope calculation to algebra.

For those who prefer the accuracy of algebra, here's the formula:

$$\frac{ATP - (LTCG \times TB)}{1 - (LTCG)} = BESP$$

ATP	After-tax proceeds from the sale at your ordinary income tax rate
LTCG	Long-term capital gains rate of 15 percent (0.15)
TB	Your tax basis in the stock
BESP	Break-even sales price

Let's fill in some numbers from Gina's example to see if it gets clearer. Gina paid $28 per share for her stock. If she sold at $372, her taxable gain would be $344 (the difference between the cost and the sales price). Multiply that amount by her ordinary income tax rate of 35 percent. She'd pay $120.40 in federal tax on each share she sold. That would leave her with net after-tax sales proceeds of $251.60. You plug that number in where it says ATP (after-tax proceeds). Now multiply the long-term capital gains rate of 15 percent (0.15) by her tax basis in the stock of $28. The result: $4.20. Subtract $4.20 from $251.60 to get $247.40.

Finally, divide $247.40 by the inverse of the long-term capital gains rate, which is 85 percent, or 0.85. The result: $291.06, which I rounded up to $292 (so you still come out ahead, even if only by pennies). That's the break-even point. As long as Gina sells her stock for more than $291.06, she's ahead by waiting for the lower capital gains rate.

Here's how Gina's formula looks:

$$251.60 - (0.15 \times \$28 = \$4.20) = 247.40 \div 0.85 = \$291.06$$

The following worksheet provides the formula for you to use with numbers from your portfolio.

 RUNNING THE NUMBERS

Calculating the Tax Implications of Selling Too Soon

1. To determine how much you would net (after tax) if you sold stock today, first compute the sales price minus the original cost of the investment, to get your net proceeds.

   _____ − _____ = _____
   (sales price)   *(original cost of investment)*   *(net proceeds)*

2. Now multiply the net proceeds by your ordinary income tax rate (0.25, 0.28, 0.33, or 0.35) to get the after-tax proceeds.

   _____ × _____ = _____
   (net proceeds)   *(ordinary income tax rate)*   *(after-tax proceeds)*

3. Put the resulting after-tax proceeds in the space marked #1 below.

   [#1] $_____ − (0.15 × [#2] $_____) =
   (after-tax proceeds) (0.20 × (original cost of investment))

   [#3] $_____
   (result)

4. Plug in the amount that you originally paid for the stock in space #2.

5. Multiply the long-term capital gains rate (0.15) by the number in space #2, and subtract the result from the number you plugged into space #1.

6. Plug the result into space #3.

7. Now divide #3 by 0.85 in the space below. The result is your break-even sales price.

[#3] $_____ ÷ 0.85 = $_____
(result from above formula) ÷ 0.85 = *(break-even sales price)*

QUICK TAKE

What You'll LEARN

Bonds and other fixed-income investments may not be exciting, but they belong in every portfolio. This chapter describes:

- Fixed-Income Investment Choices
- Bonds for Diversification
- Risks

What You'll DO

- Determine the role of bonds in your portfolio
- Set realistic return expectations, given the type of bond you choose
- Decide whether to go with taxable or tax-free investments

How You'll USE This

Getting familiar with bonds' risks and rewards will help you use these securities as a tool to fund your intermediate-term goals and to keep your overall portfolio more stable and diversified.

INVESTING IN BONDS   7

Many investors consider bonds to be the dowager aunt of the investment world. Nice, but boring. After all, this is an investment with an average annual return in the 5 percent range—5.4 percent for long-term government bonds and 5.9 percent for long-term corporate bonds. That's the type of return that will make you rich . . . well, someday when you're really, really old, if you're really, really thrifty.

Yet bonds—or at least some type of fixed-income investment, ranging from long-term corporate bonds to shorter-term government notes, bills, money markets, and certificates of deposit—are a must for every investor's portfolio. There are two reasons why.

First, fixed-income instruments address certain financial goals better than any other investment. And despite the urge to act as if investing is a high-stakes contest in which the winners are the people who post the highest gains, remember your mantra. Having the amount of money you need when you need it is the name of this game.

The fact is, while U.S. stocks have posted higher average annual returns than any other type of financial asset over long periods of time, they're a miserable place to put short- and medium-term money. That's because stock prices gyrate wildly in short periods of time. And sometimes stock prices can stay down for periods ranging from five to fifteen years. If the money you're investing is aimed at satisfying an important goal in the meantime, you're out of luck.

Fixed-income instruments are ideal for addressing those short- and medium-term goals for a couple of simple reasons. Ninety percent of the return on a fixed-income instrument comes from the "coupon," or the interest paid on your initial investment, not from price appreciation. That makes them perfect for people who need to generate cash from their investments to supplement their monthly income. And it makes them a perfect investment for someone with an important goal that must be satisfied with a set amount of cash within five years or so.

The second reason is diversification. Bond returns have almost zero correlation with stock returns. Translation: When the price of big-company stocks soared 23 percent in 1996, bond prices fell 0.93 percent.

When stocks posted another 21 percent gain in 1999, bond prices were down 8.96 percent. On the other hand, when stocks dropped 9.11 percent in 2000, bond prices soared 21.5 percent. And in 2001 and 2002, when stocks lost another 34 percent of their value, bond prices rose another 21 percent.

Stocks and bonds don't always move in opposite directions, but because they often do, bonds are a great way to provide stability for an investment portfolio.

Naturally, they're also a great choice for people who have stopped investing and are now living off their investment portfolio, which we'll talk about in Chapter 14.

What's the downside of investing in bonds? Remember those average annual returns, which are about half the average returns of investing in stocks? Over a long time horizon, that difference in return can have a dramatic impact on your wealth. Someone who invested $100,000 in stocks and earned an average annual return of 10 percent, for example, would have $1.75 million at the end of 30 years. Someone who invested that same amount in bonds and earned an average of 5 percent would have just $432,194.

Unlike your dowager aunt, bonds also aren't overwhelmingly stable. In fact, long-term bonds have almost as many money-losing years as stocks. Why would an investment that gets the bulk of its return from interest ever lose money? Whenever interest rates rise, the value of existing bonds drops. That's simply because the coupon—or interest rate—on the old bond begins to look paltry, so investors flock to higher-yielding, newly issued bonds. How much the market value of an existing bond will suffer will vary based on both the creditworthiness of the borrower—after all, bonds are essentially IOUs—and the duration of the maturity. The longer the maturity, the more a bond's value is hurt when rates rise. On the other hand, when interest rates decline, the value of old bonds can soar. In 1982, for example, when inflation had finally gotten under control and the federal government started drastically cutting interest rates, the value of long-term government bonds soared 40.36 percent.

How much of your portfolio should you devote to bonds?

The rule of thumb is to subtract your age from 100 and invest the result in stocks; the rest in fixed-income assets. If you did the calculations in Chapter 3, however, you should be able to come up with a closer estimate by adding together the amount of money you need for short- and intermediate-term goals. If you have no short- or intermediate term-goals, use the rule of thumb—or, if you're an aggressive investor, a modified rule: Subtract your age from 110. Invest the result in stocks and the rest in fixed-income investments, for the sake of diversification.

FIXED-INCOME INVESTMENT CHOICES

The fixed-income portion of your portfolio can be made up of a variety of things. The type of fixed-income investment that best serves your needs depends on your income and circumstances. For instance, if you need current income, you may want to take a look at corporate bonds or, if you're in a high tax bracket, tax-free municipals. Both offer better after-tax returns than U.S. Treasury bonds, the bellwether bond noted for the promise of complete security of your principal if you hold the bond to maturity.

At a time when thirty-year Treasury bonds would yield about 6 percent, you would expect to get 8 percent or more on higher- and medium-risk corporate bonds. Those better returns mean you can live more comfortably. It is the difference between receiving $6,000 annually on a $100,000 investment and receiving $8,000 or even $10,000. But you have to recognize that corporate bonds also pose more risk to your principal. After all, a company is more likely to have difficulty paying its bondholders than would the U.S. government, which can raise taxes or easily borrow more if it falls short of cash.

As a result, experts suggest that if you invest in corporate bonds, do it through a mutual fund, which gives you wide diversification and the benefit of professional management and clout. (When bond-issuing companies get into hot water, they often invite their biggest investors to the table to help work out a repayment plan. Individuals rarely get such invitations, and if they did, they usually lack the skill and clout to make the most of such meetings.)

Real estate investment trusts (REITs), which are actually stocks but are sold on the basis of yield, like fixed-income investments, typically yield about 2 percentage points more than Treasuries. Many professionals also suggest that individuals avoid buying REITs on their own and, instead, invest in them through mutual funds. Since

REITs aren't technically fixed-income investments, however, they're discussed in-depth in Chapter 10.

Municipal bonds, which are issued by state and local governments and agencies, offer less generous interest rates than corporate bonds, but you usually get to keep all the money. Most types of municipal bonds are exempt from federal income tax and—for in-state residents— state taxes as well. For someone in the highest tax brackets, it doesn't take much return to make this a great deal.

Consider that for those in a combined marginal tax bracket of 45 percent—this applies to those paying 35 percent in federal income taxes, plus 10 percent or more in state tax—getting a 5 percent tax-free return is the equivalent of getting a 9.09 percent return on a taxable bond. For example, if an investor in the 45 percent tax bracket plopped $10,000 into a bond earning 9.09 percent, he'd come away with $909 at year-end. However, he'd then have to pay 45 percent of that—$409—to federal and state taxing authorities. That leaves him with just $500, or a 5 percent after-tax yield on his investment. That 9.09 percent is called the "taxable equivalent yield," and it is the basis by which municipal bonds are usually sold.

To figure a taxable equivalent yield, divide the interest rate by the inverse of your combined state and federal tax rate. (You can estimate your tax rate by adding your top federal marginal bracket—ask your tax accountant, if you don't know—plus your state tax rate. State taxes are deductible, so this isn't exact, but it's close enough. A percentage point or two won't matter much.) In the above example, that means you divide 5 by 0.55—1 minus the 45 percent (0.45) combined tax rate—to get 9.09.

On the other hand, if you've got a child going to college in a year or two and you need most of the first year's tuition money ready and available without risk to your principal, you'd be better served with a money market account. Money markets offer relatively paltry yields, but they invest in short-term government and corporate securities that are both safe and easily accessible. That makes such accounts, which can be opened with mutual funds or banks, ideal places to park short-term money that you can't afford to lose.

You could also choose a Treasury note, which is like a bond, but it matures—or pays back the principal—in two to five years. Pick a note that matures when your goal needs to be satisfied.

If you are an investor who can handle a higher default risk, boost your returns by buying comparatively riskier securities, such as a junk-bond fund (also known as high-yield funds). If you're looking for lower risk, on the other hand, stick with Treasuries with short maturities—those that will pay back the principal in five years or less.

In many cases, investors would be wise to diversify their bond portfolios just as they diversify their stock holdings. For example, if you have a substantial bond portfolio, put a portion in junk or international bonds, a portion in Treasuries, and perhaps a portion in municipal bonds or mortgage-backed securities. The Treasury portion will keep a bit of your principal safe, whereas the junk portion will boost the return. The municipals can give you decent tax-free income, whereas the mortgage-backed securities offer guaranteed repayment of principal and somewhat higher interest rates than other guaranteed investments.

Bonds for Diversification

Let's say you have no specific short-term goal, but you wonder whether you ought to have a bit—perhaps just 10 percent—of your portfolio in bonds, solely for diversification's sake? Absolutely, experts maintain.

The last time the U.S. stock market went through a sustained down period, in the 1970s, the return on two-year Treasury notes—one of the dullest fixed-income investments—handily outpaced that of stocks for a full decade. In 1982, when interest rates were finally beginning to drop after hitting historic highs, the Standard and Poor's 500 stock index posted a healthy 21.6 percent return. But the return on thirty-year Treasury bonds was far better—43.6 percent—thanks to falling interest rates that sharply boosted the price of those bonds, says Joan Payden, chief executive of Payden & Rygel, a Los Angeles–based money management firm. "We are always tainted by what happened last," Payden says. "But at some point in time, bonds will do better than stocks."

It's important to realize that bonds and stocks can sometimes move in the same direction at the same time, but rarely do they move at the same pace. Sometimes returns on stocks and bonds move in opposite directions, which makes them an ideal duo for smoothing the bumps in your investment portfolio—the main point of diversification.

Risks

How do the risks and rewards of bonds compare with those of stocks? When you invest in bonds, you are effectively lending the issuer money. In return, the issuer promises to pay back your principal at some time in the future and to pay a set rate of interest for as long as the bond is outstanding. Consequently, you face two risks—default and interest rate fluctuations.

Default risk is the chance that the issuer—be it a government or a corporation—will get into financial hot water and be unable to pay all or part of the principal or interest. The amount of default risk varies dramatically with the type of security you buy. Treasury notes and bonds are believed to be virtually free of default risk, because the U.S. government is highly creditworthy. The default risk on debt issued by highly indebted companies or Third World countries, on the other hand, is fairly substantial.

Because risk and reward go hand in hand, an investor who can handle uncertainty can usually boost the yield on a bond portfolio by investing a portion of it in securities that pose some default risk. Generally speaking, junk bonds—that is, below-investment-grade securities, often issued by heavily indebted corporations—and bonds issued by Third World countries pay between 3 and 10 percentage points more than debt issued by the U.S. Treasury. (If you buy foreign bonds, you must also beware of "currency risk," which is explained in more detail in Chapter 11.)

Interest rate risk crops up when inflation and interest rates are rising. A long-term bond bought in the early 1980s, when interest rates were high, yields much more than a bond bought today, and one bought in a time of lower interest rates yields much less. Thus, the price on that higher-yielding bond will rise, and the price on the lower-yielding bond will drop.

How much it will drop depends on the bond's maturity—the amount of time the issuer has before it must pay back the principal—and the difference between current interest rates and the return on the bond. According to an analysis by Oppenheimer & Co. Inc., a New York–based mutual fund company, the estimated value of a two-year Treasury note will decrease by about 2 percent if interest rates rise 1 percentage point, but the value of a bond that matures in twenty years will decline by about 8 percent.

If you invest in bond mutual funds, which post their net asset values each day, you will see the effect of rising interest rates on your funds immediately. However, if you invest in individual bonds, you may not notice. That's simply because no one "marks their bonds to market"—that is, no one tells you the price you'd get if you were selling the bond today. Unless, of course, you ask. So if you want to stay relatively oblivious to the value bumps in your bond holdings, invest in individual bonds. If you want liquidity and don't mind knowing when the bond market declines, buy bonds through mutual funds.

QUICK TAKE

What You'll LEARN

Mutual funds make investing easy and can help small investors build far more diversified portfolios than they could cobble together on their own. This chapter discusses:

- What Is a Mutual Fund?
- Fees and Loads
- The Prospectus
- Different Types of Fund Categories
- Choosing Specific Funds in Each Category
- Fund Families
- Selecting a Fund
- The Real Cost of Fund Fees
- Exchange-Traded Funds

What You'll DO

- Consider which types of funds you want
- Call or browse the Web to get specific fund information
- Calculate how much fund fees cost you

How You'll USE This

This chapter can serve both as a primer and a reference to get specific fund information and provide the tools, Web addresses, and phone numbers to get your portfolio started.

D on't have the time, skill, or interest to pick individual stocks? There's no need to give up on investing. You can get a professional to do the stock picking for you. The easiest and least expensive way to do that is to build a portfolio of mutual funds. If you choose funds wisely, not only can you save time, you can also enjoy steady returns.

But first, a little deprogramming may be necessary for those who frequent magazine stands. There are no "Best Funds to Buy Now." There is no one-size-fits-all "Fund Portfolio for the New Millennium." Indeed, the hottest funds of today are frequently the coldest funds of tomorrow. Buy them at your economic peril. "There is more risk of loss when you buy a fund that's at the top of the performance charts than there is when you buy a fund at the bottom," says A. Michael Lipper, chairman of Lipper Inc., a mutual fund information and ranking service based in New York.

So how do you pick good funds? First, a little background on mutual funds is required.

WHAT IS A MUTUAL FUND?

Mutual funds are investment pools that collect money from many investors and use it to buy stocks, bonds, and other investments. The type of securities the fund buys is spelled out in a detailed investment document called a prospectus. Each investor owns a pro-rata share of the assets in the pool.

The fund company employs an investment manager, who chooses the specific stocks or bonds to buy and sell based on criteria spelled out in the prospectus. "Open-end" mutual funds—which make up the bulk of the industry—also calculate the value of the pool's investment holdings each day, divide that by the number of shares owned by individual investors, and report the result—the net asset value of each share. Most of these net asset values are reported in major newspapers each day, just like the prices of individual stocks. You can also get mutual fund quotes on financial websites, such as Yahoo! Finance (see "Finding Financial Data on the Web," in Chapter 5). In addition, many major fund families also provide these quotes on their websites.

Following the Money

New investors' money increases the size of the investment pool and is used to buy additional assets. Likewise, if investors pull money out of an open-end fund, the investment pool shrinks and stocks and bonds are sold to pay for these "redemptions."

However, because the net asset value has to be computed each day—and it would get complex to try to keep a running tally with investor money going in and out of the fund all day—these funds will not allow investors to trade in the middle of the day. If you want to buy additional shares of an open-end fund, your purchase will be held until trading closes. You will buy in at the close-of-business price. Likewise, if you choose to sell, your sell order will be held until the market closes.

Investors who want to react to a big rise or drop in stock prices can find this slow-paced trading frustrating. On Black Monday, when stock prices dropped more than 500 points, for example, investors in mutual funds could do nothing but watch. There was no way to bail out when the market was down only 100 points. Those who wanted to sell took the full loss.

On the other hand, "closed-end" funds sell a specific number of shares to investors at launch and don't sell additional shares. The shares of closed-end funds then trade on stock exchanges, much like the shares of individual stocks. They can be bought or sold at any time of the day. Sometimes their shares sell for more than the market value of all the securities owned by the fund; sometimes they sell for less.

Because the buying and selling of shares by individual investors does not affect the growth or contraction of the fund itself, experts contend that closed-end fund managers are able to take some calculated risks that the managers of open-end funds can't. For example, they can use leverage—borrowing—to boost returns, without worrying about investors cashing out and forcing them to sell shares in a hurry and potentially at a loss.

However, because managers are able to make these bets, closed-end funds often trade based on how much credit investors give the funds' managers. In that way, evaluating a closed-end fund is more like evaluating the purchase of an individual stock than it is like choosing a mutual fund. As a result, the rest of this section refers to open-end funds only.

Over the past decade or so, the ranks of mutual fund owners have burgeoned. Where roughly 20 million Americans invested through mutual funds in 1986, some 88 million invest this way today. Assets held by fund companies soared to nearly $12 trillion in September of 2007 from $810.3 billion in 1986.

What's made mutual funds so popular? They make investing easy. You buy a fund with a general mission and let the manager worry about exactly what stocks or bonds to buy and when to sell. After all, that's the fund manager's business—and you can feel comfortable going about your own.

The other compelling draw of mutual funds is the fact that they allow you to diversify even a small investment portfolio in a cost-effective way. When you buy a share in a mutual fund, you are buying a piece of all of the securities the fund owns. For example, a growth fund typically owns dozens—sometimes hundreds—of different stocks in different industries. An income, or bond, fund is likely to own a wide array of bonds and/or other fixed-income instruments with different maturities. Most funds also keep some assets in cash, both to pay off customers who decide to sell their fund shares and to buy better investment opportunities as they arise. For you to get the same amount of diversification that a fund buyer could get with a $5,000 investment, you would need a portfolio worth at least several hundred thousand dollars.

 FEES AND LOADS

What does it cost to get this diversification? That depends on whether you are buying a so-called "load" fund or a "no-load" fund.

In a nutshell, a load is a fee that's either charged when you buy the shares (a "front-end load") or when you sell them in the first few years (a "back-end load"). These fees go to pay the financial planners and stockbrokers who sell the fund. In the best cases, the planners and stockbrokers earn the fees by giving you good advice about which fund or funds to choose, based on your age, goals, and the other details of your portfolio. Unfortunately, in the worst cases, the planners don't give good advice—they just recommend funds that pay them rich commissions. Your portfolio suffers while the planner buys a Jaguar. (By reading this book, you'll learn enough to avoid that.)

There is one other reason that a fund might charge a load: volatility. Certain types of funds, most commonly international and market-segment or "sector" funds (see the description of sector funds in "Different Types of Fund Categories," later in this chapter), charge loads mainly to discourage investors from short-swing trading. That's because these fund managers know that the value of the fund's portfolio is likely to swing wildly simply because of the nature of the securities the fund buys. To keep investors locked in through the bad times so they can enjoy the good and the managers won't have to sell assets to raise cash to pay off selling fund holders at the worst time, they charge back-end loads that are only levied on those who sell out within a certain period—usually within the first two to five years.

No-load funds do not charge "loads," but some charge 12b-1 fees. These also go to pay the planner or broker who recommends the fund, but they are a bit more insidious. Instead of costing you a fairly obvious amount when you buy or sell your shares, 12b-1 fees are charged annually, usually in relatively small amounts. However, for long-term investors, they can cost more than even a substantial load.

Every type of mutual fund charges something called "annual management fees," which are the costs that you pay for the service of having a professional do the investment picking for you. The cost of trading—buying and selling stocks in the fund portfolio—also gets passed through to you through "other" fees.

By and large, all fund fees are charged as a percentage of your investment. If you buy a fund with a 5 percent front-end load, for example, 5 percent of the amount you invest is taken off the top. Instead of investing $100 in the fund, you actually invest $95. With a back-end load, the fee is charged when you sell. So if you sell $1,000 worth of shares in a fund with a 3 percent back-end load, the fund company will take $30 and send you $970.

With 12b-1 and annual management fees, the costs are taken out of your annual return before it's passed on to you. So let's say you pay 1 percent in annual management fees, and your fund earns 10 percent. You get a 9 percent return on your money. What happens if your fund just barely breaks even? You lose 1 percent on your money. (For an explanation of exactly how much these fees can cost you and a nifty tool to help you examine the total cost of the fees that your funds are charging, see "The Real Cost of Fund Fees" near the end of this chapter.)

The good news is that all the fees that a fund charges must be disclosed in a chart in the fund prospectus. No-load funds automatically send you a copy of the prospectus when you say you want to invest, or encourage you to download the prospectus from their website. However, if you are buying a load fund from a broker, you may need to ask for it. Make sure you do.

THE PROSPECTUS

Prospectuses are long, boring legal documents that spell out all the details about investing in a particular fund. Like most long, boring legal documents, they contain a handful of fascinating tidbits of information that can tell you whether the investment you're looking at is likely to be a boon or a bust before you put your money at risk.

Besides the fees, what else should you look for in the prospectus?

Performance

Every prospectus must summarize how the fund has performed over a variety of time periods. Somewhere in the legalese, it also tells you that "past performance is not an indication (or guarantee) of future returns." That's true. A fund that makes a fortune in one year can lose a fortune the next. What you need to know about performance is the predictable part. That's volatility.

Look at the figures that show average annual returns over one-year, five-year, and ten-year time periods. Compare those returns to the returns of an appropriate market index. For instance, the performance of a fund that invests in big-company stocks can be compared to the Standard & Poor's 500 stock market index. That tells you whether your fund manager generally does better, worse, or about the same as the markets he's investing in as a whole.

Also look for the year-by-year performance. If you can't find it, ask for a chart showing this data before you invest. Why is it so important? It tells you whether the fund you are looking at has relatively stable returns or whether the averages you've seen are masking a lot of volatility. For instance, a fund that clicks along earning 7 to 9 percent per year is significantly different from a fund that posts an "average" 8 percent return but has some years where it earns 40 percent and others where it loses half its value. This knowledge can help you determine just how likely you are to suffer a loss (or an ulcer) before you cash out.

Certainly, if you are capable of handling risk, don't eliminate highly volatile funds from consideration. But make sure you look at these figures before you invest so that you are prepared. The biggest mistake that a fund investor can make is investing in a volatile fund without understanding the swings. Then, chances are, when the fund posts a terrible year—as volatile funds are sure to do sooner or later— the unprepared investor sells out. Often that means selling at the absolute worst point, locking in a loss with a fund that's simply a roller coaster, ready to rise back after dumping the unprepared at the bottom.

Investment Objectives

Each prospectus also discloses what the fund is investing in and why. Primarily all you are looking for here is to make sure you've chosen the right type of fund for your investment objectives. For instance, if you want to put your long-term retirement money in small-company stocks, you'd look for a fund that invests its assets in the shares of small public companies. Similarly, if you want a short-to-medium-term bond fund for your teen's college account, you'd check the prospectus to determine whether the manager has such bonds in the fund's portfolio.

Risks

By and large, the paragraphs labeled *risk* in the average fund prospectus are boilerplate. In essence, they say that investments involve risk. Stocks go up; stocks go down. So do bond prices. Live with it.

Every once in a while, however, the risk disclosures tell you more. If, for example, the fund uses leverage to boost its returns, it is noted here. What that means is the fund manager is borrowing so he can buy more stock than he can afford with the cash he has on hand. Using leverage magnifies both profits and losses, so a fund that borrows to buy may appear to be more successful than its competitors when times are good. As an investor, however, you need to understand that it's likely to lose considerably more money when times are bad, too. Unless you're prepared for significant price swings, avoid funds that leverage their positions.

International funds tell you about their "hedging" strategies that are aimed at reducing currency risk (see Chapter 11). Some funds will say they don't hedge currency risk. Others say that they do and explain how. Typically, the funds that hedge earn a little less than the funds that don't when currency prices are in your favor, but they should earn more than those that don't when currency prices go the other way.

DIFFERENT TYPES OF FUND CATEGORIES

If funds will make up the bulk of your investment portfolio, you should diversify among different types of investment classes—big-company stocks, small-company stocks, international investments, bonds, and cash. That means you probably need at least five different funds.

In fund-speak, big-company stocks are sometimes categorized as "growth" or "growth and income" funds; small-company stocks are sometimes labeled "aggressive growth"; bond funds are usually listed under "income." Fortunately, there's no special code for money market and international funds. You'll find them predictably labeled. However, you should know that "global" or "world" funds differ from "international" or "foreign" funds in that the former two categories can invest domestically as well as in foreign markets. The latter are restricted to overseas investments.

You should diversify among all these categories for two reasons. The first is that a good investment portfolio addresses the purpose of your savings—the specific goals you aim to finance. Some of your goals may be short-term, some long-term, some pivotal, some discretionary. To appropriately address an important short-term goal, you need a short-term investment, such as a money market fund, that is not going to put your principal in great jeopardy. To address your long-term goals, you're better served with stock funds (either "growth" or "aggressive growth"), which swing in value but are more likely to handily outpace inflation over time.

Your fund-type choices boil down to the following options (examples of these funds are given in Chapter 14):

- **Aggressive growth** funds usually consist of stocks in small, fast-growing companies. Most of these companies do not pay dividends, and their stock prices are highly volatile.

  Risk: Very high
  Potential for capital appreciation: Very high
  Potential for current income: Low

- **Asset allocation** funds are often called "funds of funds" because they purchase shares in an array of different types of mutual funds—stock, bond, money market, and international, for example—in order to completely diversify an investor's holdings. The concept behind asset allocation funds is that one fund can be enough for your entire portfolio. Often, you're given the ability to choose between "aggressive," "conservative" or "moderate" allocations, depending on your age and ability to tolerate risks. If you filled out the risk quiz in Chapter 2, you can simply match an asset allocation fund to your result.

  Risk: Mixed
  Potential for capital appreciation: Moderate
  Potential for current income: Mixed

- **Target-date** funds are somewhat like asset allocation funds; however, the mix of their assets will vary based on the date the fund is set to "mature." These are frequently designed for retirement portfolios. Investors would thus pick the maturity date that most closely corresponds to the year they plan to retire, whether that's 2010 or 2040. The mix of assets in the 2010 fund, which is obviously for an older investor, will be far more conservative than the mix of assets in the 2040 fund. However, the mix will change as the target date nears. These are quickly becoming a favorite in company 401(k) plans because tax laws encourage companies to offer these funds and make them the default options for people who fail to choose an investment mix. There's more about target-date funds in Chapter 14.

Risk: Mixed
Potential for capital appreciation: Varies
Potential for current income: Varies

- **Balanced** funds aim for three things: income, growth of capital, and stability of principal. They do this by buying a mixture of stocks, bonds, and money market instruments. They differ from asset allocation and target funds in that the manager doesn't ask you whether you're conservative or trying to retire in 2045. Consequently, these portfolios are not going to become more conservative as you age, nor more aggressive because you're a thrill seeker. The fund manager will decide on the mix of assets based on what he or she believes to be most prudent at the time. This can make these funds more profitable than target-date funds.

Risk: Moderate
Potential for capital appreciation: Moderate
Potential for current income: Mixed

- **Fixed-income** funds invest in bonds and other fixed-income instruments, such as mortgage-backed securities. There is a wide array of different types of fixed-income funds, ranging from funds that invest in high-grade debt, such as Treasury notes and bonds, to those that invest in the debt of highly indebted companies (junk-bond funds). Obviously, the risk to your principal hinges on what type of securities your fund buys. However, all fixed-income funds face interest-rate risk, as described in Chapter 7. In a nutshell, if interest rates rise, the value of your old, relatively low-yielding bonds will fall. If interest rates drop, the value of your old, relatively high-yielding bonds will rise. But when you buy individual bonds, you're relatively blind to the changes in market direction—no one calls you to tell you that your bond is worth less or more than what you paid on a day-to-day basis. As discussed earlier, though, mutual funds report their net asset values every single day. So if you've got a paper loss on your bond fund, you'll know it. These paper losses should not negatively affect the income you receive, so if you are investing mainly for income, you shouldn't let them bother you. But expect to see them, because interest rates do change and will affect the fund's net asset values.

Risk: Moderate
Potential for capital appreciation: Low to moderate
Potential for current income: High

- **Equity-income** funds invest primarily in stocks that pay high dividends. These present some potential for capital appreciation but much less stability than a balanced fund or than many types of fixed-income funds.

Risk: Moderate
Potential for capital appreciation: Low to moderate
Potential for current income: Moderate

- **Global** funds invest in securities issued all over the world—foreign and domestic. International funds invest in non-U.S. markets. Because the cost of trading in overseas markets is comparatively high, you should expect these funds to charge slightly higher fees than domestic stock funds. Also, international markets, particularly those in developing nations, tend to be more volatile than the U.S. market, so you should expect bigger changes in your net asset values.

Risk: High
Potential for capital appreciation: High
Potential for current income: Low (except with global and international bond and income funds)

- **Growth** funds consist of stocks in larger, more established U.S. companies. Stock prices are volatile; however, the price of shares in established companies is comparatively less volatile than the price of shares in small, untested companies. Consequently, growth funds are a bit less risky than aggressive growth funds.

Risk: High
Potential for capital appreciation: Moderate
Potential for current income: Low

- **Growth and income** funds combine growth stocks with stocks in companies that pay high dividends. Some growth and income funds also invest in convertible securities and/or bonds and money market instruments. Others get the income side of the equation by selling call options on the stocks in their portfolio.

Risk: Moderate
Potential for capital appreciation: Moderate
Potential for current income: Moderate

- **Junk-bond** funds invest in the debt of companies that have borrowed heavily and thus need to pay premium interest rates to borrow more. These funds pose greater risks to your principal than traditional fixed-income funds; however, they also typically promise higher rates of return.

Risk: High
Potential for capital appreciation: Low
Potential for current income: High

- **Money market** funds invest primarily in short-term government debt, bank deposits, and short-term corporate debt. The net asset values of money market funds are usually pretty stable. However, the yields are also relatively low.

Risk: Very low
Potential for capital appreciation: Very low
Potential for current income: Moderate

- **Municipal bond** funds invest primarily in debt issued by state and local governments. Those who buy funds that invest in the debt of their home state are likely to find that the income earned on these accounts is free from both state and federal taxation.

Risk: Moderate
Potential for capital appreciation: Low
Potential for current income: Moderate

- **Sector** funds invest in specific industry groups. You would buy a sector fund if, for example, you wanted to participate in the fortunes of just the technology industry, or just the health care industry, or just Net stocks. These funds are highly volatile and relatively undiversified. They are suitable for people who want to take a piece of their assets and gamble a bit.

Risk: Very high
Potential for capital appreciation: Very high
Potential for current income: Very low

CHOOSING SPECIFIC FUNDS IN EACH CATEGORY

When it comes to choosing specific funds in each category, you have two choices: You can go with so-called index funds, or you can opt for actively managed funds. No matter which you choose, however, you should realize that most mutual funds are going to offer wide diversity within their asset category. So unlike stock investors, who have to pick lots of individual stocks, you can pick just one or two stock funds. The same is true when diversifying your bond or international holdings. If you choose wisely, a fund or two ought to be plenty.

Active Versus Passive Management

Actively managed funds are those in which a portfolio manager aims to beat the overall market's performance by carefully choosing specific investments that the manager believes are primed to excel. The fund manager then actively trades these stocks in an effort to get a better-than-average return.

Index funds, on the other hand, are "passively" managed. They simply aim to mirror the market, not beat it. They do that by buying stocks or bonds that represent the specific investments in a particular market index. For instance, an S&P 500 index fund owns the stocks that make up the Standard & Poor's 500-company stock index. An index fund that aims to mirror the Dow Jones Industrial Average buys stock in the thirty companies that make up the Dow. (Both of these index funds would also fall under the bigger category of growth funds.)

The index fund simply holds onto those investments, never trading shares unless the index components change. (Every once in a while, a company that's part of the Dow Thirty, for example, is bought out or goes out of business. At that point, another company is chosen to represent the company that fell out of the index.)

Which is the best way to go? Experts who favor the index approach say that because index funds don't actively trade shares, they generate fewer taxable capital gains. (The gains and losses realized from active trading in a mutual fund are passed on to investors at year-end. If the fund manager has sold stocks at a profit, all the investors in the fund must report—and pay income taxes on—the gains.) Of course, paying less tax as you go along leaves you with more money to invest. More important, while there are always some actively managed funds that handily beat the market at any given time, few beat the averages over long periods. If you are a long-term investor, your odds are better with an index fund. Finally, because there is very little "management" needed to buy and hold stocks that make up an index, annual management fees charged to index fund investors are low. Whereas the average actively managed stock fund may charge 1 percent of the account value in management fees each year, many index funds charge between 0.2 percent and 0.5 percent. The bottom line is that more of the investment return goes to the investor. That, too, has a beneficial effect on the value of your portfolio over time.

Why would anyone buy actively managed funds then? For the same reason that they buy individual stocks. They believe they're capable of using their knowledge about investing to beat the odds. If that describes you, actively managed funds are more your style. Remember, however, that every time you sell shares in an actively managed fund (that's not in a tax-favored retirement account), you'll pay tax on the difference between the fund's net asset value when you sell and its net asset value when you bought it. That reduces the amount you're left with to reinvest, so trade sparingly.

DID YOU KNOW?
Style Drift

Experts criticize some actively managed funds for something called "style drift." What this means is that the fund claims to be a growth fund, but the investments within it better describe an "aggressive growth" or "balanced" fund. Style drift exposes unwary investors to the risk of being poorly diversified because their funds simply aren't what they say they are. Consequently, if you invest in actively managed funds, you'd be wise to check your funds out on the website of fund-tracker Morningstar.com. Morningstar's free service allows you to plug in the ticker symbol of each fund and get a brief profile. That profile includes a "style box" that shows where your fund fits in a nine-category scale. For a stock fund, this would show where the fund fell in terms of buying big companies, medium-sized, or small; and whether its style reflected growth, value, or a blend of the two. If all your stock funds fall into the same box, you're not well diversified.

Finding and Researching Funds

No matter whether you want actively or passively managed funds, finding and researching funds has become a snap thanks to the Internet. There are a couple of sites that I find particularly helpful for the individual investor. One is www.mfea.com, which is a site operated by the Mutual Fund Education Alliance. Although the Mutual Fund Education Alliance is particularly interested in low-cost funds—those that don't charge big loads or substantial 12b-1 fees—the site offers information on virtually every fund. You can also sort funds by category and performance and get general information on investing through mutual funds.

If you want some technical analysis of your funds, you can also go to www.morningstar.com. Morningstar Inc. of Chicago is one of the nation's premier mutual fund rating services. Funds often advertise their "star" ranking, which is Morningstar's system of giving funds a performance evaluation, ranging from five stars (the best) to one. Morningstar's website also allows you to see just how many funds are in a particular fund category and where your fund's performance ranked relative to its peers.

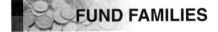 **FUND FAMILIES**

When you start trying to pick and choose among mutual funds, you are likely to feel overwhelmed. There are thousands of funds to choose from, and the performance of about 75 percent of the industry is pretty good, too. If you try to carefully examine each of your thousands of choices, you'll go crazy—or at least waste a tremendous amount of time that would have been better spent at the park. So how do you narrow your choices to a manageable number?

Look for fund families that offer services that you value. For instance, some fund companies offer twenty-four-hour access to your account via the Web or a toll-free telephone line. Some offer branch offices, where you can go and chat with a fund representative when some life event (or market move) makes you feel uncomfortable and in need of advice. Others may offer low minimum investments, which allow you to invest small amounts at a time—a pivotal feature for somebody who is starting out without a lot of money. Still others may require larger minimum investments but may charge smaller annual management fees, which is an important feature for an investor who has a relatively sizable portfolio and wants to keep costs low.

If you are looking for great convenience, you might also want to limit yourself to big fund families, which can provide you with the ability to keep all your mutual fund investments under one roof. If you're a beginning investor and feel you need lots of helpful reading material about investing, you should also know that some funds are known for their investment literature. They'll send most of it to you for free, although a few funds charge for their more sophisticated investment tools and software.

What are the big fund companies known for?

- **Vanguard Group Inc.** is noted for its low fees and index funds. The company offers dozens of stock-index, bond-index, international-index, and money market funds. If you want to put the bulk of your investment money in index funds, it's tough to do better. The company also offers a wide spectrum of asset allocation, target-date, and exchange-traded funds, as well as some highly rated actively managed funds. The only criticism savvy investors have of Vanguard is that its asset allocation and target-date funds tend toward the conservative side. That reduces their volatility, but can make them a little less profitable too. Otherwise, the company is widely respected and recommended. However, Vanguard requires relatively large investment minimums. You generally cannot open an account with less than $3,000 for a taxable account or $1,000 per fund for an IRA. Contact details: www.vanguard.com, (800) 523-0857 or (877) 662-7447.
- **Fidelity Investments** is the place to go for vast variety. The company offers hundreds of different funds, ranging from

your basic growth funds to a wide array of sector funds. Some of the company's funds are no-load; others charge either front-end or back-end sales fees. The company also has a handful of branch offices, where you can go to watch the stock ticker or talk to a representative. Contact details: www.fidelity.com, (800) 544-8888 or (800) 544-6666.

- **T. Rowe Price** offers more than ninety highly rated no-load funds, ranging from money markets to aggressive stock funds. The company also participates in a fund purchase program called Gateway that allows you to buy about 3,000 funds offered by one hundred other mutual fund families. By buying through T. Rowe, Gateway allows you to get a consolidated statement. In terms of investment minimums, you can either start with a lump sum of $2,500 or, if you don't have that kind of cash in your sock drawer, you can opt for the "systematic purchase option," whereby you simply invest at least $100 a month. (The investment minimum for IRAs is lower—$1,000 as a lump sum or a systematic purchase of at least $50 per month.) T. Rowe is also well known for wonderful investment literature, including brochures on investing for retirement and investing while in retirement. Contact details: www.troweprice.com, (800) 541-6066.

- **Charles Schwab & Co. Inc.**, once mainly a discount brokerage firm, now also offers a wide array of proprietary mutual funds. The firm continues to provide access to other companies' funds, as well, through its "OneSource" program. What makes Schwab notable, besides how it lets you do some one-stop shopping—buying your individual stocks, Schwab funds, and outside funds all from one place—is that the company offers some of the lowest investment minimums in the industry. With many of its funds, investors can buy in for as little as $100. Most other fund companies require initial investments that are at least ten times higher. This makes Schwab a great choice for a beginning investor who doesn't have much cash—yet. Contact details: www.charlesschwab.com, (866) 232-9890.

Are there other great fund companies that haven't been mentioned? You bet. Hundreds of them. But these are some of the biggest and best and should at least help to get you started on your search.

SELECTING A FUND

To pick funds that will work nicely in your portfolio, consider first how you like to invest. What services, bells, and whistles are valuable to you? Which are nice, but not necessary? Use the following worksheet to guide you.

Picking a Fund That Suits You

Contact several mutual fund families to find out whether they offer the services that mean the most to you. If they do, take the next step and ask for details, including the prospectuses, of a handful of funds that suit your investment goals.

Here are a few common fund services to jog your memory:

Toll-free telephone access	_____ yes	_____ no
Dividend reinvestment	_____ yes	_____ no
Automatic investment	_____ yes	_____ no
Low investment minimums	_____ yes	_____ no
Convenient branches	_____ yes	_____ no
Informational literature	_____ yes	_____ no
Daily switching	_____ yes	_____ no
Home-computer access	_____ yes	_____ no
Multiple fund choices	_____ yes	_____ no
Other _____	_____ yes	_____ no

Now consider the specifics of individual funds, such as the short- and long-term returns. By looking at the graphs of how a fund has performed, not only can you tell whether shareholders are better off today than when they started, you can also see how badly the fund performed in down markets and how well when times were good. These figures can give you an idea of whether the fund's returns are too lackluster or too volatile for your goals. Realize, however, that a fund that is relatively young may have too short a track record from which to draw any solid conclusions. Most observers suggest you dismiss long-term information that predates

143

the current fund manager's tenure. For instance, if the fund's very-long-term performance is great but the short-term isn't, check to see how long the current fund manager has been managing the fund's assets. If there's a correlation between the two—that is, the performance fell just as the new manager took over—you know that the long-term returns had little to do with this manager. You may want to scrap this investment, or wait until this manager's track record improves.

If, however, the management has been stable and the average performance has been good, check the year-to-year performance figures to see how volatile the fund is.

Fund's percentage gain in its best year   _____%
Fund's percentage loss in its worst year   _____%
Number of years measured   _____

Are the fees reasonable? Take a look at how the fees this fund charges compare with those of similar funds that you're considering. (Be sure you are comparing like funds—that is, compare domestic stock funds to other domestic stock funds; international funds to other international funds; bond funds to bond funds. Fee structures vary dramatically based on what the fund invests in. Generally speaking, you should expect fees on money market funds to be very low, fees on bond funds to be lower than those on stock funds, and fees on domestic stock funds to be lower than those on international stock funds.) Are they higher, lower, or about the same?

Fees
_____ higher   _____ lower   _____ equivalent

Take a look at the risk section of the prospectus. Are all of the risks noted the things you would expect? If not, why not? Now consider whether these are risks you're comfortable taking with your investments.

Risks
_____ acceptable   _____ unacceptable

THE REAL COST OF FUND FEES

When he first started investing, Charles Ackeifi liked his broker so much that he didn't worry about the price of full-service advice. Sure, a single trade might cost between $75 and $250 versus the $10 to $35 that he would have paid if he employed a discount broker. But Ackeifi liked the idea that his investments were attended by someone who had more time and expertise to devote to his account than he did.

Still, when the brokerage house took a 5 percent fee, called a front-end load, off the top of his index mutual fund investment and then informed him that it would charge a 3 percent annual fee to manage his portfolio of eight stocks—most of which Ackeifi had selected himself—he decided it was time for a change.

"I am upset with the fees they are charging," fumed the software consultant from East Granby, Connecticut. "I think these brokers are out for themselves. Your interests are not paramount."

Although the motivations of full-service brokers certainly can be debated, Ackeifi's story ought to serve as a wake-up call for investors who haven't paid a lot of attention to fees. Fees can make or break an investment. Particularly for those who invest through mutual funds over long periods of time, they can have a dramatic impact on your long-term wealth. Consider that if Ackeifi invested $100,000 in a high-cost S&P 500 index fund—one with a 5 percent load and 0.5 percent in annual expenses—and maintained that investment for twenty years, he would pay $68,197 more in total costs than if he invested in a similar no-load index fund that charges only 0.2 percent in annual expenses.

Fees, of course, are not the only consideration when choosing a fund. However, when comparing several similar funds, fees should be an important part of the equation. Yet many investors don't compare the cost of funds this carefully, partly because it's difficult. That's largely because mutual fund fees come in a great variety. As noted earlier in this chapter, every fund charges annual management fees, but some also charge annual marketing levies called 12b-1 fees. Some charge up-front fees (front-end loads) or fees when you sell (back-end loads). Some give you the option of choosing one fee structure over the other. For instance, investors might be presented with a choice of a front-end load, a back-end load, or a 12b-1 fee. Unless you are very skilled with a calculator, it's difficult to make the comparison.

On the bright side, if you have a computer and Web access, the Securities and Exchange Commission (SEC) will help you do the math. The agency has posted a "Mutual Fund Cost Calculator" on its website, www.sec.gov. When you get to the site, look for "Investor Information," and click on the link "Calculators." The top calculator link on that page is the mutual fund cost calculator. This calculator allows you to figure the total cost of investing in a fund—adding in the cost of loads, if any, 12b-1 fees, annual management fees, and the like—over the entire time you expect to own the fund. The amount of time you expect to own the fund is important when comparing fees because certain fee structures are expensive at first but become less so over time. Meanwhile, other types of fees that may appear innocuous can rob you of solid long-term performance. This calculator allows you to make apples-to-apples comparisons with funds that promote apple, orange, and banana-style fees.

For instance, let's say you want to figure out whether it makes more sense to buy fund ABC, which charges a 5 percent load and 1 percent in annual management fees, or a similar no-load fund, XYZ, that charges 1.75 percent in annual management and 0.25 percent in 12b-1 fees. Just for example's sake, we'll say that you have $100,000 to invest in either fund.

By using the SEC calculator, you can see that the better choice hinges on whether you plan to own the fund for two years or twenty. If you plan to hold this investment for just two years, the front-loaded ABC fund will cost you nearly twice as much—$8,337.51 versus $4,792 for XYZ. But if you're going to own this fund for twenty years, ABC is significantly less expensive, costing $150,015 versus $223,617 for XYZ. Over thirty years, XYZ will cost you a quarter of a million dollars more than ABC. Why? That insidious extra 1 percent in annual expenses eats up a tremendous amount of your return over time.

Notably, these numbers are higher than the raw amount of fees that you would get if you simply added the amount you expect to pay in fees year after year. That's because the SEC calculator takes into account forgone earnings. In essence it accounts for the fact that the money you paid out in fees in year one was not there to earn a return for you in year two. That's a significant cost.

EXCHANGE-TRADED FUNDS

After the 1987 market crash—dubbed "Black Monday" and commemorated by those in the know on Wall Street as the worst one-day percentage decline in the history of the U.S. stock market—investors started thinking about the problem with mutual funds. Sure, they were diversified. Sure, they were simple. But, if you wanted to trade in a hurry—if you wanted out on a really bad day—you were stuck. You had to wait hours and hours until the end of that really bad day to sell your shares. Those who are convinced that they could be quick on their feet (or phone) and get their brokers to sell before they took that big loss find the traditional fund delay frustrating. On Black Monday, that meant investors had to sit idly by while the value of their stock portfolios plunged 22 percent in a single day.

Now, set aside the notion that the people who did sell during the 1987 crash proved to be stupid. The market had completely rebounded within three months. Those who stuck it out recovered their losses and went on to earn considerably more. Those who sold in a panic locked in their losses and often didn't get back into stocks for years. But Wall Street is a land of optimists—people who are sure that they can beat the market, that they are fleeter of foot and mind than the average Joe, and that they can avoid losses and predict gains. These people needed a mutual fund product that allowed them to buy and sell at a moment's notice. They needed to buy mutual funds like they bought stocks.

In 1993, they got a new product. It's called an exchange-traded fund, or ETF. Although ETFs started slowly, they are now one of the hottest products ever to hit the mutual fund industry. By the end of 2006, the industry bragged 359 ETFs with $422.6 billion in assets, according to the Investment Company Institute, a trade group for the mutual fund industry. That compares with just 80 ETFs, holding $65.6 billion in assets, a mere six years earlier—nearly a five-fold increase in the number of funds and a more than six-fold increase in assets.

While there are some technical differences, ETFs resemble closed-end funds. They trade on an exchange and are bought and sold through brokers. Theoretically, they could trade at a discount or premium to their net asset value. However, usually they don't. That's mainly because the vast majority of ETFs reflect a market index, such as the S&P 500 Index. Essentially, they're index funds that can be bought and sold at any time during the day.

What are the advantages to an ETF? There are no trading restrictions. Where mutual funds won't let you trade in the middle of the day, you can trade an ETF at any hour that the market is open. Moreover, some fund companies bar investors from buying their shares shortly after they've sold them. Why? It's annoying, for one thing. Because you're buying mutual fund shares generally directly from the fund, your purchases and sales boost (or restrict) the amount of money the fund has to invest. If a lot of people did that, the value of the fund's assets would move so much that it would become challenging to properly invest the assets. Besides, fund companies have to keep track of your account information and send you statements when you are a shareholder. If you're a shareholder one day, not the next, and then back to being a shareholder, you boost the fund company's work and administrative costs. That costs all shareholders. Funds are designed to be long-term investments, so they stop you from doing short-swing trading.

But, with ETFs, the fund is not keeping track of you on a day-to-day basis. Like buying or selling shares of closed-end funds, you are buying shares from another investor, not the fund itself. Consequently, your open-market purchase has no impact on the amount of assets the fund manager has to invest. The fund doesn't have to keep track of you. You can trade at will.

Although the assets of an ETF should reflect the value of the index it's tracking—just like an index mutual fund—the structure of ETFs makes them relatively cheap to offer. Consequently, the annual management expenses charged to investors are usually a touch lower than for similar index funds, which are already inexpensive. Consider, for instance, the Vanguard Total Stock Market Index fund, which charges 0.19 percent in annual management fees to investors. The company offers an identical ETF, which charges just 0.07 percent. On a $100,000 investment, you'd pay $190 for the mutual fund and pay just $70 for the ETF.

However, you'll pay brokerage fees each time you buy or sell the ETF, which do not apply when you're buying or selling mutual fund shares directly from Vanguard. So the ultimate cost to the investor of ownership can be higher (if you trade a lot and pay a substantial amount in brokerage fees) or lower (if you buy them through a discount broker and defy the selling point of ETFs and hold them for the long term). Or about the same.

Consequently, the best choice for a long-term investor who is weighing an ETF and an index fund that are otherwise identical will depend on how you purchase shares. If you want to purchase a fairly large stake in one fell swoop and leave it alone, the ETF is the best choice because your trading costs will not be significant and your annual management fees will be cheaper than those for the index fund.

But if you buy shares on a monthly program, or if having the ability to trade will cause you to trade frequently, you'll end up paying more with the ETF.

QUICK TAKE

What You'll LEARN

If you want to put your investments where your values are, you now have plenty of choices. There are roughly 200 different socially screened funds to choose from. You'll learn about:

- Evolving Influence
- Promising Performance
- Social Fund Screens
- Finding Mutual Funds with a Socially Responsible Bent

What You'll DO

- Decide whether socially screened funds work for you, or if you want to support causes in another way
- Be cognizant of the additional costs of social investing
- Screen social funds, based on ethical and economic criteria

How You'll USE This

Life's full of tough choices. Do you invest your money so it follows your values—or do you invest the cash that your investments produce to support your values? Because socially screened mutual funds can be more costly than funds that don't provide social screening, you could potentially earn better returns on other investments, leaving you more to support your cause. But social investing can work. What do you do? Decide what works best for you.

I n the beginning, there was a guiding principle: Thou shalt not make money from industries that do harm.

From this sprang a small cadre of so-called ethical investors. Primarily well-heeled religious folk, ethical investors followed their creed by sidestepping investments in tobacco, alcohol, and gambling companies. In the 1960s and 1970s—during the Vietnam War—the movement expanded to add agents of war, such as manufacturers of guns, bombers, and nuclear weaponry, to the list of "shalt-nots." And they quietly invested, secure in the knowledge that even though they couldn't change the world, ethical investors would at least sleep knowing that their money was not being used to do harm.

EVOLVING INFLUENCE

A cry for help changed everything. In the early 1980s, bishops of the Anglican Church in South Africa appealed to their brethren in the American Episcopal Church to help them end apartheid. When a decade of quiet urging proved fruitless, the ethical investors got more boisterous and started enlisting powerful allies, including managers of multibillion-dollar pension funds and city and state treasurers.

When they flexed their collective muscle by divesting themselves of investments in companies doing business in South Africa, that country's economy went into a tailspin. Suddenly, South Africa's white minority government sat down to bargain with the black majority, which helped lead to a complete overhaul in the system of government. And it also changed this segment of the investing world forever.

"It was a watershed period," said Amy Domini, author of several books on the topic and founder of Domini Social Investments in New York. "Until then, we called ourselves 'ethical' investors because we didn't want to imply that what we were doing was going to make a difference. It turned out that we could be part of the solution."

Little more than a decade later, ethical investing was renamed socially responsible investing to reflect the industry's newfound power and tactics. Now, instead of sidestepping companies with questionable track records, some social funds invest in these companies to press for change. They're not just looking at "sin" stocks anymore either. They're involved in an array of environmental and employee-relations issues, from sustainable logging to sweatshops and the treatment of women in the workplace.

Indeed, the category has grown so much in the past decade that virtually every big mutual fund family now includes a socially screened fund. And there are funds to address broad social concerns, as well as narrow ones. For instance, there are funds that promote Catholic or Muslim values and those that concentrate on workforce equity or women's issues. One indication of how mainstream these funds have become is they've even inspired a backlash. A few years ago, the "Vice Fund" launched to invest in all the things social funds screen out, such as alcohol, tobacco, firearms, and gambling concerns.

The movement continues to grow and collect new causes. The latest target: Darfur, where the Sudanese government is accused of perpetrating a massive genocide that's killed hundreds of thousands and has displaced more than 2 million people. Already, several states and many universities have cleared their investment portfolios of offending stocks. Websites such as www.savedarfur.org urge investors to pressure their companies, governments, and investment firms to do even more.

PROMISING PERFORMANCE

The long-held belief that investing with your heart will pinch your pocketbook has proved a myth. A series of studies conducted over the past decade indicate that socially screened mutual funds perform on par with their unscreened counterparts—both actively and passively managed.

"The thought was that if you invested socially, you sacrificed return. But in fact you can win, lose, or draw, just like anyone else," says Tim Grant, president of the Pax World Fund family in New Hampshire, which uses social screens. "We've gotten a market return. There are some funds that are winning, some are losing, and some are in the middle."

Other experts note that the social funds that had performed poorly had suffered for the reasons that other funds suffer—they picked bad stocks. Sometimes, the screen that's used can affect performance, however. For instance, the Domini Social Equity Fund, which was a passively managed index fund until recently, performed better than most of its peers in the 1990s. The reason: It screened out sin stocks, including oil companies and defense contractors which were doing poorly at the time, and it leaned fairly heavily on new-economy stocks. But when the technology sector took a dive, the Social Equity Index fund did too. Now the fund's performance—once the envy of the industry—lags the Standard & Poor's 500 market index by about 1 percentage point.

The social-investment movement continues to grow rapidly. From 1995 to 2005, assets in socially screened investments surged from $639 billion to $2.29 trillion, according to the Social Investment Forum's ten-year report. There were only fifty-five socially screened mutual funds in 1995, which held $12 billion in assets. There are now more than 200 socially screened funds with $179 billion in assets.

But because the category has grown so rapidly and in so many different directions, individual investors who want to get involved in social investing might want to do a little soul-searching first.

Consider the things you value and the things that would make you uncomfortable to support. Then contemplate whether your ethical and social concerns are addressed by a mutual fund, or if they're so specific that you ought to consider investing in individual companies rather than a fund.

SOCIAL FUND SCREENS

Almost all social funds screen out investments in "sin" stocks—companies that produce and sell alcohol and tobacco or facilitate gambling. Most also avoid defense contractors and gun manufacturers. Some avoid the purveyors of nuclear power. Many use "positive screens" to buy into companies that appear to have progressive work practices or particularly good environmental records. Some focus on investing within underserved communities—areas that may be economically blighted and thus bereft of some of the financial and social services that other communities take for granted. However, only a small number have looked at other tricky issues, such as animal testing. And their positions on issues such as the environment, for example, can vary.

There is, however, now nearly universal agreement that social investing can make a difference. Domini says her view on the movement's impact is summed up by a fable that is reflected in the company's logo—and virtually everything it does:

Thousands of starfish washed ashore. A little girl began throwing them back in the water so they wouldn't die.

"Don't bother, dear," her mother said. "It won't make a difference."

The little girl stopped for a moment and looked at the starfish in her hand. "It will make a difference to this one," she said.

FINDING MUTUAL FUNDS WITH A SOCIALLY RESPONSIBLE BENT

Think you're ready to put your money where your values are? The toughest part of social investing has always been finding the companies and funds that have values that match yours. However, this process has been made easier thanks to several resources that are now available on the Web.

For instance, www.socialinvest.org, the Social Investment Forum, a Washington, D.C.–based nonprofit, provides information about what social investing is all about and where you can go to find investments that suit your needs. This site concentrates on mutual funds that screen out investments in certain types of companies. Your job is to determine the types of investments you want to avoid and then match your concerns to a fund that has similar goals.

For instance, if the environment is your primary concern, you will want to make sure that you don't invest in companies that are major polluters or destroyers of the rain forest or the ozone layer. If social-equity issues are your bag, you will want to avoid companies that employ sweatshop laborers or have discriminatory hiring practices. Hate war? There are funds that won't invest in defense contractors and weapons manufacturers. There are also screens for companies that manufacture or promote alcohol, tobacco, and gambling—and a few for companies that do animal testing.

In fact, if you click on "Mutual Fund Performance Charts" on the Social Investment Forum's home page, you'll flip to a page that lists roughly one hundred socially screened funds and offers several tabs to get more detailed information. The first page of this listing shows these funds' financial performance over one-year, three-year, five-year, and ten-year time frames. It also shows the funds' assets and expenses. (A word to the wise: Expenses of social funds are generally higher than those of unscreened funds, which can hurt performance. Make sure you consider the fees just as carefully as you consider the fees of any other funds. After all, you can support causes with your investment dollars—or, if you pay less for your investments, you can support them with the cash you save. Either way, you can ensure that causes you care about win.)

Want to know what types of social ills each of these funds aim to address? Click on "Screening & Advocacy." Another tab takes you to a listing of investment minimums, which tell you whether you can afford to invest in any given fund, and another will allow you to pull up more detailed profiles of the funds you're interested in.

Clearly the chart doesn't provide enough detail on the funds' philosophies, social criteria, and investment performance to make it one-stop shopping. However, it gives investors the ability to whittle down their list of possibilities to a few before researching further.

Serious investors will want to know more, such as year-by-year performance and information about fund managers and risks. But in most cases that information is only a click away. The site offers links to the home pages of the vast majority of funds listed. Click on the fund you're interested in, and you zoom through cyberspace to another Web page that provides more detailed information.

It's important to note that only about half of the socially screened funds are listed on the Social Investment Forum's site. These are the fund companies that are the trade group's sponsors. A more complete listing of social funds—although without the nifty performance charts—can be found at www.coopamerica.org, which links to the fund providers' websites, where you can find detailed information about fund performance and prospectuses.

Notably, the Co-op America Foundation Inc. site provides a far broader look at all things "green"—giving tips on everything from investing to recycling and planning an environmentally friendly wedding. The organization also publishes the *National Green Pages*, which is a listing of some 3,000 socially and environmentally screened businesses, including banks, mutual funds, and financial planners. The guide is free with membership to the nonprofit organization, which can be had for a donation as small as $20. If you don't have Web access, you can contact Co-op America by mail or phone at 1612 K Street NW, Washington, D.C., 20006; 800-58-GREEN (800-584-7336).

QUICK TAKE

What You'll LEARN

Real estate investment trusts (REITs), created in 1960, allow individuals to invest in commercial real estate. You'll learn:

- What REITs Are
- The Risks, Performance, Volatility, and Rewards of REIT Investing
- How to Invest in REITs

What You'll DO

- Familiarize yourself with an investment category that's young and not well understood
- Consider how much you might want to invest in this category

How You'll USE This

Like many unfamiliar things, REITs could appear either perfect or horrible if viewed in isolation. But, like most other investments, they have some real benefits and real risks. You'll use this chapter to understand both and determine what percentage, if any, of your assets should be devoted to REIT investments.

REAL ESTATE INVESTMENT TRUSTS

10

In the investment world, real estate investment trusts (REITs) are a relative newcomer. Established as a way of allowing individual investors to buy into commercial real estate, REITs have become popular in recent years because they bridge the gap between stocks and bonds, exhibiting qualities of both.

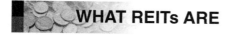 WHAT REITs ARE

REITs are companies that invest in commercial real estate, from shopping centers and office buildings to apartment complexes and hotels. Like other companies, they issue stock through initial public offerings, or IPOs, after which the stock is traded on major stock exchanges and sold through brokers. The market price of the stock generally reflects the underlying value of the real estate the company owns and the income it produces from that real estate, as well as market perceptions of the company's management and prospects. As a result, REIT shares can sell for a premium or a discount to the company's net asset value—just like the shares of any other publicly traded company.

Over the past thirty-five years, the average annual returns for REITs have been similar to those of big-company stocks. REIT returns have averaged 10.75 percent over this time, according to the National Association of Real Estate Investment Trusts. Big-company stocks have returned roughly 10.4 percent over the eighty-one-year period tracked by Ibbotson Associates of Chicago.

Income

REITs also resemble bonds in that they throw off a relatively steady stream of dividend income. The dividend income generally comes from two sources: rent from the real estate the company owns and profits from selling the real estate.

U.S. tax laws dictate that REITs pay out at least 90 percent of their income to investors each year in the form of dividends. Most pay out 100 percent of income because the tax law encourages them to, says Brad Case, vice president of research and industry information at the National Association of Real Estate Investment Trusts. REITs typically pay their managers fees that are set by contract. These fees reduce the net returns to investors and are reflected in the average returns of any given fund.

As with bonds, the amount of income that a REIT produces will vary by both company and market conditions. Recently, REITs were paying between 4 percent and 5 percent annually—about the same as a ten-year Treasury note. More commonly, their yields have been in the 6 percent to 8 percent range.

Taxes

Does all that income get taxed to the recipient? Unless you own a REIT within a qualified retirement plan or college savings plan, yes. However, REIT managers try to reduce the unpleasant nature of the tax bite by at least ensuring that some of the dividends are "qualified" to receive preferential tax treatment. A portion of the income returned to REIT investors reflects capital gains income from selling properties at a profit. A portion can reflect a return of principal. The rest is ordinary income, taxed at ordinary income tax rates. REIT managers will tell investors what's what when they report taxable dividends at year-end.

Risks

There are several risks involved in investing in REITs.

- **Decline in property values.** If property values decline, so does the value of a REIT's underlying assets. Worse, because REITs use leverage—they borrow to buy properties—their stock prices can fall twice as fast as the value of their real estate.
- **Dearth of renters.** Generally REITs secure long-term leases with their corporate clients, who agree to rent out their properties at a set rate for long stretches—five or ten years or more. However, in a bad economy, some of these renters can end up strapped and unable to pay. Unless the economy is

healthy enough to allow more companies to launch and fill up the space, the REITs' income stream can suffer.

- **Glutted markets.** When the economy is booming, some markets go through building booms, increasing competition among purveyors of property. That can increase vacancy rates and depress REIT returns.
- **Geographic ills.** Many REITs concentrate their properties in set geographic areas, such as the Northeast or the Southwest. That allows the managers to become expert on what's needed in an area, but it also subjects the properties to regional downturns in local economies.
- **Industry ills.** Certain REITs specialize in particular industries. Some might buy only office buildings, for example. Others might concentrate on medical buildings, or shopping malls, or apartment complexes, or manufactured homes. A small segment of the REIT market concentrates on making loans on commercial properties. If any of these businesses or industries suffers, the REIT can suffer too, and often in a magnified way. One case in point: When the All REIT Index was down just 5.92 percent for the first nine months of 2007, the Mortgage REIT Index was down a whopping 44 percent in reaction to the subprime mortgage crisis and rising concerns about delinquencies.
- **Management.** Just as public companies can sometimes go sideways because of a manager run amok, so can a REIT. But, again, because REITs are often highly leveraged investments, management gaffes—that range from picking the wrong properties to paying managers too much for their services— can be magnified in the company's stock price.

Performance

As a whole, REITs have earned an average of 10.75 percent over the past thirty-five years, according to the National Association of Real Estate Investment Trusts, which has been tracking REIT returns since the 1970s. However, professionals caution investors from reading too much into those numbers. Why? Thirty-five years may seem like a long time, but as far as investment data goes, it's a drop in the bucket. Stock returns have been tracked since 1926 by Ibbotson Associates in Chicago. However, Roger Ibbotson has said that he's not sure that even eighty-one years is enough time to draw statistically valid conclusions about normal returns.

Volatility

Then, too, the overall returns mask a tremendous amount of volatility. The All REIT Index, which reflects the performance of 153 companies, has lost money in seven years of thirty-five—that's performance that appears to be a little less volatile than stocks. But that's total return, including dividend yields. Take out dividend yields to look solely at stock price, and REITs have lost money in twelve years of thirty-five. The preliminary data from 2007 appear to increase the total to thirteen years of thirty-six in which REITs have declined.

Rewards

So why even bother with this volatile and risky investment category? A study by Ibbotson Associates indicates that REITs have an enviable impact on investment portfolios: Adding a modest exposure to REITs boosts returns and reduces overall volatility. That's because REIT returns are not closely "correlated" with either stocks or bonds.

"They tend to zig when the market zags," says Mike Kirby, chairman and director of research at Green Street Advisors Inc., a Newport Beach–based investment firm that specializes in the REIT industry.

How does that help you? A portfolio made up of 40 percent bonds, 10 percent Treasury bills, and 50 percent stocks would have earned about 10.7 percent on average annually from 1972 through 2006. But if you had shaved a touch off both the stock and bond portfolios to add a 10 percent exposure to REITs—now the portfolio is 10 percent T-bills, 10 percent REITs, 35 percent bonds, and 45 percent stocks—you would have earned 11.1 percent. And, if you had boosted the REIT exposure to 20 percent by shaving another 5 percent off each of the stock and bond portfolios, you would have earned 11.5 percent.

Real Estate Exposure

But what if you feel like you're already loaded up on real estate because you own a home and it makes up such a large portion of your net worth? Wouldn't investing in REITs make you less diversified? Commercial real estate—the type that's rented out—is different from residential real estate, Case contends. Unless you're charging people to live in the guest room, you aren't exposed to the commercial property market by owning a home.

If you own rental real estate on your own, however, you may well have enough exposure to this segment of the market. In this case, you'd want to look through Chapter 14 to determine whether you could use more exposure, or if real estate is dominating your portfolio.

 HOW TO INVEST IN REITs

That said, experts suggest that individuals buy REITs through mutual funds rather than individually. The reason is summed up in the risk section above. Buying individual REITs is a lot like buying any other type of individual stock. To be properly diversified, you'd need numerous REITs operating in different industries and various geographic areas. You can do that, but only if you have quite a lot of money to invest. That's because REITs ought to make up no more than 10 or 20 percent of your overall portfolio.

Kirby also believes that this is a particularly difficult segment of the market for an individual to analyze because some of the information about property values is simply not easily accessible.

"If you have access to a high-quality evaluation of net asset value, you have a good anchor on where a company's stock should trade," he says. "But most individual investors don't have that. If you go it alone, you are at a big informational disadvantage."

On the bright side, individual investors can easily find mutual funds that specialize in real estate and that are often made up exclusively of REIT shares. Such funds are offered by most of the major fund companies, including Vanguard, T. Rowe Price, Fidelity, and Schwab.

"There are a group of very dedicated investors who do nothing all day but focus on this niche," Kirby says. "This is a segment where hard work delivers benefits. An active manager can do quite well."

QUICK TAKE

What You'll LEARN

International markets offer myriad opportunities for U.S. investors, but many of these markets are more volatile than our own. You'll learn about:

- The Effects and Risks on Diversified Portfolios
- International Mutual Funds and Related Investment Vehicles
- All About Currency Risk

What You'll DO

- Determine how much of your assets to devote to international investing
- Calculate the impact of currency swings and decide whether that's a risk worth hedging
- Decide whether to invest in a country or region or the globe

How You'll USE This

Every investor ought to have some international exposure in his portfolio. But the type of exposure can vary from relatively stable global or international funds to the far more volatile, but potentially more lucrative, regional and country funds. You'll learn enough about the risks and rewards of each in this chapter to decide how you want to invest, which will help you find funds that match your strategy.

INTERNATIONAL INVESTING  11

The foreign labels on the things you buy should signal two things to you as an investor. One, to maintain your current buying power, you need a certain amount of international exposure. Two, there are some great companies producing world-class products overseas. That spells opportunity.

"It used to be that the United States dominated the world economy, so it was appropriate for U.S. investors to ignore the rest of the world," says James J. Atkinson Jr., chief executive of Guinness Atkinson Asset Management Inc. in Woodland Hills, California. "But you can't make that claim anymore."

Indeed, though the U.S. stock market remains the biggest in the world, foreign markets now account for about 55 percent of the world's stock market capitalization. Concentrating all your dollars in the domestic markets means you are ignoring more than half of the world's investment opportunities.

In an environment of global companies, global distribution, and global consumerism, many experts maintain that every investor ought to have a portion of his portfolio invested globally, too.

THE EFFECTS AND RISKS ON DIVERSIFIED PORTFOLIOS

What may be the most compelling reason of all to invest in foreign markets is this: A host of independent studies suggest that international investments have had an unusual effect on diversified portfolios. They reduced overall risk and modestly increased the potential return, according to Ibbotson Associates in Chicago. Ibbotson has tracked a historical link between the performance of U.S. and foreign stock markets for almost forty years.

Like bonds and real estate investment trusts (REITs), international stocks benefit a portfolio by being only loosely correlated with U.S. stocks. In other words, when U.S. stocks are rising, foreign stocks could be rising, falling, or clicking along without change. Big international markets sometimes move in tandem, but often they don't. The practical impact on investors is that even though foreign markets are more volatile than the U.S. stock market, adding them to your portfolio makes the overall portfolio more stable. Go figure.

That does more than save you money on antacids. It actually improves your portfolio's overall performance over time.

But even the biggest advocates of foreign investments agree that they are best taken in moderation because many foreign markets are subject to violent swings in value. In addition, currency risk can magnify these swings.

Volatility

Since you should always know about the risks of your investments, as well as the potential rewards, let's first talk about volatility. While some of the more established foreign markets—those in Britain, Germany, and France—aren't overwhelmingly more volatile than U.S. markets, the stock markets in less-developed countries can be terrifying roller coaster rides.

To illustrate, let's take a look at the performance of T. Rowe Price's Latin America Fund. Keep in mind, by the way, that T. Rowe is an excellent fund company, with excellent managers and comparatively low costs. Additionally, this fund is investing in several Latin American countries. All those factors should make the fund less volatile than the underlying markets as a whole.

Over the twelve months that ended Oct. 31, 2007, the fund earned a stunning 78.39 percent. Over three years, it's earned an average of 65.22 percent, and over ten years, it's still got an enviable average annual return of 21.64 percent. You're probably calling T. Rowe right now to buy some, since it seems like the volatility of this fund is all on the upside. But, as we explained in the chapter on mutual funds, the average returns mask a lot.

The calendar returns: In 1997, the fund earned 31.88 percent; in 1998, it lost 35.43 percent. In 1999, it earned 59.38 percent; in 2000, it lost 11.2 percent. The fund lost 0.23 percent in 2001 and posted another 18.10 percent loss in 2002. In 2003, the fund came roaring back with a 57.92 percent return, followed by a 38.35 percent return in 2004, a 60 percent return in 2005, and a 51.24 percent return in 2006.

Why do you need to know that detail? If you're not prepared for the volatility, you would have sold out in '98, or at least by 2002. And then, of course, you would have missed the good years that made up for it.

More broadly diversified foreign funds—those that can invest all over the world, rather than limiting themselves to one geographic region—are a touch more stable. Naturally, that also makes them less lucrative. (You learned that in Chapter 4.) Average returns with T. Rowe's International Stock Fund, for example, were 28.12 percent over the past twelve months; 22.5 percent over the past three years; and 7.49 percent over the past ten years. Why was the ten-year performance so rotten? Because this fund lost 17.09 percent in 2000, 22.02 percent in 2001, and 18.18 percent in 2002. Since then, however, the fund has posted nothing but solid gains—31.28 percent in 2003, 13.89 percent in 2004, 16.27 percent in 2005, and 19.26 percent in 2006.

The moral of this story is that when you invest overseas, you've got to be prepared for a wild ride and you've got to be ready to hang in for the long haul.

Currency Risk

The second risk investors need to contemplate when buying into foreign markets is currency risk. What's that? All world currencies, whether U.S. dollars, euros, or yen, fluctuate in value when measured against one another. When you buy stock in a foreign company, you normally buy the shares with that country's currency, after converting dollars to the currency at that day's exchange rate. When you sell, you get paid in that country's currency, and you then must convert it back to dollars at the going exchange rate.

If the exchange rate is significantly different between the time you buy and the time you sell, it can either add to or reduce whatever return you earned on the stock itself. In some cases, the change in currency values can be more significant to your total return than the actual appreciation or depreciation of the particular stocks you purchased.

If the dollar weakens in value against another currency, you make money on the currency exchange, because each unit of foreign currency translates into more dollars. If the dollar strengthens against another currency, you lose on the currency exchange, because each unit of foreign currency translates into fewer dollars.

To illustrate, consider a hypothetical individual, John, who invested $10,000 in Japanese stocks in April 1995—a time when the Japanese yen was at record strength against the dollar—and sold them in October 1996.

When John bought, his $10,000 was converted into 843,000 yen worth of stocks, because $1 equaled 84.3 yen at the time. In terms of yen, his stocks appreciated a solid 20 percent over the period as the market rose, making the securities worth 1,011,600 yen when he sold.

But in the same time period, the dollar strengthened considerably against the yen. Instead of 84.3 yen needed to equal $1, it took 114 yen to equal $1 when John sold. So after converting his yen to dollars, John came home with just $8,874—a $1,126 loss, caused solely by currency swings.

On the other hand, a U.S. investor who bought Japanese stocks in 1990 and made no return on the stocks at all would have earned a tidy amount when converting Japanese currency back to dollars ten years later, because the dollar's value had weakened considerably against the yen over that time. Where $1 bought 140 yen in 1990, it bought about 104 yen at the beginning of 2000.

Volatility and currency risk aren't the only worries for Americans investing abroad. Investing directly in international markets can be prohibitively expensive and inconvenient if you try to do it alone. Fees are high, some stocks cannot be sold quickly, and there are many delays in transferring funds. This is particularly true of the smaller stock markets in less-developed nations.

Of course, it is possible to buy some foreign stocks on U.S. exchanges. Such issues trade as American Depositary Receipts (ADRs) and are quoted in dollars. Although it is increasing, the number of such stocks is still limited.

INTERNATIONAL MUTUAL FUNDS AND RELATED INVESTMENT VEHICLES

For the most part, the simplest and most economical way to invest in international markets is through mutual funds. Although fund companies also must pay the brokerage settlement and exchange fees involved, they're able to get better rates because they are buying in bulk. The costs are also spread among a larger group of investors.

International mutual funds are not all alike. Some invest in single foreign markets, others invest in specific regions (such as the Pacific Rim), and others invest all over the world. Some try to hedge away currency risk, while others embrace it. Then, too, some funds take a top-down approach to stock picking, choosing the countries first and the specific stocks second, while others pick the stocks of companies they like no matter what country the company is based in. By and large, these differences are clearly delineated in each fund's prospectus—a detailed legal document provided to investors that spells out the fund's risks, strategies, fees, and historical returns (see Chapter 8, on mutual funds, for more details).

Savvy investors analyze whether a fund's investment strategy meshes nicely with their own. Consider, for example, whether you want your fund to bank on one country's economic strength or if you'd prefer a fund that has a broader reach. Does currency risk make you cringe, or can you handle extra risk with the potential for better rewards? Do you want to invest in so-called emerging markets—less-developed countries, where stocks may experience tremendous volatility over the short run but could provide more generous returns over long time periods? Or are you more comfortable investing in mature economies with track records—the Germanys and Japans of the world—because their markets tend to be more predictable?

Another option is so-called global funds, which differ from · international funds in that they have the flexibility to invest a substantial portion of their assets in the U.S. market when fund managers think that's where the best opportunities lie. International funds, on the other hand, are generally required to invest the bulk of their assets overseas.

Foreign stocks also can be purchased via closed-end funds and exchange-traded funds (ETFs). Unlike open-end mutual funds, closed-end funds and ETFs raise capital once and invest it. Their shares, which trade on major exchanges, can sell at a discount or premium to the true value of the underlying portfolio.

After you decide which type of fund is best for you, the only question is how much money you want to invest overseas. There's no pat answer, but experts advise individuals to dedicate anywhere from 5 percent to 25 percent of their portfolios to international investments. The more time you have, the more exposure you can handle in volatile—but potentially rewarding—foreign markets.

The "Buy American" Approach to Foreign Investment

When the U.S. markets were relentlessly breaking records in the late 1990s, a segment of the investment community took a different approach to global diversification. They argued that because big U.S. companies often have operations overseas, you can diversify internationally by doing nothing fancier than buying shares in Coca-Cola Co. and General Electric Co.

Admittedly, those who had done just that between 1996 and 1999 would have done far better than the intrepid investor who stepped into the international markets. Between currency crises and economic and political scandals and upheaval, one market after the next has toppled, while residents in these countries suffered crippling inflation and diminished living standards. Investors, particularly those who participated in the big late 1990s declines of the once-bright stars of Latin America and Southeast Asia, were understandably gun-shy.

But those who were able to talk themselves into taking their profits out of U.S. markets and investing them overseas would have done far better than investors who took the U.S.-only approach. It boils down to age-old market wisdom: "Buy low, sell high."

In other words, if you are going to chase performance, chase the losers, not the winners.

"If you got out of America when it was popular [in the 1960s, when U.S. stocks were rising much like they did throughout the 1990s] and into Japan when it was unpopular [around the same time], you would have made a fortune," says Thomas S. White Jr., president of Thomas White International LTD and manager of the Thomas White International Fund in Chicago. "But it doesn't feel comfortable, because you think you know which country is going to do best. Then everybody thought that Japan was perfect in 1989. They did everything right; we [the United States] did everything wrong. Then they had a bear market for ten years."

Of course, such a move requires fortitude on the part of investors. Going against the crowd means you must be confident enough to handle the ridicule of your friends (or even the cocktail-party guy). On the bright side, fundamental economic indicators suggest that such fortitude will pay off over time.

Consider how the value of various countries' stock markets contrasted with the goods and services that these economies actually produced—two figures that in theory, at least, should move more or less in tandem, since stock prices follow corporate earnings. In market-speak, this compares market capitalization (the value of all of the stocks trading on a particular exchange) to that country's share of global gross domestic product (a measurement of all of the goods and services a country produces). U.S. equities accounted for more than 50 percent of the value of every stock trading on every exchange in the world in 1999. But U.S. companies produced less than 30 percent of the goods and services bought and sold around the world.

By contrast, Japan, which went through a decade of slumping stock prices, produced about 14 percent of the goods the world consumed in 1999, but the value of companies traded on Japan's stock exchange accounted for less than 8 percent of the global market value.

This comparison was reversed two decades ago. In 1988, Japanese stocks accounted for 40 percent of the value of the world's corporate shares, while the country produced less than 20 percent of the goods and services consumed around the globe. At the same time, U.S. stock values and its domestic product were nearly in sync.

ALL ABOUT CURRENCY RISK

Jane Smith decides she wants to get into the foreign stock markets. She buys $1,000 in Mexican stocks and $1,000 in German stocks at a time when each U.S. dollar buys one Mexican peso and one euro. The value of the shares she purchased rises 10 percent over the course of the year in both countries. However, because Jane must bring the proceeds back into the United States to spend the money, her final return will hinge on just how many euros and pesos will be required to buy a dollar. In this case, let's say the value of the Mexican peso dropped, so it now takes 1.3 pesos to buy a dollar. Meanwhile, the value of the euro rose, so it takes just 0.9 euros to buy a dollar.

Investments	Mexican	German
Purchase price	$1,000	$1,000
Appreciation	+$100	+$100
Proceeds from sale (in foreign currency)	$1,100	$1,100
Divided by the cost of a U.S. dollar	÷1.30	÷0.90
Net proceeds in U.S. dollars	$846	$1,222
Total return	−15.4%	+22.2%

It may seem daunting to have to keep track of companies, countries, and currencies for just one piece of your portfolio, but in the end, it's likely to be worth it. Remember those Latin American fund returns? Don't you want a piece of that? During 2007, investors would have been wise to have a significant piece of their portfolios overseas for no better reason than currency swings. The U.S. dollar dropped dramatically against many major currencies, and while U.S. investors were getting relatively lackluster returns, those who were repatriating their dollars from Europe and Britain were seeing double-digit returns. Were the companies better? Not necessarily. They just took an additional risk—in this case currency risk—and were able to reap an additional reward.

QUICK TAKE

What You'll LEARN

If you're able to shelter your investment income from tax, your savings will build up faster and you are likely to end up richer. Fortunately, the government provides vast tax-favored options for those saving for future college and retirement costs. You'll learn about:

- Decreasing the Tax Burden
- Tax-Favored Versus Taxable Investing
- Saving Options
- College Savings Accounts (Coverdell Accounts, 529 Plans)
- Retirement Accounts (401(k) Plans, IRAs, and More)

What You'll DO

- Calculate the benefit of investing in a tax-favored account
- Consider whether the rewards are worth the potential tax penalties, if you use the money for an unintended purpose
- Weigh the relative benefits of Roth vs. traditional IRAs

How You'll USE This

This chapter should give you a clear read of your tax-favored savings options and the benefits and drawbacks of using them. By understanding the benefits and potential penalties, you can avoid the problem of the tax-wise but bottom-line foolish investor and use these strategies only when they pencil out nicely.

TAX-FAVORED INVESTING  12

The tax tail should never wag the investment dog. You know that this saying remains true. And yet if you can get the dog and the tail going in the same direction at the same time, you may have the best of both worlds—a good return that you get to keep.

"It probably shouldn't be your No. 1 investment criterion, but [taxes] ought to be in your top three or four," says Philip J. Holthouse, partner at the Santa Monica tax law and accounting firm Holthouse Carlin & Van Trigt LLP. "If you don't take the tax consequences into account, you are cheating yourself."

There are plenty of opportunities to combine investing and tax management in profitable ways. But the increasing array of choices is making the process complicated for the average investor. And that can lead to costly mistakes.

Holthouse has seen dozens of them. He's had clients—sophisticated, high-income types—fail to realize that they triggered taxable gains when they sold one mutual fund and bought another within the same fund family. He's seen high-income individuals sell a stock one month too soon—within eleven months of the purchase, which precludes them from claiming preferential capital gains tax rates on the profit. Their federal tax hit jumps to about 35 percent from 15 percent on such a transaction. He's seen people put variable annuities and municipal bonds in retirement accounts—an unnecessary and costly doubling up of tax-favored vehicles.

Worse still, he's seen individuals pull money out of retirement plans to pay off bills or buy luxury items. The hit—taxes and penalties—is crushing, usually about half of the amount withdrawn, and these individuals forever lose the benefit of allowing that money to grow for long periods on a tax-favored basis.

So what are the wise ways to minimize the taxes on your investments?

DECREASING THE TAX BURDEN

- **Invest in tax-managed accounts.** Mutual fund companies are increasingly offering funds that promise to manage the taxable income passed on to you. One of the more effective strategies they use is simply not to trade shares often. Index funds, which buy and hold all the stocks in a particular index, are among the most tax efficient. Generally the only gains they pass on to investors are dividends and an occasional long-term gain from selling shares in a company that's been bought out or has otherwise fallen out of the index.
- **Trade sparingly.** The best way to manage your capital gains bills is not to trigger any gains. After all, you have to pay capital gains taxes only if you sell shares at a profit. If you buy stocks because you think the company has great long-term potential, and nothing dramatic has occurred to make you change your mind, sit tight.
- If you must trade, **trade in tax-favored accounts.** There are options galore—Roth IRAs, traditional IRAs, Keogh accounts, and 401(k)s, for instance—that shelter your gains from tax until you pull the money out at retirement. The first three types of accounts allow you to completely self-direct your invest-ments. (You also self-direct your investments with a 401(k), but your options are usually more limited.) You can buy individual stocks, mutual funds, bonds, certificates of deposit, and so on. And if you decide you want to alter your investment mix, you can sell any or all of your holdings without triggering a taxable gain. Of course, you also can't use capital losses realized within a retirement account when figuring your taxes. So do your best to trade wisely.
- **Fully fund any tax-favored account** you have available. Start with your 401(k) at work. Contributions to 401(k) plans and similar plans, such as 403(b) plans for teachers and 457 plans for other government employees, are deducted from your taxable income, so they reduce your federal income tax when you contribute. Additionally, most employers match anywhere from 25 percent to 100 percent of their workers' 401(k) contributions, up to set amounts. So if you put in $100, the

employer kicks in an additional, say, $50. You make a 50 percent return on your money before you've invested a dime. You don't pay current income tax on either the company contributions or the investment income you've earned on the account, either. It grows and compounds on a tax-deferred basis until you withdraw the money. It doesn't get much better than that.

DID YOU KNOW?
Opportunity Cost

Oftentimes, it's more effective to contribute to your 401(k) retirement account than pay down debt. For example, let's say you're in the 28 percent federal tax bracket, like many working Americans. If you contribute $5,000 annually to a 401(k), or $417 per month, that reduces your taxable income by the same amount. The result is that you pay $1,400 less in federal income tax that year. Or to put it another way, your $5,000 contribution has a net cost to you of $3,600. Now your employer kicks in, say, 25 percent, or an additional $1,250 a year ($104 per month). Then you earn an average of 10 percent on your money. At the end of year one, you have $6,545. Considering that your net (after-tax) cost was $3,600, that's an 82 percent return. That beats the 20 percent interest savings you would get by paying off your credit card debt by a wide margin.

You can take this one step further and reduce your debt as well as increase your savings. Assume that you have $5,000 annually to spend. Because a $5,000 401(k) contribution is going to cost you only $3,600 after tax, use the remaining $1,400 to pay down your debt. Keep it up, and you would pay off your $5,000 debt in less than five years. Your 401(k), assuming you keep earning that average annual return of 10 percent, will be worth a tidy $40,332.

What about buying variable annuities and municipal bonds? If you are very wealthy—paying income taxes at the nation's highest rates—municipal bonds can make sense for a part of the fixed-income portion of your portfolio. Unfortunately, many people with scant taxable income buy munis so they don't have to pay income tax on the investment income. But because municipals generally pay significantly less interest than taxable bonds, these people often get a lower after-tax return than they'd earn on a taxable-bond investment.

As for variable annuities, if you find an extremely low-cost annuity, they might work for high-income individuals who have maximized their other tax-favored retirement account options but still want to save more. But they're a sorry substitute for investing in a 401(k). And some tax advisers argue that they're less attractive than simply investing in stocks or tax-managed mutual funds for the long term. Annuities are less flexible than taxable investments, these advisers note. And when you permanently withdraw money from an annuity, your investment gains are taxable at ordinary income tax rates rather than at the lower capital gains rates.

■ RUNNING THE NUMBERS

TAX-FAVORED VERSUS TAXABLE INVESTING

How much of a difference does tax-favored investing make? Frankly, the precise figure depends on a number of variables that are impossible to predict accurately—such as your tax rate at retirement and the rate of return you'll earn on your money each year. But making a few guesses and running them through an example or two can help illustrate.

Consider an investor, Sam Smart, who puts $100 a month into mutual funds in his company's 401(k) plan—a tax-deferred retirement account—and earns 10 percent on average annually over a forty-year period. At retirement, he has $632,408.

His friend, Sue Savvy, invests in a taxable mutual fund instead and pays income tax from her fund account each year. Even though Savvy invests the same amount and earns the same investment return as Smart, she accumulates much less—just $349,101. (To simplify matters, we've assumed that the fund has realized 100 percent of its capital gains, and she pays federal income tax on all of it at a 20 percent rate. In reality, most mutual funds would defer at least some gains, and individual tax consequences can vary.)

When Savvy retires, she doesn't have to worry much about taxes. Smart, on the other hand, must pay tax on the 401(k) when he withdraws the money at retirement. If he takes the money out in one lump sum, he'll push himself into the highest marginal tax bracket, but he'll still end up with about $411,065 after surrendering 35 percent of his savings in federal income taxes.

If, in a more likely scenario, he takes money out over time, the money withdrawn from the 401(k) will be taxed at a more modest rate.

In any event, Smart is somewhere between $60,000 and $100,000 (depending on his tax rate at retirement) richer than Savvy simply because he was able to collect investment returns—and allow them to compound year after year—on money that otherwise would have been paid to the government.

Which is all to say, tax-favored compounding is a powerful force. Just how powerful it will be depends on other considerations. Tax rates that are much higher at retirement will reduce Sam Smart's advantage, while lower tax rates at retirement could cause his advantage to multiply. Unrelated capital losses might reduce the taxes on gains Sue Savvy would pay along the way. And tax law changes are, of course, unpredictable.

SAVING OPTIONS

Congress, in its infinite wisdom, has decided that there are two types of savings goals that are so important that they should be supported with tax dollars. Consequently, they have created a myriad of accounts that can be used to save for these goals—college and retirement—in a tax-favored way. There are also a handful of other investments, from growth stocks to municipal bonds, which offer tax advantages as well. Here's a look at the options, starting with the special-purpose plans.

COLLEGE SAVINGS ACCOUNTS

There are three different tax-favored ways to save for college. However, the oldest way—using so-called Uniform Gift to Minors Accounts (UGMAs) and Uniform Transfer to Minors Accounts (UTMAs)—has lost a lot of its appeal in recent years because there are frankly better options. The two best: 529 plans and so-called Coverdell Accounts.

Generally speaking, your contributions to these plans are not tax-deductible. However, the investment income earned within the account is not taxed until the money is pulled out. If the money is used for qualified education expenses—generally that's tuition, fees, books and

get more conservative as your child gets older to reduce the chance that you'll have blown the tuition money on a flyer in the stock market right before tuition is due.

There are literally dozens of these plans available. Most advisers suggest you look at your own state's plan first to see if it offers good investment options, and whether your state is one of the generous few providing state tax deductions. If you don't like your state's plan, you can invest in any plan offered by any state. A good way to check out viable plans is through a website operated by an accountant named Joseph Hurley. (He's also written a book about 529 plans, *The Best Way to Save for College*.) His website rates plans on a graduation-cap scale that aims to compare the returns, investment options, and tax breaks on a one-to-five scale, one cap being the worst and five caps the best. The site is www.savingforcollege.com.

Where Have All the UTMAs and UGMAs Gone?

They were once the best tax-favored savings strategy. Parents put money in their kids' names through UTMAs or UGMAs. That allowed any investment income in the account to be taxed at the child's rate, rather than the parents'. But these accounts have lost favor in recent years as Congress has authorized the tax-free Coverdell and 529 options, and as parents discovered the other compelling drawback of using these to finance college. Namely, money in an UGMA or UTMA account is considered the child's asset. The child can use the money for school or to buy a Porsche. Moreover, federal financial aid formulas weigh children's assets more heavily than the assets of the parents. Simply put, each dollar in a 529 plan will cost a child about 6 cents in aid eligibility. Each dollar in an UGMA will cost the child about 20 cents in aid.

 **RETIREMENT ACCOUNTS**

Generally speaking, traditional retirement accounts (this excludes the Roth individual retirement account, or IRA) have two major advantages. Contributions are tax-deductible, so, as an incentive for saving, you pay less current income tax. In addition, investment income earned in your retirement account is not taxed until you start to withdraw it.

But there are two major disadvantages: When you withdraw the money, every dollar—including your principal—counts as taxable income (assuming you took the deductions up front as you contributed). And withdrawals are taxable at your ordinary income tax rate, which may be higher than the capital gains rates that might otherwise apply to long-term investment gains.

In addition, if you take your money out before retirement, you'll get hit with penalties—hefty ones. The federal government generally imposes a 10 percent tax penalty on retirement funds withdrawn before age fifty-nine and a half. And many states impose their own penalties besides. California, for example, imposes a penalty amounting to 2.5 percent of the withdrawn amount.

A variety of tax-deferred retirement accounts are offered to different groups of people and are subject to different rules and regulations. For example, there are Keogh plans for self-employed individuals; traditional individual retirement accounts; Roth IRAs, which don't offer up-front deductions but promise tax-free withdrawals; 403(b) plans for teachers and employees of nonprofit organizations; and so-called 457 plans for government workers. Here's a quick rundown of the options.

401(k) Plans

These are among the most flexible and attractive retirement plans available. The vast majority of large employers offer these company-sponsored retirement programs. In 2007 they allowed workers to set aside up to $15,500 of their wages annually (if their company program rules allow it) and to deduct this amount from their taxable earnings. Someone contributing $15,500 would reduce his or her annual tax bite by $4,340 if that person was in the 28 percent federal tax bracket. (This person would save on state income taxes, too.)

If you are age fifty or over, you can make an additional "catch-up" contribution of up to $5,000. (The amounts that can be contributed to these plans are periodically adjusted for inflation.) So someone who was fifty-five in 2007 would be able to contribute a tidy $20,500 to savings, cutting his taxable income by a like amount and saving him $5,740 in federal income tax. He'd likely also save money on his state tax bill.

Better yet, contributions to retirement plans are "before the line" deductions, which mean they reduce "adjusted gross income." In today's Byzantine tax system, that's pivotal because many popular tax breaks, such as the child tax credit, the Hope and Lifetime Learning Credits, and the dependent care credit, are all income-tested. The test pivots on AGI, so reducing your AGI with a retirement plan contribution boosts your chance of being able to qualify for these income-tested tax breaks too.

But what really differentiates 401(k) accounts from other tax-favored retirement options is that most employers match worker contributions, kicking in $0.25 to $1 for every $1 the employee saves. That supercharges the returns, making it far easier to save a substantial sum.

Equally attractive is the fact that many companies allow workers to borrow as much as $50,000 or 50 percent of their 401(k) savings, whichever is less, to finance anything from a home purchase to a college education. This reduces the need to make actual withdrawals (which would incur penalties). Other retirement plans don't offer this kind of flexibility.

Because these are employer-sponsored plans, the employer determines what investment options are within the plan. Workers must choose among the given options. Usually these options include a host of mutual funds that invest in different portions of the market— big company stocks, small company stocks, international stocks, bonds, cash, and, sometimes, real estate through real estate investment trust (REIT) funds. Increasingly companies are offering so-called "target date" funds, too, which automatically diversify worker savings among asset classes based on their age and projected retirement date.

Employees' ultimate returns on the 401(k) will depend on how much they save, whether their employers match contributions, and whether they've invested wisely. How should you choose investments in these accounts? Chapter 14 provides a simple guide.

Roth IRAs

These retirement accounts don't offer up-front tax deductions, but they promise big tax breaks in the end. The way they work is this: Qualifying individuals can contribute up to $5,000 per year as of 2008. Those who are age fifty and over can make an additional $1,000 contribution. Your contributions are not tax deductible, but if you leave your money alone for at least five years and then withdraw only for a "qualified purpose," such as retirement, death, disability, or the purchase of your first home, all the money you take out—principal and interest—is tax free.

There are, however, some restrictions. Your ability to contribute to a Roth IRA is limited if you earn more than $99,000 when single or more than $156,000 when married. Once your income exceeds $114,000 when single or $166,000 when married, your ability to contribute phases out completely. (The income thresholds are occasionally adjusted for inflation.)

However, if you meet all the restrictions and have a very long time to save, Roths can be tremendously powerful tools. For example, if a twenty-year-old woman started saving $2,000 a year and kept it up for ten years, and then left the money alone until she retired at age sixty-five, how much money would she have? She would have saved a total of $20,000 of her own money, but at an average 10 percent annual return on her investment, she would have accumulated a stunning $1.1 million at retirement. If that money was in an ordinary retirement account, it would all be taxable at her ordinary income tax rate. Assuming that she paid tax at 28 percent, it would cost her about $300,000 in federal income tax. But if it were in a Roth, none of that tax would be due.

Traditional IRAs

If you are not covered by a qualified retirement plan at work, you can deduct contributions of up to $4,000 in 2007 and up to $5,000 in 2008 to a traditional IRA. (If you are age fifty or over, you can deduct an additional $1,000 in contributions.)

If you are covered by a company retirement plan, you can only deduct traditional IRA contributions if your income is below set thresholds. These thresholds change modestly each year to reflect inflation. However, for a single filer or head of household, contributions are fully deductible to $52,000 in annual income and partially deductible for those earning up to $62,000. If you're married, filing jointly, you can fully deduct contributions until your income exceeds $83,000 and partially deduct contributions until your adjusted gross income hits $103,000.

Tough Choices

How do you choose whether to contribute to a Roth or a traditional IRA, when you qualify for both? It's tough. Frankly, the best choice will depend on how your tax rate today compares with at retirement—which you can't possibly know now. And it will hinge on your investment returns in the interim, and that, too, is tough to call in advance.

Here are a few rules of thumb:

- If your tax rate is likely to be the same in retirement as it is now, it's likely to be an economic wash—the accounts will generate roughly the same after-tax income. The question you need to ask is: Do I trust Congress? If not, do you think they're more likely to raise regular tax rates (which would argue for the Roth) or take away the tax benefit for big savers—arguing that "millionaires" shouldn't be able to avoid tax? That would argue for taking the tax benefit today.
- If your tax rate is likely to be higher in retirement than now, use the Roth.
- If your tax rate is high now—and you haven't saved that much, so you figure it will be lower later—use the traditional.
- If you are very young and in a low tax bracket, but already saving, you're likely to be in a higher bracket later. Use the Roth.
- If you started saving late in life, and are still finding it tough to scrape together enough to save, use the traditional. It will make today's job of saving more affordable.

403(b) and 457 Plans

These are employer-sponsored retirement accounts for government workers and employees of nonprofit organizations. They're similar to 401(k) plans. All contributions are taken out of paychecks before tax is computed, cutting the contributor's taxable income and income tax. The amount that can be contributed is $15,500 per year in 2008, but those over the age of fifty can make additional contributions of up to $5,000 annually.

However, far fewer employers match contributions to these plans. In addition, you may need to be wary of the fees and investment choices offered through your plan. Why would you need a warning about investment choices in a 403(b) and not a 401(k)? The Employee Retirement Income Security Act imposes something called "fiduciary duty" on the plan administrators of 401(k) plans. What that means is your plan administrator is bound by law to act in your best interest—not his own. If he acts unreasonably, if he fails to give you good investment choices, you can sue and potentially force your employer to take more responsibility for your economic health in retirement.

But 403(b) and 457 plans are mostly public-employee plans, and the government rarely applies the same rules to itself that it applies to everyone else. Employers are able to get out of their fiduciary duty to employees fairly simply with these plans. With 403(b) plans, employers sometimes don't choose the investments at all—they simply tell workers that they can pick any plan from any company on their approved vendor list, and these lists can include hundreds—or just a few—vendors. You need to look at the choices fairly carefully.

What should you avoid?

- **Annuities.** Annuities are tax-favored investment vehicles that charge a fee for their tax-favored status. When you are investing in a 403(b) or 457, you already have tax-favored status. Investing in an annuity means you're paying twice for the same benefit. (Some sales people will tell you there are other benefits with an annuity. There are, but the benefits are relatively modest and are seldom worth the often exorbitant price. You can compare the prices at the Securities and Exchange Commission site at www.sec.gov, using the mutual fund calculator described in Chapter 8.)
- **"Load" funds.** Unless you need a lot of hand-holding and advice, load funds will cost you more and get you little in the way of additional value. If you do need hand-holding and advice, check out Chapter 16 on hiring financial help.
- **Wrap accounts.** With a wrap account, you pay an investment adviser a fee, which is calculated as a percentage of your assets, to select investments for you. Theoretically, the advisers are supposed to earn that fee by selecting investments that are so profitable for you that they more than make up for the fees charged. In reality, this rarely happens, and wrap fees can gobble up as much as 2 percentage points of your return each year. That, over time, is an astounding cost.

What should you select?

- **Index funds.** These funds reflect the performance of an entire market index and usually charge exceptionally low fees. Check the prospectus to ensure that your fund charges 0.50 percent or less in annual management fees.
- **Brand names.** Options that include respected low-cost fund companies, such as Vanguard and T. Rowe Price, should give you some confidence that whoever is doing the selecting wants you to have some good choices.

Simple Plans

Simple plans are a cross between a traditional IRA and a 401(k). They were designed for small employers who couldn't handle the copious recordkeeping requirements of a 401(k) plan. Indeed, there are two types of Simple (which stands for Savings Incentive Match Plan for Employees of Small Employers) plans—a Simple 401(k) and a Simple IRA.

With a Simple 401(k), workers can contribute up to $10,500 annually in 2008. A worker who is age fifty or over can contribute an additional $2,500 annually. Your employer is required to provide some sort of contribution, too. Employers can either contribute 2 percent of pay to all workers, or they can provide matching contributions of at least 3 percent to those who contribute to their own savings accounts. The Simple IRA follows these same guidelines.

In other ways, the Simple plans work just like 401(k)s. Employees choose among a select number of investment options—usually a group of mutual funds. Their account grows by virtue of their contributions, their employer's contributions, and the wisdom of their investment choices. (Hopefully, reading the rest of this book will help you to make choices that are wise.)

Simple IRAs, SEP IRAs, Keoghs, and Self-Employed 401(k) Plans

If you are self-employed, the government gives you a number of retirement savings options to choose from. These plans can allow self-employed individuals to set aside a substantial portion of their income. However, each has a series of benefits and detriments. The plans that allow you to set aside the most money, for example, are also usually the most complex, and require monitoring and complex tax filings. Because it's impossible to do these plans justice here—there are entire books dedicated to this topic alone—suffice it to say that if you make any reasonable amount of money with your self-employment, you should spend the time, effort, and cash to talk retirement plans over with a seasoned tax adviser. It will certainly be worth your while.

Retirement Savings Contribution Credit

If you earn a modest income but contribute to a tax-favored retirement plan anyway, the government will give you an additional tax break in the form of a credit of up to $1,000. And it's worth mentioning that a credit is far more valuable than a deduction. Deductions reduce your taxable income. That saves you tax at whatever your income tax rate is. In other words, if you get a deduction of $1,000 and you're in the 25 percent tax bracket, it will save you $250, or 25 percent of $1,000. But a tax credit reduces your tax on a dollar-for-dollar basis. So, for somebody in the 25 percent bracket, a $1,000 credit is worth $4,000 in deductions.

What does it take to get this retirement savings credit?

- You must contribute to a traditional or Roth IRA, 401(k), 403(b), 457, Simple IRA, or simplified employee pension (SEP).
- You must earn less than $52,000 if married, filing jointly; $39,000 if your filing status is "head of household"; or $26,000 if you are single or married, filing separately.
- You must be over the age of 18; cannot be a full-time student; and cannot be claimed as a dependent on somebody else's tax return.
- If you have otherwise tax-free income from a foreign job, or imputed income from somebody paying your foreign housing costs, it must be added in to figure your adjusted gross income for this credit.

The exact value of the credit will depend on how much you contribute to a qualified retirement plan and your income. To figure your credit, you'll need to fill out an Internal Revenue Service form 8880, which you can download directly from the IRS website at www.irs.gov.

Tax-Deferred Annuities

Like standard retirement accounts, annuities are essentially "shells" through which you can invest in securities such as stocks and bonds, deferring taxes on earnings until you begin withdrawing the money at retirement.

But unlike standard retirement accounts, the money you contribute to an annuity is not tax-deductible. What's more, if you pull money out before retirement, you'll get hit with federal and state tax penalties. If you pull the money out before your annuity contract allows it, you may also get hit with a so-called surrender fee from the insurer, and all the investment income pulled out of an annuity at retirement is taxed at ordinary income tax rates, not preferential capital gains rates.

On the bright side, annuities get their special tax treatment because they're "wrapped" with a life insurance policy. By and large, that insurance policy guarantees only one thing: If you die and the market crashes at the same time, the insurer will make sure your heirs get at least as much as you contributed to your account. But the cost of the insurance policy boosts the annual fees imposed on your annuity account, and that depresses your total return.

Because there are limited tax benefits and the cost of annuities can be high, experts suggest that consumers maximize every other qualified retirement plan—401(k), 403(b), Simple, SEP, or traditional IRA, for example—before even considering a tax-deferred annuity. Even then, many people would be better off saving in a taxable account and simply attempting to manage the taxable gains by trading sparingly.

Growth Stocks

Another tax-favored investment alternative is to buy and hold stock in companies that grow and appreciate. What will that get you? Until you sell, you won't have to pay tax on the stock's price appreciation.

Let's say you put $100 a month into the stock of a fast-growing company, and the stock appreciates 10 percent a year on average. At the end of the fortieth year, you have $632,408 in stock—just as much as Sam Smart has in his 401(k). But Sam pays taxes on his 401(k) at ordinary income tax rates. And he pays tax on the entire amount in the account. You, on the other hand, are going to pay tax at a 15 percent capital gains rate, and only on the appreciation, not on the principal. Subtracting your principal investment of $48,000 made over the forty years, if you sold your stock worth $632,408, you'd pay $87,661 in federal capital gains taxes, leaving you with $544,747.

That's more than Sam Smart ends up with, unless he is in a very low tax bracket at retirement. And if you end up leaving money to charity or heirs, there are significant tax advantages to giving appreciated stock rather than trying to give away 401(k) funds. On the other hand, Smart got up-front tax deductions that you didn't get when investing directly in stocks. And if he got matching funds from his employer, he's probably ahead.

Municipal Bonds

These bonds, which are debt issued by cities, states, and counties, pay interest that is tax free to residents of the state in which the bonds are issued. If you are in the highest federal and state tax brackets, municipal bonds can be a good bet. Although they pay relatively low rates of interest, all the interest earnings are free from federal and state income taxes.

QUICK TAKE

What You'll LEARN

You don't need to be rich to invest in stocks. You just need to have a few hundred dollars and a commitment to earning more. You'll learn:

- How to Start Small
- Other Options for Small Investments
- The Cost of Delays

What You'll DO

- Decide whether you want to invest in individual stocks or through mutual funds
- Find a fund company that suits you
- Get started

How You'll USE This

If you've been telling yourself that you're too poor to invest, this chapter will debunk that myth and give you practical ways to get started. Even if you can't invest a lot, investing a little for a long time can make you rich—or at least a heck of a lot better off than you were before.

Think you're too poor to invest in stocks? Many people do, partly because they know that most brokerage firms and mutual funds require at least $1,000 or $2,000 to even open an account. However, there are several ways that you can get started with as little as $25 to $50 a month. Better yet, new opportunities are arising daily, thanks to cheap online trading services, which are increasingly accommodating to individual investors who don't have a lot of cash.

Two Web-based brokerages, for instance—found at www.sharebuilder.com and buyandhold.com—allow investors to buy individual stocks with no investment minimums and at a minimal cost. Both of the companies encourage a strategy called dollar-cost averaging, which is one of the most successful, time-proven strategies on Wall Street.

Dollar-cost averaging works like this: You decide to invest a set amount in a particular security each month, every month. You set it up in advance and, aside from funding the purchases with either a deposit or an automatic transfer from your bank account, you forget about it. You don't watch stock prices. You don't trade quickly when the market is rising or falling. You let the company trade for you, based on the schedule you've prearranged, no matter what.

The reason dollar-cost averaging works is that it takes the emotion out of investing, and it naturally enforces age-old market wisdom—buy low, sell high. Let's say you choose to buy $100 in XYZ stock each month. In month one, XYZ is selling for $10 a share. Your $100 investment gets you ten shares. In month two, XYZ is selling for $15, so your $100 gets you just 6.67 shares. In month three, when its stock price plunges and XYZ is now selling for $5, you're loading up. Now you get twenty shares for your $100 investment. Assuming that this company will eventually grow and prosper because you picked wisely, dollar-cost averaging simply takes the emotion out of the day-to-day purchase decisions, reducing the chance that you panic and do something harmful to your wealth.

HOW TO START SMALL

Assuming you're willing to go with this program, either company will make investing simple and inexpensive. With BUYandHOLD, you can spend $6.99 per month to get up to two trades per month. If you want to trade more often, you can get an "unlimited" investing plan for $14.99 per month.

At ShareBuilder, you can open a basic account with no fee and pay $4 per trade. Or you can pay $12 per month to get up to six free trades per month, paying just $2 per trade after that. Neither company imposes an investment minimum.

If the amount you've chosen to invest won't buy you a full share of stock, these companies will buy you a fractional share. In other words, if you can afford to invest just $20 per month but want to buy stock in a company that sells for $60 per share, they'll buy you roughly one-third of a share each month.

If you want to trade in "real time"—in other words, buy a share of stock instantaneously—you can do that too, but it will cost you more. BUYandHOLD charges $15 for the service. ShareBuilder's costs range from $12 to $16 based on the type of account you have.

Still, if you are a long-term investor looking for a way to accumulate shares, being able to trade in the blink of an eye isn't a huge issue. It is more likely to hurt you than help, in fact, because investors rarely manage to trade at exactly the right time. Savvy investors say they don't even try—particularly not after the Psychic Network went bankrupt, without ever predicting it. At the same time, the ability to trade in small amounts gives virtually any working American the chance to start investing—no matter how little he or she earns.

How much of a nest egg can you accumulate with these small regular investments? If you save just $20 a month and earn 10 percent on your money, you could have $45,210 socked away in thirty years. If you save $25 a month, earning the same 10 percent on average, you'd have $56,512; $30 a month would generate $67,815 in savings; and $40 a month would net you $90,420. You can save $50 a month, you say? Great. You'll have more than $113,000 in thirty years, assuming you earn an average annual return of 10 percent on your money.

DID YOU KNOW?
SIPC

Think you found the perfect discount broker because some website promises trades for free? Maybe you have, but be wary of investment firms that appear too good to be true. Any firm you deal with should be Securities Investor Protection Corp. (SIPC) insured. SIPC does not protect investors from a risk of investment loss, but it ensures that investors get their stocks back—and up to $100,000 in invested cash—if a brokerage firm fails without providing the securities to investors. To find out if your broker is SIPC insured, go to www.sipc.org. Under the heading "Who We Are" is a "Member Database." Click on that, and you can look up your broker. If he or she is not listed, find out why and consider taking your business elsewhere.

 ## OTHER OPTIONS FOR SMALL INVESTMENTS

Notably, the services offered by ShareBuilder and BUYandHOLD are only the most cost-effective offerings in a wide array of options available to those who don't have a lot of money to invest. Many mutual fund companies also allow you to make small monthly investments. However, they generally require investments of at least $50 per month. There are also dozens of discount brokerage firms that charge relatively small commissions for trading. Charles Schwab, for example, charges $12.95 per Web-based equity trade; Scottrade Inc. charges $7 for Web-based trades, $17 for trades done over the phone, and $27 for broker-assisted trades.

Additionally, you can participate in so-called direct stock purchase programs that are now offered by more than one thousand companies nationwide. Direct stock purchase plans often allow you to buy stock in the company of your choice without paying any brokerage fees at all. Typically, you'll need to buy one share of stock first. But after that, you can enroll in the company's dividend reinvestment plan and buy more shares at your pleasure, usually without paying any commissions.

However, small investors have to realize that there are two shortcomings to this approach. Specifically, to have a diversified portfolio, you need shares in at least ten different companies, operating in ten different industries. If you're buying one share at a time, it can take a long time to build this diversity. The other shortcoming: If you are buying just $20 or $30 in stock each month, even a $4 commission takes a big bite out of your investment, in percentage terms. You'd be wise to invest at least $50 per month and, ideally, $100.

Think you can't afford that? You might be right. But, before you decide for sure, check out the advice in Chapter 1 in the section "Saving too little—or not at all."

If you can afford $100 per month, you can buy into a no-load mutual fund. Charles Schwab offers several that boast investment minimums this low. A fund helps you by providing automatic diversification of your investment, without the fuss of having to pick each share and determine whether it's different enough from the other companies you own. A professional manager is doing that analysis. And unless his or her performance is consistently miserable, you can figure they're probably at least as skilled at the job as you would be.

Once you build up assets of $2,000 to $3,000, you can invest with virtually any mutual fund company and enjoy the ability to buy more shares without paying trading commissions.

How do you get started?

First, decide whether you want to buy individual stocks, or if you want to go the mutual fund route.

Mutual Funds

If you opt for the mutual fund route, I'd recommend you start with Charles Schwab funds. The reason: Most mutual funds that offer superlow investment minimums charge relatively high fees. Frankly, they have to. The reason is simple. Mutual funds charge fees as a percentage of your investments. If they charge a 1 percent fee and you've invested only $100, they earn $1 on your account each year. They'd lose money each year by simply buying stamps to mail your quarterly statement.

Although Schwab's low-minimum investment funds charge more than some of the lower-cost companies, such as Vanguard and T. Rowe Price, they're considerably less costly than many of the insurance companies that offer similarly low minimum investments to get into their mutual funds.

Schwab is banking on the idea that once you've built up a reasonable portfolio with their less-expensive funds, you'll decide to stay—and maybe you'll use their discount brokerage services or their OneSource mutual fund purchase plan too. To reach them, go to www .schwab.com, or call 866-232-9890.

To find out about other low-minimum plans, go to www.mfea.com and run your cursor over the "Fund Selector" menu. This will bring up the link "Fund Quicklist." Click on that to bring up several choices, including the link "Low Initial Investment." Click again and you'll get a long list of funds that allow you to get in with $500 or less. This chart also shows the funds' recent performance and provides their rankings via Morningstar. Morningstar ratings go from a high of five stars to a low of one. Anything that gets three stars or more is a reasonable choice. Avoid funds with lower ratings, and be wary of funds that aren't rated.

Individual Stocks

If you choose the individual stock route, you have three options:

1. Go to both buyandhold.com and www.sharebuilder.com to compare costs and benefits. Consider which site you find friendlier, and consider the way you might trade to determine which company's fee structure might work best for you. Both companies are good and reputable and have been in business for the better part of a decade.

2. Check out www.directinvesting.com, which is a site that explains how to invest in corporate dividend reinvestment plans directly. Subscribing to Direct Investing costs $199 per year, but it can provide a discount on buying individual shares and provide advice on which shares are best for your portfolio. Some of these services are also available through BUYandHOLD and ShareBuilder.

3. Go directly to the company that you want to buy and see if they offer a direct stock purchase plan. Roughly one thousand companies nationwide offer investors the ability to buy their shares directly from the company. By and large, you must have one share of the company's stock registered in your name to start. After that, you can buy additional shares directly from the company either at no cost or at a very low cost.

The downside to most of these plans is speed. Normally, share purchases are done just once a week or once a month (depending on the plan), so you can't time your buy or sell to correspond with some news event that's had a big impact on the stock price.

In addition, while most plans allow you to buy shares very cheaply—for about $0.03 per share or even for free—they often charge substantially more when you want to sell. It's not uncommon for companies to charge $0.10 to $0.12 per share on sales, for example. In other words, while it would cost you about $30 to buy one thousand shares of stock, it could cost you $120 to sell those same one thousand shares. Then, too, many of the companies that investors are interested in buying don't offer direct stock purchase plans.

On the bright side, if a company you're interested in does offer such a plan, and you don't mind the processing delays, getting started is easy if you have Web access. Generally, you can go directly to the company's website and click on "Investor Relations," which tells you how to get started.

THE COST OF DELAYS

Whichever plan you choose, remember one thing: Every moment you delay costs you money.

The most powerful word in all of finance is *compounding*. Compounding means that the longer you leave your money invested, the more money you have in the long run.

Consider this little financial riddle: Who would have more money saved at retirement, the woman who socked away $2,000 a year for ten years—a total of $20,000—between the ages of twenty and thirty, or the man who saved twice as much for twice as long but didn't start until he was forty?

You guessed it: the woman. But how much more she would have might just surprise you. Because she left that $20,000 alone to compound for thirty-five additional years, until she turned age sixty-five, she landed a nest egg of $1,114,310. That's right—she would have more than $1.1 million.

Her male counterpart, who saved four times more of his own money—$80,000 total—would generate a nest egg worth just $416,465. (These figures assume that they both earned 10 percent on average on their money and they both retired at age sixty-five.) In other words, if you start early, it's easy to save even vast amounts. Wait and the work becomes increasingly harder.

The moral of this story is that it doesn't matter how little you've got. Get started now and make your money grow.

QUICK TAKE

What You'll LEARN

Investing wisely doesn't require a PhD or unlimited time and patience in picking the perfect investments. You can do well quickly and easily with the Lazy Investor's Portfolio detailed in this chapter. You'll learn to:

- Determine What You Have
- Determine What You Need
- Choose Specific Investments
- Rebalance Your Portfolio

What You'll DO

- Fill in the worksheets to establish how much you have
- Determine whether your assets are currently wisely allocated between cash, stocks, and bonds
- Adjust your portfolio where necessary
- Compare your mix of investments to a handful of sample portfolios

How You'll USE This

This chapter is designed to give you an action plan that you can live with in good markets and bad, with a minimum of time and effort. It allows you to take everything you've learned in the previous chapters and apply it to a hands-off portfolio.

Now let's just say, for argument's sake, that investing is not your life. Sure, you want to have money, both now and later. And you know you have to invest in order to accumulate that money. But you don't get a huge thrill from considering the relative strengths of stocks versus bonds; the international markets versus the domestic. And the idea of spending every waking hour poring over financial statements and analyzing price/earnings ratios makes you want to hide out in the wine cellar—even if you don't have one.

Good news. You can invest as well as anyone and spend only about an hour or two *a year* doing it. Seriously. Give me ten minutes a month and I'll give you a portfolio that will stand the test of time.

What's the catch? There are two. First, the initial setup will take you a little longer than an hour—maybe even two hours. But you'll find that even the setup delivers benefits in the end. After that, it's just a matter of monitoring, and the monitoring is easy.

Second, this portfolio will not strive to beat the market. It will meet the market, and that's not half bad. But, if your goal is to brag at cocktail parties, this portfolio will be too boring to talk about. You'll have to brag about your kids' baseball skills. Or your spouse's cooking. Or your daughter's SAT scores. If somebody asks you about your portfolio, you should respond with a Mona Lisa smile and say, "It's clicking along, like it's supposed to." That, in truth, is what it will be doing. (If you manage to look smug enough, this mysterious approach might convince the cocktail-party set that you have some sage investing secret that they don't have—but you don't want to share.)

Will your investments suffer bad years if you follow this program? Of course. You will also be subject to the laws of gravity and physics—and traffic, for that matter. Having a good investment plan does not mean you'll never have an investment that performs poorly, or a year in which your overall portfolio loses ground. In fact, there will probably always be at least one underperformer in your portfolio. Ideally, that dog will hunt when your other investments languish. But unless you completely ignore the instructions, your bad years will not derail your plans. With the wisdom of someone who actually understands your investments, you will learn to weather those years because they often lead to years when investments do stunningly well. (Reread "Why a Bad Market Could Be Good for You" in Chapter 2.) Meanwhile, your money will be invested in a way to produce the amount you need when you need it.

Now, if you're still with me, let's get started.

To do this right, you have to do three things: figure out what you have, figure out what you want, and consider what mix of investments is most appropriate to serve those goals. Next year, at this time—or at any time you set aside for your once-annual, hour-long checkup—you'll need to think through whether your goals have changed, or become more urgent, which would suggest a change in your investment mix. If they haven't, you'll simply "rebalance," which I'll explain later.

■ STEP ONE: DETERMINE WHAT YOU HAVE

Pull out your bank statements and investment records and start filling out the worksheets below. You can use this in two ways: first it will give you a picture of your net worth—your assets minus your liabilities. This is your baseline. Measure again a year from now to see how far you've come and whether you're satisfied with that progress.

Second, it will show what categories your current investments fall into. After this is all noted, we'll take a look at your goals and risk tolerance to see if you should adjust. Make sure to read through the charts before filling them out, so that you put investments in the right categories. Certificates of deposit, for example, are listed twice—once under "cash" and once under "income." You'd put only the short-term CDs—those with maturities of less than two years—in the cash category; the longer-term CDs go in the income category.

Incidentally, there's space here to note the banks, brokerages, and mutual fund companies you're dealing with and your account numbers. If you choose to list these, you can use this book as a one-stop shop whenever you need to fill out a detailed financial statement. It can also serve as a guide for your heirs, in the unlikely event that something happens to you and they need to piece together your finances. But if you do list the account numbers, make sure you put this book in a safe place where the information isn't likely to be stolen.

■ CASH

Checking account balance: $_____

Bank: _____ Account #: _____

Checking account balance: $_____

Bank: _____ Account #: _____

Savings account balance: $_____

Bank: _____ Account #: _____

Savings account balance: $_____

Bank: _____ Account #: _____

Short-term certificate of deposit: $_____

Bank: _____ Account #: _____

Maturity date (within 2 years): _____/_____/_____

Short-term certificate of deposit: $_____

Bank: _____ Account #: _____

Maturity date (within 2 years): _____/_____/_____

Treasury bills: $_____

Broker: _____ Account #:_____

Treasury bills: $_____

Broker: _____ Account #:_____

Savings bonds (total): $_____

Bond numbers: _____

Total amount in safe, short-term investments: $_____

(Add the numbers above and enter the result here.)

■ INCOME INVESTMENTS

Long-term certificate of deposit: $_____

Bank: _____ Account #: _____

Maturity date (more than 2 years): _____/_____/_____

Long-term certificate of deposit: $_____

Bank: _____ Account #: _____

Maturity date (more than 2 years): _____/_____/_____

Municipal bonds: $_____

Broker: _____ Account #: _____

Maturity date: _____/_____/_____

Municipal bonds: $_____

Broker: _____ Account #: _____

Maturity date: _____/_____/_____

Treasury notes and bonds: $_____

Broker: _____ Account #: _____

Maturity date: _____/_____/_____

Treasury notes and bonds: $_____

Broker: _____ Account #: _____

Maturity date: _____/_____/_____

Mortgage-backed securities: $_____

Broker: _____ Account #: _____

Maturity date: _____/_____/_____

Mortgage-backed securities: $_____

Broker: _____ Account #: _____

Maturity date: _____/_____/_____

_____Bond fund: $_____

(List fund type in the blank above, i.e., Treasury, corporate, junk bond, etc.)

Fund company: _____ Account #: _____

_____Bond fund: $_____

(List fund type in the blank above, i.e., Treasury, corporate, junk bond, etc.)

Fund company: _____ Account #: _____

_____Income fund: $_____

Fund company: _____ Account #: _____

_____Income fund: $_____

Fund company: _____ Account #: _____

_____Balanced fund: $_____

Fund company: _____ Account #: _____

_____Balanced fund: $_____

Fund company: _____ Account #: _____

_____REIT fund: $_____

Fund company: _____ Account #: _____

_____REIT fund: $_____

Fund company: _____ Account #: _____

Other (type and amount) _____

Company/broker: _____ Account #: _____

Total amount in income-oriented investments: $_____

■ GROWTH INVESTMENTS

Individual stocks $ _____

Use the worksheet in Chapter 15 to tally up your investments in individual stocks. Only list the total here. If you've taken care to diversify and know which of your holdings are in big companies, small companies, or midsized firms, use the break-outs below to list them separately. But when you're done, still total it up, and note it above.

- Big company stocks: $_____
- Small company stocks: $_____
- Midsized companies: $_____
- Foreign stocks/American depositary receipts (ADRs): $_____

_____Growth fund/ETF: $_____

Fund company: _____ Account #: _____

_____Growth fund/ETF: $_____

Fund company: _____ Account #: _____

_____Growth fund/ETF: $_____

Fund company: _____ Account #: _____

_____International fund/ETF: $_____
Fund company: _____ Account #: _____
_____Global fund/ETF: $_____
Fund company: _____ Account #: _____
_____Sector fund/ETF: $_____
Fund company: _____ Account #: _____
_____Sector fund/ETF: $_____
Fund company: _____ Account #: _____
_____Other fund/ETF: $_____
Fund company: _____ Account #: _____

Total amount in growth investments: $_____

■ REAL ESTATE

Estimated value of your home: $_____
Mortgage amount: $_____
Net value: $_____

Estimated value of rental real estate: $_____
Mortgage amount: $_____
Net value: $_____

Total assets: $_____
(Add together all the previous totals.)

■ DEBT

Auto loan balance: $_____
Payment: $_____ Interest rate: _____
Lender: _____ Phone #: _____
Auto loan balance: $_____
Payment: $_____ Interest rate: _____
Lender: _____ Phone #: _____

Student loan balance: $_____

Payment: _____ Interest rate: _____

Lender: _____ Phone #: _____

Student loan balance: $_____

Payment: $_____ Interest rate: _____

Lender: $_____ Phone #: _____

Credit card balance: $_____

Payment: _____ Interest rate: _____

Lender: _____ Phone #: _____

Credit card balance: $_____

Payment: _____ Interest rate: _____

Lender: _____ Phone #: _____

Credit card balance: $_____

Payment: _____ Interest rate: _____

Lender: _____ Phone #: _____

Total liabilities: $_____

(Add up all your debts.)

Net worth: $_____

(Subtract your assets from your liabilities.)*

*Chances are, you're worth a little more because we haven't accounted for the value of your car and your personal property. But since you're probably not planning to sell your car or your personal property, unless you replace them, we're going to call that a wash.

STEP TWO: DETERMINE WHAT YOU NEED

Now flip back to Chapter 3 and go through the worksheets on which you calculated what you needed for your goals, from emergencies to retirement. If you already had money set aside for those goals, compare that amount to what you have. For long-term goals, use the worksheets in Chapter 3 (if you haven't already) to determine whether what you have and what you're saving will be sufficient to fund a long-term goal.

If there are more goals than money, prioritize. What goals are most precious? What goals are coming up the quickest? Are the goals that are coming soon more precious or less precious than those that are farther away? If they're less precious, are they precious enough to require funding at all?

Now start comparing goals to the amount of money you have set aside in appropriate "baskets."

Short-Term Goals

Goals that are immediate to two years away need to be funded with "cash" investments. Naturally, it's smarter to fund the goal that's two years away with a two-year CD than a money market account, since it's likely to pay more and still be available when you need it.

Read through Chapter 3 and do the calculations, if you haven't already. Record the amount of money that you need for short-term goals—emergencies, urgent car and home repairs, and a little slush fund for the potential of losing your job—here: $_____. Record the amount of money you already have in cash investments (from above) here: $_____.

Compare the above numbers: If you have more in cash investments than you figure you need for short-term goals, you're either very conservative and fearful about losing your money or you're over-allocated in cash. If you don't have nearly enough here, you'll want to create a plan to start feeding the cash basket either by moving other investments or by contributing to it over time.

Medium-Term Goals

Now go through Chapter 3 to identify your medium-term goals—anything that's between two and ten years away. This could be a goal of buying a car or a house, or sending a teenager to college. Or, if you're in your mid-50s or 60s, a medium-term goal is to fund the first few years of your retirement. The end of your retirement is still a long-term goal.

Goals that are within five years generally need to be funded with income investments. That's simply because you know the amount they're going to pay and you know roughly what they're going to be worth when your goal comes due. The more precious and near the goal, the more conservative you need to be about the income investments you choose.

Consider, for example, a sixty-four-year-old whom we'll call Suzy. She is set on retiring at age sixty-five, so her medium-term goal is to fund those first several years of retirement. Because this is a precious goal, she doesn't want to fiddle with uncertainty. She'll put at least three years of living expenses in fairly safe, fixed-income instruments, such as Treasury notes, conservative intermediate-term bond funds, and certificates of deposit. Why three years' worth of living expenses? Because this year she's working, so that takes one of the next five years off the table. The following year should be funded as a short-term goal. The remaining three years are the years that need secure, but somewhat higher-yielding income. (How much do you need for living expenses? Go back to Chapter 3 and run through the math in the Goal: Retirement table. But because the goal is so near in this case, you can dispense with the fancy inflation calculation and just use a back-of-the-envelope figure that reflects the current inflation rate. In other words, use this year's expenses, and if inflation averages 5 percent, add 5 percent to that figure for the second year, 10 percent for the third year, and so on.)

Suzy has another five years—years five through ten—of intermediate-term goals that will need funding. But because that's on the longer end of intermediate, she can take a little more risk with those funds. She has the ability to wait out some market fluctuations, so with this money, she's going to look for ways to boost yield. The five-to-ten-year bucket can be funded with real estate investment trust (REIT) funds, mortgage-backed securities, corporate bonds, and corporate bond funds. These investments are likely to produce better returns over time, but they can also fluctuate in value. The bottom line is the pot of money that Suzy sets aside for intermediate-term goals is in a mixture of fixed-income investments—about 40 percent of them safe, the rest divvied up among fixed-income investments that are a bit more risky.

When Suzy does her annual checkup, she'll need to replenish her one-to-five-year income basket, since this is the money she's using to live on. To do that, she'll first look at her five-to-ten-year basket and see if the appreciation on those investments has been sufficient to result in a pot of cash that's more than enough to fund five years of expenses. If so, she'll take a little of that money off the table and leave the rest alone.

Second, she'll look at her "growth" basket and see which of those investments she'd like to lighten up on. Ideally, she should take money out of the investments that have done the best in the past year. It's counterintuitive—everybody wants to let their winners ride and dump their losers. But, we're back to the age-old wisdom: buy low; sell high. If you take money out of the investments that are doing the best, you're selling high. Those investments may go higher, but you don't care. You're not selling all of them; you're just lightening up a bit. Remember, you're not trying to brag; you're using your money as a tool to fund your life. That's what it's for.

What about other medium-term goals, like buying a car or a house, or funding a teen's college bills? The process is largely the same. The closer the goal, the more conservative your income investments. But you should always have a mixture. The risk you choose in this mix will depend on just how precious the goal—and how capable you are of punting if the investments don't turn out like you planned. For instance, the goal of sending your child to college is certainly precious. But you might choose to take more risk if you'd be willing to tighten your belt and find another way to finance tuition, if the investments didn't yield as much as you'd hoped.

Now, tally up the amount you need to fund intermediate-term investments (from Chapter 3) and enter the amount here: $_____. How much do you have in income investments, according to your calculations in the worksheet earlier in this chapter? $_____.

If you have more need than investments, you should either move some money from a category that's overfunded, or start contributing on a monthly basis to this bucket of investments until you have what you need.

Long-Term Goals

All your other goals are long-term. They can be addressed with long-term investments, which are typically more volatile, but more lucrative. These are the investments shown in the growth category above.

What if funding the short- and medium-term investments left you with no money in growth investments? If you're under the age of thirty, that's probably not surprising. You're still starting out and have a fair number of short- and medium-term goals. But you need to start shifting your focus, because this long-term category is exceptionally important and funding it now will save you a lot of heartache and struggle later. Particularly if a good portion of your savings is in the short-term category, you might also be wise to consider if there are better ways to protect yourself from short-term emergencies—like disability insurance or a bus pass—than a fat savings account. Remember that most companies allow you to borrow from a 401(k) in an emergency. If your company allows that, consider shifting some of your emergency money into the 401(k). Certainly, if you haven't already, start funding this category.

What if you're over the age of thirty? Let's say, for example's sake, that you are Suzy, and that ten years of living expenses is pretty much all the money you have to retire on? Then, unless you're in terrible health, you're not ready to retire. In a case like this, Suzy would have three options: save more—and quickly; spend less, pretty much for the rest of her life; or retire later or incompletely.

The first option is possible if Suzy wins the lottery or moves in with her children, while she saves money for her retirement. (Hey, they probably moved in with her when they were saving to buy a house. It's only fair.)

The second option may be reasonable if Suzy has a home and doesn't mind selling it to free up cash and to reduce her monthly mortgage and maintenance expenses. She'll still have to pay rent, of course. But, assuming that's less than the mortgage, property tax, insurance, and maintenance costs of the home, she still reduces her expenses relatively painlessly (assuming she's not overwhelmingly attached to the home) and frees up cash from the home's equity to live on. She'd then recalculate her annual living expenses and see if she now has more money to put into the long-term category.

Option three is probably the least painful. Let's say that Suzy opts to work a couple of extra years. This has the impact of shortening her retirement, thus her retirement savings needs. She also pays into the Social Security system for those extra years, which boosts her Social Security earnings and wins her a relatively higher monthly benefit later. (She can also take her monthly benefits at age sixty-five and simply bank them, boosting her savings.) If she has a company pension, the same holds true there. In a matter of two or three years, Suzy's financial picture is substantially stronger—and she hasn't annoyed her children by moving in needlessly.

What if Suzy hates her job so much that she can't stomach the idea of working a few years longer? She might consider finding a part-time job that she enjoys to defray a portion of her living expenses. If she's able to earn 50 percent of her living expenses, her ten years' worth of living expenses now becomes twenty years of living expenses, which is considerably closer to what she needs. And, if she chooses this route, she still has the house that she can sell later, if she finds herself short of cash in her late retirement years.

STEP THREE: CHOOSE SPECIFIC INVESTMENTS

Okay, now you've got your investments in categories. How about the nitty-gritty of picking specific investments? Because this is a guide for a lazy investor, I'm mostly going to recommend index funds, rather than individual stocks or bonds. These get you broad diversification and they're low cost.

Because index funds are Vanguard's specialty, I'm going to focus my search here. But if you have a relationship with T. Rowe, Fidelity, or Schwab, you'll find that they have many similar offerings. If you have trouble figuring out which they are, call and ask the telephone representative. They're usually pretty helpful and smart.

Cash

For your cash investments, pick a bank—any bank. Well, actually, start with the one where you have your checking account. First put enough in your checking account to ensure that you're not charged fees on this account and that you'll never bounce a check. Then, check out the bank's short-term CD rates. If they're pretty good, you might choose to put some of the remaining cash stash there. If they're not good, check out www.bankrate.com. This website publishes average rates as well as the specific rates offered by individual federally insured banks and thrifts operating all over the country. You may be able to easily boost your yield by a percentage point or two by rate shopping here.

Another option if you have several thousand dollars in this category: go to www.vanguard.com and continue to the site for personal investors. Click on "Research Funds & Stocks." Then click on "By asset class," in the left-hand panel. If you're not in the highest federal tax brackets (you'd know it, if you are), look under "Taxable Money Market" accounts. Pick one. There's not a bad option among the four listed there.

If you're in the highest federal income tax bracket and live in a high-tax state, look under "Tax-Exempt Money Market" funds and see if you see your state listed. If you don't, you may want to switch your search to www.fidelity.com, where they have more state municipal bond funds. You'll click on "Mutual Funds" and then "Money Market Funds" and finally "State Municipal Money Market." Find your state and go. Of course, you can also simply invest in a money market that's free of federal income tax and not stress over the relatively small state tax burden.

Income

If your main intermediate-term goal is funding a child's college education, you may want to choose a 529 plan, with an age-based investment portfolio. That fund will automatically diversify your assets based on when your child plans to enroll in college. (See Chapter 12.) If you didn't already do this when reading through Chapter 12, go to www.savingforcollege.com to pick a good option, based on where you live and what you want.

For your other intermediate-term goals, go back to "Research Funds & Stocks" and click on "By asset class." Scroll down to "Taxable Short-Term Bond" and pick one or two of those funds for the money you're setting aside for goals you expect to reach in the next two to five years. I'd recommend the Short-Term Bond Index or the Short-Term Investment-Grade bond fund. The index fund is made up of short-term Treasuries and the debt of federal agencies—all very safe investments. The investment-grade fund is made up of high-quality corporate bonds. Both pay a little more than Treasuries, but aren't substantially riskier.

For the money that you want for goals that are between five and ten years away, you'll want to divide your money among the following:

- One of the options under "Taxable Intermediate-Term Bond" or, if you're concerned about inflationary pressures, the Inflation-Protected Securities fund. You should expect these funds to pay about 4 percent to 6 percent on average. The exception: The High-Yield Corporate fund is a so-called "junk-bond" fund, which is about as volatile as a stock. If you choose this fund, use it for the money you need last and be sure to be cognizant of the risk of loss.

- And a balanced fund. Some I'd recommend: STAR, Wellington, or Balanced Index.
- And, maybe, put 5 percent to 10 percent of this money in the REIT Index Fund. (This is listed under "Domestic Stock—Sector-Specific.") Why do you have a stock fund in your income basket? Frankly REITs are such a mixture of stock and bond qualities, I figured it was toss-up whether to put them under "income" or "growth." If you're more comfortable putting a REIT fund in your growth portfolio, go for it. You probably want at least a little REIT exposure somewhere in your portfolio, though.

Growth

Choosing specific funds for your growth investments is complicated by the fact that the bulk of your savings in this category is likely to be in your retirement plan. If that plan is a 401(k), you've got a limited number of options. However, most plans include a broad stock index fund, an international fund, and/or a target-date fund. Some also include a REIT fund.

If you have a target-date fund option, you can choose this one fund and be done. It will make your portfolio a touch more conservative than necessary because this fund will divvy your retirement assets among stocks, bonds, and cash, and you've already got some bonds and cash in your overall portfolio. But you can reduce that too-conservative bent by picking a target date that's past your actual planned date of retirement. In other words, if they have a target date 2020, which is when you plan to retire, but you've already done a pretty good job of diversifying into bonds and cash, you could instead choose the target date 2025 or 2030. Or, if you're particularly conservative, you can simply go with it. You'll likely give up a percentage point or two in annual return, but your portfolio will be easy and you'll sleep nights.

No target date fund? Divide your retirement assets among the stock index, international index, and REIT fund. If you're like Suzy, and a portion of your intermediate-term goals are going to be funded by your retirement plan, put that portion in an intermediate-term bond fund, too.

How much should go into each fund? That will depend on your age, assets, and ability to tolerate risk. But, generally speaking, at least half of this money should be in domestic stocks. Between 10 percent and 25 percent should be in international funds. Between 10 percent and 25 percent should be in bond funds; and the remaining amount— somewhere between 10 percent and 20 percent—could be in REIT funds.

If you are managing your own retirement portfolio, I'd recommend a selection of Vanguard funds:

- The Vanguard Total Stock Market Index fund, for the domestic stock portion of your portfolio.
- The international pick would depend on age: if I were forty or younger, I'd likely choose the Vanguard Emerging Markets fund. If I had less time, I might go for Developed Markets, Global Equity, International Value, or Total International Stock Index. If I had lots of cash, I might invest in two of these choices.
- For the REIT segment, the Vanguard REIT Index fund.
- For the bond segment, if I were young, I'd choose the High-Yield Corporate fund—if I needed bonds in my retirement portfolio at all. (A young person would need bonds in their retirement portfolio if they had decided they had few or no intermediate-term goals, and didn't own bonds elsewhere in their portfolio. Otherwise, you diversify your entire portfolio, not the individual pieces.)

How Should This Look?

Let's consider a few hypothetical investors to illustrate.

• **Young Investor.** Jessie is twenty-four and less than a year out of college. She earns $30,000 annually and works for an employer who offers a 401(k) plan. For each dollar she contributes to the 401(k), her employer contributes 50 cents. She has total assets of $5,000.

She figures she needs $500 in emergency savings, just in case her car breaks down. If she loses her job, she figures she'll move back in with Mom. She hasn't yet contemplated buying a house, getting married, or having children, so she has no intermediate-term goals at the moment. Her emergency savings is in her checking account, which allows it to serve the dual purpose of eliminating her monthly checking account fees and ensuring that she never bounces a check. The rest of her money is in her 401(k) plan, which she is building up by contributing 10 percent of her income—$250 per month, or $125 per paycheck. Her 401(k) is invested in the company's target-date 2050 retirement fund.

Her portfolio looks like this:

10 percent cash

90 percent target-date 2050 retirement (which is made up of mostly domestic and international stocks)

• **Young Family.** John and Jane are thirty-somethings with two children, ages three and five, and $65,000 in annual income. They save 10 percent of their income in 401(k) plans and are setting aside $50 a month for each child's future college bills. They have $10,000 in emergency savings, $2,000 in each college account, and $40,000 in their retirement plans. They realize their emergency savings wouldn't be sufficient to cover a long job loss, but they have borrowing power on their credit cards and great families that they figure they could lean on in a pinch. Their portfolio looks like this:

Cash

$1,000 in checking

$2,000 in a five-month CD, paying 5.25 percent

$3,000 in Vanguard's Federal Money Market fund, which is yielding about 5 percent

$5,000 in Vanguard's Short-Term Federal fund, a bond fund that is yielding about 5.5 percent

Income

$4,000 in two college savings accounts, which is diversified based on the children's age

Growth

$20,000 in the Vanguard Total Stock Market Index fund

$10,000 in the Vanguard Total International Stock Index fund

$5,000 in the Vanguard High-Yield Corporate fund

$5,000 in the Vanguard REIT Index fund

This mix puts about 65 percent of their assets in stocks (counting the REITs as stock); just under 20 percent of their assets in cash; and the rest in bonds and 529 plans, which have been diversified without their input.

Is this too conservative for a couple in their early 30s? The cash portion is theoretically high on a percentage basis, but they need that safety net. However, as they continue to contribute to the retirement plans, their retirement and college portfolios will grow and begin to dwarf the emergency savings portion. In other words, if it's too conservative now, it's not drastically so and is likely to balance out over time.

• **Midlife Investor.** Tom and Karen are in their mid-forties. They have one child in college, and one is a senior in high school. They are a dual-income family with plenty of life, disability, and health insurance, and earn $150,000 annually. They contribute $15,000 annually to their respective retirement plans, which are worth a cumulative $300,000. Their college accounts are worth an additional $50,000. They've chosen to put only $20,000 in emergency savings because they have the ability to borrow against their 401(k) plans and both feel secure in their jobs—as well as in their ability to live on less, if one of them is temporarily out of work. Their portfolio looks like this:

Cash

$5,000 in checking
$15,000 in Vanguard's Federal Money Market fund

College accounts

$20,000 in Vanguard's Short-Term Bond Index fund
$30,000 in Vanguard's Wellington fund, which is a balanced fund
　　　that invests in both stocks and bonds

Retirement assets

$100,000 in Vanguard's Wellington fund
$150,000 in Vanguard's Total Stock Market Index fund
$25,000 in Vanguard's Total International Stock Index fund
$25,000 in Vanguard's REIT Index fund

Overall, they have about 5 percent of their assets in cash investments; about 23 percent of their assets in fixed income (that's the $20,000 in the short-term bond index, plus half of the amount they have in the Wellington fund in both the college and retirement accounts). The remaining 72 percent of their assets is in growth investments with 7 percent in REITs, 7 percent in international, and 58 percent in domestic stock.

Is this too risky for a couple in their 40s? Not for a couple that's comfortable enough in their lives and jobs to accommodate a little extra investment risk. But as they get closer to retirement, they'll want to move more of their investments into the Wellington Fund, or add a bond fund to their mix.

• **Preretiree.** Now, let's consider a solvent Suzy, who has $500,000 saved for retirement. After accounting for her pension and her Social Security income, she figures she's going to want to tap her savings to the tune of $25,000 annually. That's going to cause her to put roughly half of her assets in some sort of income-oriented investment. The rest of her assets will be invested much like Tom and Karen's—in a mix of domestic stocks, international stocks, and REITs. Her portfolio:

Cash

$5,500 in checking
$30,000 in Vanguard's Federal Money Market fund
$12,500 in an 18-month Certificate of Deposit
(As she taps her checking account to pay bills, she'll replenish that
    account with money from the Money Market fund.)

Long-term

$100,000 in Vanguard's Wellington fund
$150,000 in Vanguard's Total Stock Market Index fund
$12,500 in Vanguard's REIT Index fund
$12,500 in Vanguard's Total International Stock Index fund

DID YOU KNOW?
Vanguards

You may be wondering why I've chosen to mix just Vanguard funds here. They're low cost and well respected. They also have a wide array of index funds, which allows you to diversify easily and know precisely what you're getting. If, on the other hand, you choose actively managed funds, you'll have to do more work to make sure that there's not too much overlap in your portfolio. (See the Greta story in Chapter 4.)

STEP FOUR: REBALANCE YOUR PORTFOLIO

Once your investment mix is set up, you need to do just one thing once a year. That's to simply look at your portfolio, calculating how much you have in each investment basket, and how those figures relate to the size of your portfolio as a whole.

For instance, you may have started with $100,000—10 percent in cash, 40 percent in bonds, and 50 percent in stocks. Your stock portfolio might have been 50 percent domestic, 25 percent international, and 25 percent REITs.

But because investment returns in each of these categories are likely to vary, the percentage of your assets in each category will vary too. If those percentages were well thought out, you might want to adjust to take money out of the highest-returning investments and put some in the lowest-returning investments. This gets your investment mix back into the balance you decided on at first, and it forces you to "sell high" with at least a portion of your portfolio.

Let's say, for example, that the most unpredictable portion of this investor's portfolio was in his growth basket. He wanted half of those investments to be domestic stocks, but because the international fund he bought earned a huge return, he now has only 40 percent of his assets in domestic stocks and 35 percent in international stocks. To rebalance, he can sell some of the international stocks and use the proceeds to buy domestic stocks. Or, if he continues to contribute to this portfolio, he might simply stop making regular contributions to the international fund and shift that money into the domestic stock fund.

If all your investments have performed essentially as expected, you may not need to rebalance at all. In that case, pat your portfolio nicely and go out to dinner, take in a movie, or call a friend. Your investing responsibilities are done for the year. You get to relax and focus on the rest of your life, which is decidedly more fun.

QUICK TAKE

What You'll LEARN

Even the savviest investors can fail to keep good records and that can cost them. You'll learn about:

- Getting Organized
- Keeping Tabs on Your Investments

What You'll DO

- Copy the worksheets to track your investments
- Get your brokers to fill in the blanks, if you've failed to keep good records in the past
- Fill out the charts so you won't have wonder about your capital gains and losses

How You'll USE This

The first thing you'll do with this is get your tax records in order, which will lower your taxes, and probably fees if you have your taxes professionally prepared. Good records can also help signal when you have a long-standing dog in your portfolio that ought to be reevaluated or dumped.

HOW TO FIX YOUR BROKEN RECORDS

Barbara knows exactly how much she paid for one hundred shares of stock way back in 1962. It's what's happened since then that she is fuzzy about. That's because she's been reinvesting dividends for the past twenty-six years. She never stopped to calculate how much extra money that amounted to. But now that she's considering selling the stock, she's in a quandary.

Going through twenty-six years of records to tabulate her total investment, including reinvested dividends, will be a horrible—maybe even impossible—job. But if she doesn't do it, she may pay too much in tax.

Her story is by no means unique. Investment professionals maintain that record keeping is one of the most important and most widely ignored steps in wise investing. Good records help you monitor your portfolio and help you determine when to buy and sell. They're also pivotal when you're determining how much tax you have to pay. And they can signal whether something is wrong with the way your broker or other financial advisers are handling your accounts.

Record keeping is the financial equivalent of getting an annual physical, experts contend. It helps you keep up with fees and performance, and can save you a fortune if you pay by the hour to have your tax return professionally prepared.

Yet many investors fail to do it because the process can be ponderous. But it doesn't need to be. If you start early and do it right, keeping good records will save you time and money—and won't burden you with too much additional work.

 GETTING ORGANIZED

Ellen Norris Gruber, author of *The Personal Finance Kit* suggests that you buy a large three-ring binder, a three-hole punch, and some colored binder tabs. That will set you back $15 to $20, but these materials can serve as a basis for your investment records for decades, she says.

Next, divide the binder into sections for specific investments or types of accounts. Some people, particularly those with large, diverse portfolios that have actively traded investments, set their records up by date instead, keeping track of trades on a month-by-month basis. But an investment-by-investment approach works nicely if you have a manageable number of investments that you hold for long periods.

With taxable accounts, you should label each segment with the name of the investment—"XYZ Company," for instance, or "XYZ Mutual Fund." If you have tax-favored retirement accounts, such as 401(k)s, IRAs, or Keoghs, you may want to label them by the name of the account instead. You might have a section called "John's 401(k)" or "Mary's IRA," for example.

The retirement accounts only need the "IRA" or "401(k)" label because one of the primary reasons that you keep these records is to determine your taxable gains and losses. Investments held in a retirement account all have the same tax properties. You can sell IBM at a profit and buy a new stock—or keep the profit in cash—and as long as the money stays in the IRA, there is no tax consequence. The only time you'll have to determine your tax bill when selling investments in a tax-deferred IRA, Keogh, or 401(k) is when you pull the money out of the account to spend it. Then the tax will be assessed on the entire amount—principal, interest, and capital gains.

With other investments, taxes are due in any year that you collect income or sell them at a profit. On the other hand, you can generate a capital loss if you sell when the stock price drops below your purchase price, which can offset other gains. You cannot deduct capital losses in tax-deferred accounts from capital gains or ordinary income.

The third step is to create a page that summarizes that particular investment. This summary should include how much you initially invested, your cost of investment—such as brokerage fees—and any subsequent investments you've made in that stock, bond, or mutual fund. The initial costs (including brokerage fees or mutual fund loads and sales commissions) as well as the amounts of subsequent investments will all determine your tax basis—the total cost of the investment—when it comes time to determine your taxable gain when you sell. Those who fail to keep track of the brokerage fees and reinvested dividends, or of the initial cost of the stock, may pay too much tax.

When you sell shares, the custodian or transfer agent will send both you and the IRS a 1099 showing the proceeds from the sale. Barring information to the contrary, the IRS assumes that the entire amount is profit. You must establish your cost by maintaining investment records. If you can't establish your cost basis in the investment, you could end up overtaxed.

After you've got your system set up, all you need to do is file the periodic account statements behind the summary page for each investment. It's wise to briefly review each statement when it comes in to make sure there are no errors or other discrepancies.

Once a year, you should update your summary page to indicate additional investments or sales and taxable profits. The summary page serves as a quick reference guide for you or your tax accountant when you want to determine your tax obligation for the year. It should also give you a good idea of how your individual investments and your portfolio as a whole are faring.

Can you delete a section when you sell an investment? Not immediately. You should save those records for at least four years, just in case you're audited by federal or state tax authorities.

What if you're in Barbara's situation—you've been investing for years without keeping good records and are now uncertain about where you stand?

You could estimate and hope you aren't audited, of course. If you are going to do it right, though, ask your broker, mutual fund company, or investment adviser to help you reconstruct your account history. In some cases, you'll be charged a fee for copies of old account statements or for the adviser's time. If the account isn't terribly old, the fees are likely to be modest, and the job will be manageable. But the longer you wait, the more difficult it becomes.

KEEPING TABS ON YOUR INVESTMENTS

If you start early and do it regularly, keeping good investment records is a snap. Here's a sample worksheet. Use one for each security you own in a taxable account.

■ INVESTMENT RECORD

Investment: _____

Per-share purchase price: $_____

Date purchased: _____ /_____ /_____

Number of shares: _____

Total initial investment: $_____

Brokerage/trading fees: $_____

Total invested, initial year: $_____

Subsequent investment: _____

Year:_____

Additional amount invested: $_____

Shares acquired/new total: _____ /_____

Reinvested dividends: _____

Brokerage/trading fees: _____

Total invested to date: $_____

Subsequent investment: _____

Year:_____

Additional amount invested: $_____

Shares acquired/new total: _____ /_____

Reinvested dividends: _____

Brokerage/trading fees: _____

Total invested to date: $_____

Subsequent investment: _____

Year:_____

Additional amount invested: $_____

Shares acquired/new total: _____ /_____

Reinvested dividends: _____

Brokerage/trading fees: _____

Total invested to date: $_____

Subsequent investment: _____

Year: _____

Additional amount invested: $_____

Shares acquired/new total: _____ / _____

Reinvested dividends: _____

Brokerage/trading fees: _____

Total invested to date: $_____

QUICK TAKE

What You'll LEARN

After reading this book, you probably don't *need* to hire a financial planner, but you may still *want* to hire a planner. If so, the following steps will help guide you to selecting an adviser.

- Choosing Among Financial Planners
- Understanding Professional Designations
- Finding a Planner
- Hiring a Planner

What You'll DO

- Determine whether you want help or prefer to go it alone
- Decide how you want to pay for a planner's services
- Sidestep planners with bogus credentials

How You'll USE This

You know how to mow your lawn and scrub your toilets, but you may have decided to hire a gardener or housekeeper because you choose to use your time in other ways. If you've decided you want to do the same thing with your finances, this chapter will help you find a planner, check out his credentials, and be as comfortable with the person who is handling your money as you are with the people who handle the yard work.

GETTING HELP

16

Okay. You've read the book. You know that you probably can invest on your own. But what if you don't want to? What if you prefer to hire someone to help you allocate your assets, pick individual stocks, and occasionally just hold your hand when the market activity makes you nervous?

Then you need to hire a financial planner to help. However, choose your planner carefully. Get recommendations. Look for important professional designations. And check out the planner with state and federal securities regulators to make sure he or she doesn't have a criminal record or a history pockmarked with investor complaints. After all, your future comfort may hinge on just how well this planner serves your best interests.

CHOOSING AMONG FINANCIAL PLANNERS

Before you start looking, it is also important to know how financial planners earn their money. There are three different options: commissions, fees, or a combination of both.

Commission-based planners are usually paid out of what you invest. For example, if you invest $10,000 in a mutual fund with a 5 percent load, only $9,500 is actually invested. The other $500 is paid to the planner who recommended this fund to you. Commission-based planners also make money from commissions generated from selling you life and disability insurance, limited partnerships, and other investments.

Unfortunately, many consumers are drawn to commission-based planners simply because it appears that their advice is free. That's because the commissions paid on many of these products are hidden or subtle. You don't see the commission that's paid on a whole life insurance policy when you purchase it, but it will certainly affect your long-term return. In fact, the commission on a whole life policy often amounts to 100 percent of your first-year premium. If a planner sells you a limited partnership or a viatical settlement, a big portion of what you've paid has also been eaten up in commissions paid to the planner that are largely invisible to you. By the same token, you may not pay a lot of attention to them, but the loads and 12b-1 fees charged by mutual funds can also dramatically reduce your long-term returns.

If, on the other hand, you go to a fee-only planner, you will pay to have a plan drawn up for you. For a comprehensive plan, it's not unusual to be charged between $1,500 and $2,500 for the service. However, a fee-only planner has no financial incentive to steer you toward a product that pays the planner better than it pays you.

Meanwhile, a planner who is paid through both fees and commissions usually charges less up front but will recommend some products that will pay the planner a commission. A planner in this category may recommend no-load funds, for example, but get commissions for selling you life and disability insurance. Commissions are typically computed as a percentage of what you spend.

It has become popular to say that you should never hire a commission-based planner. That's simply because a planner who charges by commission may sometimes be tempted to sell you a product that's less attractive for you but pays the planner a fat commission. After all, even planners have to eat. Instead, many financial journalists steer their readers solely toward fee-only planners because of the apparent conflicts of interest with commission-based planners.

This is easy but not always helpful advice. There are many good commission-based planners who have been in business for decades because they offer good advice that isn't influenced by whether or not they're earning a commission. Moreover, although you must realize that commission-based advice is not free, this payment system may simply work better for some families.

Plopping down $2,000 to pay a planner up front may leave you with nothing left to invest, for instance. So it may make more sense for you to invest the $2,000, knowing that a portion of that amount and of your subsequent investments will pay the planner. Yes, that may cost you more over time than simply paying up front. But you'll also have gotten started, which you might not have done if you had used up all your money buying advice.

If you do seek advice from a commission-based planner, you should make sure that you are sophisticated enough to evaluate whether the promise of a commission is affecting your planner's advice. If you find your planner is constantly pushing insurance, high-load funds, limited partnerships, or other unfamiliar investments, you should start asking questions.

On the insurance side, you need to consider just how much insurance you need and compare that to the amount your planner wants to sell. You should also know that term insurance is almost always a better deal than whole life insurance, particularly if you have a young family that needs lots of financial protection. But whole life insurance pays far higher commissions to the planner. If insurance is a big-ticket item for your family, check out a series titled "Insurance 101" that is posted on the *Los Angeles Times* website, at www.latimes.com. If your planner is pressing you to buy more insurance than you think you need, ask how he or she arrived at that number. Your planner may have thought about some valid expense that didn't occur to you or may simply not understand your family as well as you do. If you can't come to a meeting of the minds, look for another planner.

If your planner is recommending high-load funds, ask him or her to explain precisely why this fund is better than similar low-load or no-load funds. Expect data, including year-by-year returns, background on the fund manager, and Morningstar rankings on how the fund's peer group has performed. If your planner cannot give you this information, view the advice skeptically.

If your planner is recommending limited partnerships or viatical settlements, think very seriously about finding another planner. These are not investments that are well suited to beginning investors. And some might argue that these investments are not well suited to anyone. Yet they pay hefty commissions to people who sell them.

The ADV Form

How do you know how your planner is paid? Ask.

Registered financial advisers are required to fill out an extensive form called an ADV-Advisers form. The planner must file this form with securities regulators, and regulators expect planners to make at least the second part of it available to their clients. The ADV, Part II, discusses how the planner is paid, the type of business he or she specializes in, and other facts about the financial planning firm. However, the first part of the ADV form includes the planner's disciplinary history—little tidbits of information like whether the planner has ever been fined or suspended for absconding with customer money or making inappropriate investment recommendations to clients. Obviously, this is information you ought to know before you hire somebody.

Ask for this form—both Part I and Part II. Read it. Make sure you understand the pertinent sections before you entrust your financial life to a planner. If the planner doesn't want to give you the first part of the form, consider it a warning sign. Then call the public disclosure hotline (800-289-9999). They should have a record of your planner's disciplinary history. (You can—and should—call the broker check line if you want to check the disciplinary history of a stockbroker, too.)

UNDERSTANDING PROFESSIONAL DESIGNATIONS

When interviewing planners, you should also look for their professional designations, which are often listed in an alphabetical jumble after their names on their business cards. There are literally dozens of professional designations that planners can and do trot out—CFP, ChFC, CLU, CPA, EA, CFS, CMFC, and PFS, to name a few. Some of these designations are important—a sign that your planner has more education and skill than the average Joe. Some, though, are insignificant. And some designations are simply made up.

Which are the important designations?

- *CFP* stands for *Certified Financial Planner*. This designation means that the planner has taken an extensive course of education, has passed exams, and has worked in the industry for at least three years. CFPs are monitored by the Certified Financial Planner Board of Standards, which requires that they adhere to rules of ethical conduct and continue their education. If they don't, their designation is pulled. It is one of the first, and most important, professional designations you should look for when hiring a planner.

- *CPA* stands for *Certified Public Accountant*, which indicates your adviser has a financial background, has passed a grueling examination, and has at least two years of public accounting experience. A CPA who also has a *PFS* designation (for *Personal Financial Specialist*) has taken some extra training in personal financial planning. These designations are also policed by the American Institute of Certified Public Accountants, which requires CPAs to continue taking classes to keep their skills up-to-date.

- *CFA* stands for *Chartered Financial Analyst*—another prestigious designation that requires training, testing, and licensing. CFAs must undergo rigorous training in portfolio management, securities analysis, and economics, among other things. However, CFAs typically don't set up shop to deal with individual clients. They typically work for mutual fund companies, where they manage large portfolios for mutual funds and for other big institutions. However, if you're checking out a fund manager's credentials, this is one to look for.

- *CLU* and *ChFC* are designations given to people who have taken financial training concentrated on insurance issues.

- The National Association of Personal Financial Advisors, a trade group made up of fee-only planners, has created a special designation, *F-O (fee-only)*, to indicate that the planner doesn't take commissions. Don't attach too much significance to the absence of this designation, because you're going to find out how your planner is paid by reading his or her ADV form.

What about the ten zillion other acronyms? Some of them indicate that your adviser has taken a special class. Some of them indicate that he or she has passed a test. Some indicate that he or she specializes in some specific area, such as estate planning. (However, if you're wealthy enough to have to worry about estate planning—that would be if you had assets in excess of $2 million as a single person, or $4 million as a married couple in 2007—you'll need to be concerned about other qualifications, such as law degrees, too. But that's a topic for another book.)

There is a burgeoning trend to collect impressive-sounding designations—and even "publish" articles about various financial topics—in order to woo new customers. But as one of those prospective customers, you need to take particular care. There are marketing firms that sell generic articles on various financial topics to planners, who then publish this pap under their names, often with their contact numbers and photographs attached, making it appear that the articles are their work.

Some planners will also take worthless classes to gain additional titles, many of which mean nothing. When confronted with an alphabet soup of unfamiliar professional designations, ask what they're all about. If somebody is touting these initials, they should certainly be able to explain why they're important. Make sure you know who gives the designation, what kind of training and/or experience is required to get it and keep it, and whether the designations are permanent or if they can be pulled if the planner breaches the group's rules or ethics. Obviously, designations that require continuing education and monitoring are more significant than ones that don't.

Beware the "Senior Specialist"

The latest trend among the ethically challenged planner set is to collect titles that intimate they've gotten special training in investments that are the most appropriate for seniors. Calling themselves "certified senior advisors" and "senior specialists," these planners often sell seniors wildly inappropriate investments. A series of regulators testified about this before a Senate panel in late 2007.

William Francis Galvin, secretary of the Commonwealth of Massachusetts, told the U.S. Senate's Special Committee on Aging about "a widespread pattern of purported senior specialists using sophisticated marketing tools to give senior citizens the impression that they are acting as their unbiased, knowledgeable and independent adviser, when the real objective is to convince them to purchase a product that the specialist offers." Often the investment is a high-commission annuity that is unsuitable for senior citizens because the investment imposes lengthy lock-up periods and large surrender fees to pull money out early.

What made these advisers "specialists"? In some cases, they filled out a five-minute online application with the National Ethics Bureau, a for-profit company that purports to certify a salesperson's ethical caliber with its "Seal of Trust," Galvin said. One salesman who had been awarded the seal had a long record of regulatory sanctions, customer complaints, liens, and a bankruptcy. Another had been fired by his broker-dealer for selling unapproved products.

The "certified senior advisor" moniker issued by the Society of Certified Senior Advisors also is "primarily a marketing tool" that doesn't require meaningful training, Galvin testified. The society defended its training and designation in testimony to the panel, but said its program didn't qualify anyone to give investment advice.

"Our office has been flooded with countless stories of harm to seniors resulting from the unscrupulous use of these questionable credentials," Galvin said.

Massachusetts recently adopted a regulation that bars broker-dealers and financial advisers from using a designation that has not been accredited by a reputable national accreditation organization. Other states have no such measures. The organization of state securities regulators intends to adopt a "model rule" that encourages other states to take similar action, but that process could take years. In the meantime, it's buyer beware.

Seniors are believed to be vulnerable to fraudulent investment pitches for a variety of reasons, including a high incidence of cognitive ailments and an upbringing that makes many seniors too polite to hang up on aggressive, cold-calling salespeople. Con artists have targeted that vulnerability for decades, but the problems may be getting worse. A survey by the North American Securities Administrators Association suggests that fraud against seniors has risen 44 percent in the past year. About 28 percent of all investor complaints received by the group in 2005 were from seniors, reports Joseph Borg, the organization's president.

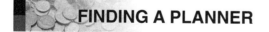 **FINDING A PLANNER**

If you want some help finding a planner, there are several good resources available. All of these organizations will happily provide you with lists of professionals in your area.

- The Financial Planning Association at www.fpanet.org (800-322-4237) offers referrals to planners in your area, who might be paid through either fees or commissions.

- If you're looking for a fee-only planner, contact the National Association of Personal Financial Advisors at 847-483-5400 or at www.napfa.org. If you want a CPA with a Personal Financial Specialist designation, contact the American Institute of Certified Public Accountants (888-777-7077 or visit their website at www.aicpa.org).

HIRING A PLANNER

When you get down to the business of hiring a planner, assume it's going to take some time. You should get the names of at least three to five planners, check their professional designations and their disciplinary histories, and if those look good, interview them in person.

Realize that choosing a planner is a lot like choosing a doctor. Part of the process is objective—the training and professional designations, for example. Part of it is subjective. Do you feel comfortable pouring out the details of your financial life to this person? Are you comfortable with the type of advice he or she is giving? Is the planner willing to explain things to you clearly and in detail, so that you know not only why he or she is making the recommendation but also how it fits into your life and your portfolio?

Planners should be willing to sit down with you and discuss what type of clients they normally work with, how they charge for their services, and what they charge for and what you get for free. (For instance, some fee-only planners charge by the hour; others will have you give them a retainer that allows you to call and ask advice numerous times throughout the year at no additional charge.)

They should be willing to show you plans they have done for others (with the other clients' names removed, of course) so you can get an idea of what kinds of recommendations they make and why.

During this interview process, you should be looking for a couple of things: Is the planner candid? Is there any area that he or she seems unwilling to discuss? Does he or she handle a lot of people like you? It's helpful to deal with planners who specialize. For instance, if you're a teacher, it's good to deal with a planner who has many other teachers as clients, because he or she is likely to have more experience with the particular issues that affect your profession—such as 403(b) plans, which are likely to be your main source of retirement savings, and the "government pension offset" that can reduce or eliminate your Social Security benefits.

Make sure the planners you're considering pass all the objective tests. But also subject them to your own inner voice—the one that normally tells you whether you trust someone. All too often, individuals get intimidated by financial professionals, so they ignore the uneasy feeling they have when dealing with them. They get talked into investments they don't understand because they assume the planner is smarter or more educated. Don't. Remember this and only this: This is your money. What happens to it will determine how well you and your family live in the future. Make sure that you feel very comfortable—both personally and professionally—with anyone who gives you financial advice.

GLOSSARY

ADRs. American Depositary Receipts, which are securities traded on U.S. stock exchanges that represent the shares in a foreign concern. Generally, these are similar to owning shares in a foreign company; however, they bear less currency risk. (See Chapter 11.)

ADV. A financial adviser form required by the Securities and Exchange Commission, the chief regulator in the securities industry. The form discloses a financial adviser's training, background, and employment arrangements, including whether the adviser has been disciplined by regulators and how the adviser is paid.

Call date. The point when the issuer of a bond can redeem (or pay off) outstanding bonds prior to the bond's maturity date.

Calls. Or *call options*, securities that give the holder the right to buy a particular security at a set price by a specific date in the future.

Capital gain. A profit earned on a capital asset, such as stock or real estate. The term is also used to describe the favorable tax rate you pay when earning a profit on capital assets. (Where ordinary income is taxed at a 10 percent, 15 percent, 25 percent, 28 percent, 33 percent, or 35 percent federal rate, capital gains are taxed at either 5 percent or 15 percent, depending on your ordinary income tax bracket.)

Certificate of Deposit. A contract with a bank, whereby you agree to deposit a set amount for a set period of time. In turn, the bank agrees to pay you a set rate of interest. CDs, like other bank deposits, are insured by the federal government to $100,000 per depositor.

Closed-end funds. A type of mutual fund that offers just a fixed number of shares and trades on a major exchange, much like the stock of individual corporations. (See Chapter 8.)

CMOs. Collateralized mortgage obligations are a hybrid form of mortgage-backed security aimed at defining and dividing the risk of mortgage securities among different investors. (See Chapter 4.)

Commodities. Bulk goods, such as food, coffee, grain, livestock, and metals, which are traded on the commodities exchange.

CPI. The Consumer Price Index is a cost-of-living benchmark aimed at measuring inflation in America. The statistic, which is published by the Bureau of Labor Statistics, determines cost-of-living adjustments on everything from Social Security benefits to tax schedules.

Corporate bonds. IOUs issued by individual corporations. When you buy a corporate bond, you are lending that company money in exchange for the promise that the company will pay you interest on your loan at regular intervals.

Currency risk. The chance that an investor in a foreign security will lose buying power when converting the proceeds of his or her stock sale to U.S. dollars from a foreign currency. (See Chapter 11.)

Default. When a company (or government entity) is unable to pay regularly scheduled principal or interest payments to bondholders.

Defined benefit plan. A type of pension that promises set monthly payments for the life of the pensioner (or the life of both the pensioner and his/her spouse).

Derivatives. A hybrid security that's formed by taking a traditional investment and turning it into a nontraditional security through the magic of investment banking. By and large, derivatives are designed to solve some specific problem or reduce some specific risk with the underlying investment. Unfortunately, with every risk that's eliminated, a new risk is created.

Dividend. Payments of cash or stock that represent a distribution of corporate earnings to shareholders.

DRIPS. Really geeky people, or dividend reinvestment plans, depending on context. DRIPS automatically reinvest shareholder dividends at set intervals, providing the investor with additional shares in the company's stock.

Dividend yield. The annual percentage return earned by an investor from the payment of cash or stock through dividends. The dividend yield is calculated by comparing the market price of the stock to the annual per-share dividends. In other words, if a company pays $1 per share in dividends each year and the stock sells for $50 per share, that stock would have a 2 percent dividend yield.

Earnings per share. The amount of earnings allocated to each share of a company's outstanding stock. (A company with 1 million shares outstanding and $1.2 million in profits would report $1.20 in per-share earnings.)

Exchange rate. The price at which one country's currency can be converted into another country's currency. (In other words, you might get 100 Japanese yen for each U.S. dollar.)

Fannie Mae and Freddie Mac. Quasi-governmental entities that buy mortgages from lenders, consolidate them into "pools" of loans with like interest rates and maturity dates, and then resell them to investors. Technically, Fannie Mae is short for the Federal National Mortgage Association, while Freddie Mac is the nickname for the Federal Home Loan Mortgage Corp.

Ginnie Mae. The cute name for the Government National Mortgage Association, which functions much like Fannie Mae and Freddie Mac.

IRA. Individual retirement accounts are personal, tax-deferred retirement accounts that allow qualifying individuals to set aside up to $5,000 per year in retirement savings and deduct that amount from their income in the current tax year.

Inflation. The rise in the cost of goods and services.

Initial public offering. The first offering of a company's stock to the general public.

Money market account. A bank account that pays somewhat higher interest, but imposes certain restrictions on depositors such as a requirement to maintain a high minimum balance.

Money market mutual fund. An open-end mutual fund that invests in relatively safe, short-term investments such as short-term commercial paper, bank deposits, and Treasury bills.

Municipal bonds. IOUs issued by state and local governments. Generally, these bonds pay relatively low rates of return, but the interest paid is free from both federal and state income taxes.

Portfolio. The combined investment holdings of an individual, which may include stocks, bonds, real estate, cash, and other investments.

P/E. The price/earnings ratio is a method of measuring a company's market price relative to its earnings. (See Chapter 5.) It's calculated by dividing a company's current market price by its annual earnings per share. A company that sells for $50 per share and earns $2 would have a P/E of 25.

Puts. A security that grants the holder the right to sell shares in a specific security at a set price by a certain date in the future. If I own a $35 put on XYZ Co., for example, I can sell that stock on or before the expiration date for $35 per share, even if XYZ's market price declines to $30.

Real-return bonds. A type of bond that is aimed at keeping direct pace with the U.S. inflation rate. (See Chapter 4.)

REIT. Real estate investment trusts are companies, often publicly traded, that manage a portfolio of rental properties, passing on the profits from both real estate sales and rents to investors.

Share. A unit of equity ownership in either a corporation or a mutual fund.

Tax basis. Your cost, for tax purposes, in a capital asset, such as a stock or real estate. In other words, what you paid for your holdings in a particular stock, inclusive of commissions and fees, which gets deducted from the sales price, to determine your taxable profit.

Trading volume. The number of shares of stock that are traded during a given period—usually one day.

Treasury bills. Short-term government debt issued to investors. Treasury bills mature in one year or less.

Treasury bonds. Long-term government debt, which take more than ten years to mature, or pay back principal to investors.

Treasury notes. Medium-term government debt, with maturities ranging from two to ten years.

Viatical settlements. Life insurance policies sold by old or ailing policyholders for a fraction of the death benefit. (See Chapter 4.)

INDEX

ABOUT THE AUTHOR

Los Angeles Times business writer **Kathy Kristof** is nationally known for her weekly syndicated personal finance column, which reaches 40 million readers online and in more than fifty major newspapers. Cited as "maybe the best reporter of all the personal finance columnists" in the TJFR 1999 Blue Chip Newsroom ranking of the top 100 American business journalists, she has received numerous writing awards and honors, including the title of 1998 Consumer Advocate of the Year by the California Alliance for Consumer Education. She is a sought-after lecturer at investment conferences and appears regularly on radio and television news programs. Kathy lives in Los Angeles with her two children.

ABOUT BLOOMBERG

Bloomberg L.P., founded in 1981, is a global information services, news, and media company. Headquartered in New York, the company has sales and news operations worldwide. Serving customers on six continents, Bloomberg, through its wholly-owned subsidiary Bloomberg Finance L.P., holds a unique position within the financial services industry by providing an unparalleled range of features in a single package known as the Bloomberg Professional® service. By addressing the demand for investment performance and efficiency through an exceptional combination of information, analytic, electronic trading, and straight-through-processing tools, Bloomberg has built a worldwide customer base of corporations, issuers, financial intermediaries, and institutional investors.

Bloomberg News, founded in 1990, provides stories and columns on business, general news, politics, and sports to leading newspapers and magazines throughout the world. Bloomberg Television, a 24-hour business and financial news network, is produced and distributed globally in seven languages. Bloomberg Radio is an international radio network anchored by flagship station Bloomberg 1130 (WBBR-AM) in New York.

In addition to the Bloomberg Press line of books, Bloomberg publishes *Bloomberg Markets* magazine.

To learn more about Bloomberg, call a sales representative at:

London: +44-20-7330-7500
New York: +1-212-318-2000
Tokyo: +81-3-3201-8900

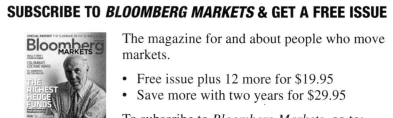